From my kitchen to yours along with a piece of my heart ~
Carol Ann Kates

Grocery Shopping Secrets

Cooking is an art that requires a nurturing spirit, fresh ingredients, careful shopping, and love. Love of food and love of those you invite to your table.
—Author Unknown

Carol Ann Kates
author of *Secret Recipes from the Corner Market*

Grocery Shopping Secrets

published by:
Penny Lane Press of Colorado
6620 Crooked Stick Drive
Windsor, CO 80550-7079

CarolAnn@CarolAnnKates.com

design by:
Rebecca Finkel, F + P Graphic Design, FPGD.com

ISBN paperback: 978-0-9773485-1-0
ISBN eBook: 978-0-9773485-2-7

Library of Congress Control Number: 2023920183

First edition
Printed in USA

This book is dedicated in loving memory of:

My father, **Merrill Seth Steele,** a simple, hard-working grocer, who taught me the importance of using only the freshest ingredients in the meals I prepare.

My mother, **Ellen Pauline Allen Steele,** an accomplished cook, who taught me the satisfaction of perfecting simple recipes.

My aunt, **Beryl Mae Allen Henry,** a woman with class and style, who taught me to nurture the food I prepare with tender loving care.

My uncle, **Edgar Parkins Henry,** an expert butcher, who taught me to appreciate a good steak and cook prime rib to perfection.

My grandmother, **Olive Amelia McNary Steele,** a consummate hostess, who taught me the joy of having special treats tucked away to share with company.

My grandmother, **Gladys Loveall Finch,** whose playful spirit taught me the joy of having secret ingredients.

and in loving devotion to: My husband, **Russell Keith Kates,** who has always been a pleasure to cook for.

These bits of food wisdom are gifted to my children: Jennifer Ellen Kates-Fore (Ryan Daniel Fore), Brian Merrill Kates (Kelsey Adele), Alisa Anne "Leelee" Kates (Joshua James Olson), and my grandchildren: Aliyah Jordan Kirkes, Aiden Russell Luttes, Calder Grey Kates, and Hayden Lamar and Carson Daniel Fore.

Acknowledgments

With thanks to my team:

I extend my heartfelt appreciation to:

Judith Briles, the Book Shepherd, who encouraged me to compile these bits of food wisdom into a book and from whom I have learned so much.

Rebecca Finkel, my book designer, whose patience and perseverance helped me see this project to completion. This book was a long-time coming. Rebecca's creative flair gave this book personality and style.

Randa Dubnick, my editor, whose thorough attention to detail scrutinized my manuscript with tender, loving care.

Sheralyn Luplow, Nancy Hansford, and Holly Manley, members of my critique group, who carefully read and reviewed every page.

Bobby Crew, my assistant, who helps me navigate the world of social media.

Mike Daniels, the Publisher's Coach, whose advice, guidance, and wisdom I value.

Christy Martell, a talented artist, who created the "Shopping", "Selecting," and "Availability" icons to help readers identify pertinent information more quickly.

Dale Crawford, a talented caricaturist, who created my shopping cartoon, adding a sense of playfulness to the chore of grocery shopping.

And lastly, but not least, *Russell Keith Kates,* my husband, whose undying support never faltered through the thick and thin of compiling my wisdom into a book.

Contents

Author's Note

Supermarkets are changing. Some changes have been positive ... and some haven't. When you want to make your favorite recipe, the ingredients you need might not be available. Grocery stores have had, and still have, their own set of problems with inventory supplies. What do you do?

You may discover the produce at your local supermarket is not as fresh as it used to be. Food costs have increased, and package size has been reduced. What do you do?

It has never been more important to be an informed food shopper–for quality–for quantity–for your budget.

I grew up in a corner market, living and breathing the grocery business. My father founded a small family-owned chain, Steele's Markets. Merrill Steele was a perfectionist and quite picky about the products he sold, insisting on stocking only the freshest perishable products and best brand names. The legacy he left me was "how to shop."

Papa taught me to select superior food products much like other children learned the alphabet. Exceptional perishable products—produce, meat, deli, bakery—were of utmost importance at Steele's Markets.

After the death of my parents, I inherited co-ownership of Steele's and spent the majority of my adult life owning and operating supermarkets and delis in Northern Colorado. My family carried on Papa's legacy of hand-selecting only the finest foods for our customers. My experience as a grocer and deli operator taught me the ins and outs, dos and don'ts of supermarket shopping. Although I absorbed what my father taught me about quality food, I have continued to expand my expertise as the culinary world has changed and as supermarkets have changed as well.

By following my grocery-insider wisdom in selecting and storing produce, meat, fish, dairy, and deli, you will save money because your perishables will be fresher and last longer. With my advice, you will be able to survive the health and economic chaos that the 21st century delivered globally.

I learned my most valuable lesson about cooking from a simple grocer..... my father. He bluntly said, "Garbage in. Garbage out." Stated more poetically: *Great meals begin with shopping. The quality of the ingredients used when preparing a meal can be more important than the recipe.*

My favorite responsibility at Steele's was creating recipes for our ads, which provided our customers with creative ways to use everyday ingredients. I compiled the recipes I perfected for our weekly ads into the best-selling, award-winning cookbook, *Secret Recipes from the Corner Market.*

Thousands of copies were embraced by cooks and kitchens; my book was seen as a practical and usable collection of family-tested, customer-approved recipes. Readers loved the grocery-insider tips about selecting and storing food. *Secret Recipes from the Corner Market* was selected as "Top Ten Favorite Cookbooks" by the *Denver Post* Food Staff.

ONE

24 Strategies to Reduce Your Food Budget

Are you struggling with
increasing prices at the supermarket?

It is all over the news: food costs have been on a roller coaster ride.

As I write this, my friends with teen-age sons claim their grocery budgets have doubled from the previous year. The price of beef is up 16 percent; milk and chicken prices are up more than 13 percent; and the cost of fresh seafood is up 12 percent. Even the price of items once considered low-cost sources of protein—like dried beans and lentils—are up more than 10 percent. The good news is that the cost of fresh fruits and vegetables has only risen 6 percent.

Are you struggling with increasing prices at the supermarket? When I was a little girl, my mother, who grew up during the Great Depression, often said, "Waste not, want not." These words resonate with today's gyrating food costs.

There are many strategies to help reduce your food budget. Some are no-brainers. Changing your shopping and cooking habits may be difficult. In my home, my family is chipping away at the suggestions below one or two at a time. We don't want to be overwhelmed. And most likely, you don't either.

1. **Pay attention to prices.** This is particularly hard for me as I am a brand-name shopper and always want to purchase the best quality products. Now, I am looking at prices and comparing prices, not only between brands but between stores.

2. **Plan meals in advance and make a shopping list of what is needed.** Planning meals in advance, making a list of what is required for each recipe and meal, and shopping from the list helps you resist those impulse items that you do not need but are tempted to put into your cart. My husband struggles with this, always coming home from the store with something he couldn't resist that is not on the "list." If this is also hard for you, consider limiting your splurge items to one or two each shopping trip.

3. **Keep the pantry organized.** Keeping your pantry organized helps prevent canned and package goods from expiring. I check expiration dates and rotate newer items to the back, using older dated items first. Before I head to the grocery store, I check my shopping list. If chicken broth is on the list, I make sure a can of chicken broth isn't hidden away somewhere in my pantry.

4. **Keep your refrigerator tidy.** Take a regular inventory of the fresh, perishable foods in your refrigerator and attempt to use them before they pass their prime.

5. **Don't throw out leftovers.** Find inventive ways to use leftovers. When I have leftover mashed potatoes, I love making potato pancakes and serving them with fried eggs for breakfast. Topping a baked potato with leftover chili creates a whole new meal. Soft strawberries can go into your morning smoothie, and ripe bananas are perfect for banana bread. As my mother said, "Waste not, want not."

6. **Get creative with what you have.** My husband loves scoping out what's in the fridge and creating a unique, delicious breakfast from what he can throw together. Don't get too tied to following recipes. Eat what you have and enjoy experimenting.

7. **Get a loyalty card.** Most supermarkets and even larger independent markets have a loyalty card program which provide discounted prices to members.

8. **Investigate all the savings programs available at the supermarket you patronize.** Every supermarket chain and even larger independents will offer a variety of incentive programs that can save you money. Some offer extra fuel points with the purchase of gift cards. Check your supermarket's website for different ways to save.

9. **Shop the ads.** Most supermarkets come out with their weekly ads on Wednesdays. Many of them post their ads several days in advance. Read them and plan your meals around what is on sale. If something you use frequently is on special, stock up if you have the extra cash. Recently, King Soopers had Red Bird® boneless, skinless chicken breasts on sale, my favorite brand of chicken. I purchased several packages and froze them.

10. **Buy the store brands:** they are normally cheaper. I grew up in the grocery business. Papa would often bring home different brands of the same product, like corn. Samples of each brand were laid out, and testers—all of us—evaluated the differences. We always had a favorite brand. If you are a brand-name shopper, like I am, it can be painful to substitute. I personally struggle with giving up my favorite brands. My husband is different. He always buys what is cheapest.

11. **Avoid pre-cut fruits and veggies in the produce department.** I have purchased these as a time saver; it's also a money waster. Pre-cut apple slices can cost three times more than apples you slice yourself and will have a shorter shelf life. In checking prices at King Soopers today, I found that loose broccoli cost $1.49 a pound, where prepackaged broccoli florets cost $4.99 for 32 ounces, or almost 50 cents more per pound. To save money, avoid pre-cut, pre-washed produce.

12. **Save money the old-fashioned way—use coupons, both paper and digital.** When I first started working at Steele's, shoppers would come in with stacks of coupons. Checkers had to pair each coupon with an item in the cart. I must admit, I hated dealing with coupons. Today, most coupons are digital. Check your supermarket's website for digital coupons. Also, by downloading their app, you may find additional discounts and sale items.

13. **Buy in bulk.** Consider a Costco or Sam's membership for items you consume on large scale. For example, if your children love Nature Valley Sweet & Salty Granola Bars, Costco sells a 48-count (1.2-ounce) package for $17.49 or 36 cents per bar. Sam's sells a 36-count package for $11.28 or 31 cents per bar. King Soopers sells a 12-count (1.2-ounce) package for $5.49 or 45 cents per bar. You save buying this item in bulk.

14. **Check unit prices.** Sometimes we are fooled into thinking larger package sizes are cheaper per ounce, but that's not always the case. Looking at unit prices will help you find the real deals on the shelf.

15. **Buy from local farmers and producers.** Seek out farmers and producers that sell at your local farmers' markets. Their costs may be lower due to lack of transportation costs and middlemen. Find a Community Supported Agriculture (CSA) group to join.

16. **Cook with seasonal produce.** Learn what produce is in season and cook seasonally. Produce that is in season is cheaper.

17. **Don't avoid the freezer aisle.** I have always been a cook who prefers to put fresh food on my table. Any produce destined for the freezer section of the supermarket is ripened until it reaches its peak and then flash frozen. Frozen produce is cheaper than fresh but will also last longer.

18. **Learn to properly freeze.** Learn to properly freeze expensive foods like meat, cheese, and nuts. With proper freezing, you can buy these foods in bulk, freeze them in small portions, and not worry about waste. This book offers many tips on properly freezing fresh foods.

19. **When you buy fresh, select the best.** Papa taught me my most important lesson about cooking: "Garbage in. Garbage out." I am a real stickler for selecting only the freshest perishables. My cookbook, *Secret Recipes from the Corner Market,* and the information in this book, *Grocery Shopping Secrets,* include grocery-insider wisdom on selecting the very best. The fresher the food you take home from the supermarket, the longer it will last, and the more money you will save on your grocery bill.

20. **Use products beyond the sell-by date.** Don't throw food out just because it has past its "Sell-By" date. Supermarkets remove product from their shelves it if has past the "Sell-By" date; however, these foods are safe to consume after that date. Eggs are good for three to five weeks after the "Sell-By" date; ground beef and poultry are good for 1 to 2 days; and beef is good for 3 to 5 days. If you have questions, you can find more information online about how long products are consumable after their "Sell-By" dates.

21. **Cut back on meat, poultry, and seafood.** Meat, poultry, dairy, and seafood are the foods most impacted by rising food costs. Typically, the price of fresh fruits and

vegetables is more stable unless there is a massive crop shortage. You can cut back on your consumption of meat, poultry, seafood and eat vegetarian meals a few days each week. This will, no doubt, make your doctor happy as well.

22. **Plant a garden.** If you have the room in your yard to plant a vegetable garden, you will save money growing your own food. Even growing a few high-priced vegetables, like tomatoes, in containers near a sunny window can help reduce your grocery bill.

23. **Learn to can and preserve food.** Your grandparents canned and preserved what they grew. I remember with fondness my Grandmother Steele's basement shelves stocked with food she had lovingly preserved. Even if you don't have a garden, you can purchase items, like peaches and pickling cucumbers, in bulk from farmers' markets and preserve them for future consumption.

24. **Never purchase dented cans or packages that are opened, torn, or punctured.** Damage to the exterior packaging may affect the quality of the interior product.

TWO

Understanding Food Labels

Food labels will list total sugar, which is a combination of both added and naturally occurring sugar.

Food labels are confusing. Understanding the information in the nutritional box can be overwhelming. Many commonly used terms, like "free range", have no USDA legal definition; and their true meaning can be a mystery. I have put together the following information to help you unscramble what is in the nutritional label and to understand other terms commonly found on food labels. I'll start with date labeling.

Dates

The "Sell-By" date indicates that retailers must sell the product by that date or remove it from their shelves. All products bearing a "Sell-By" will be good for a limited time after that date. "Best-If-Used-By" indicates when a product will be at its peak for both taste and quality. It is not a safety date, and the product will be good for a limited time after this date. "Best-By" or "Use-By" dates are the last date the product will be at its peak. This is also not a safety date, and food will be good for a limited time past this date. If you are using products past any of these dates, you should ensure that the product is still good by examining its appearance. Does it look fresh? Does it have an odd color? How does it smell? A bad odor indicates food is spoiled. How does it taste? Does it still taste good?

Nutrition Labels

Since 1994, food manufacturers have been required to provide nutritional information on food labels. You can find the following information on those labels:

Servings

The first listing under nutritional facts lists the number of servings in the container; for example, 3.5 servings per container. This is followed by the serving size, which is calculated in common household measurements like cup, tablespoon, piece, or slice. The label will also list the size by its metric amount in grams (g). By law, serving sizes are estimated by how much a normal person would eat or drink, not how much they should eat or drink. Remember, calories or other nutritional information on labels is for a single serving, not for the entire package.

Nutritional Facts

The nutritional facts listed on the nutritional label are based on a 2,000 calorie per day diet. The Daily Value refers to the recommended amount of nutrients you should consume each day. The %Daily Value (%DV) is the percentage a single nutrient contributes to your daily diet. Nutritional labels will list the nutritional values of the product according to total fat, cholesterol, sodium, total carbohydrates, and protein. The Daily Value and the %Daily Value for each of these nutrients must be listed on the label.

Calories

A calorie is a way to measure how much energy food provides to your body. The calorie intake listed on food labels is for one serving. Most healthy adults need 1,600 to 3,000 calories per day, though this will vary based on age, gender, height, weight, and physical activity. Some labels will indicate how many calories come from fat.

Fat

Nutritional information on food labels will list total fat, saturated fat, and trans fat. Total fat includes all the fat.

Saturated fats are found in animal products, like beef and pork; in full-fat dairy products, like milk and cheese; in eggs; and in tropical oils like coconut and palm. Saturated fats are typically solid at room temperature and are often called "solid fats."

There are two types of trans fats: one occurs naturally in animal-based products, and one is artificial. Artificial trans fats are created by an industrial process that adds hydrogen to liquid vegetable oil to make it more solid. Trans fats are usually found in processed foods, fried foods, baked goods, and snack foods. Trans fat is the worst fat for your health.

Unsaturated fat is not listed on food labels. There are two types of unsaturated fat: monounsaturated and polyunsaturated. Monounsaturated fats are found in olive and peanut oils; avocados; nuts, like almonds and pecans; and seeds, like pumpkin and sesame. Polyunsaturated fats are found in sunflower, corn, and flaxseed oils; walnuts; flax seeds; and fish. Unsaturated fats are considered healthy fats. To calculate how much unsaturated fats in a product, subtract the saturated and trans fats from the total fat.

Some claims on food labels regarding fat may be:

1. *Fat free* means the food has less than 0.5 grams of fat per serving. You may find the letter FF on fat-free products.

2. *Low fat* indicates the product will contain 3 grams of fat or less per serving. You may find the letters LF on low-fat products.

3. *Reduced fat* means the food has at least 25 percent less fat than a traditional serving.

4. *Light* indicates the product must have one-third fewer calories or 50 percent less fat than a traditional serving.

Cholesterol

Cholesterol is both made by your body and is eaten as dietary cholesterol. Only meat and dairy products contain cholesterol; plant products do not. Diets high in cholesterol may lead to health problems.

Sodium

Food labels will indicate the percentage of sodium in a single serving. Other names for sodium are salt, monosodium glutamate *(MSG)*, sodium citrate, sodium phosphate, sodium alginate, and sodium chloride.

Some claims made on food labels regarding sodium may include:

1. *Unsalted* means there is no sodium added to the food product, but it may contain natural occurring sodium.

2. *Sodium-free* or *salt-free* means the products contains less than 5 mg of sodium per serving.
3. *Low sodium* or *low salt* means a single serving has 140 mg or less of sodium. You may find the letters *LS* on low-sodium products.
4. *Reduced-sodium, lower in salt,* or *lower in sodium* means the product contains 25 percent less sodium than the traditional product.

Total Carbohydrates

Nutritional labels will list dietary fiber, total sugars, and added sugars.

Dietary fiber, also known as roughage or bulk, includes the part of plant foods your body cannot completely digest or absorb. Good sources of dietary fiber are fruits and vegetables, whole grains, nuts and seeds, and legumes.

There are two types of sugars found in food—added sugar and naturally occurring sugar. Any product that contains fruit (fructose) or milk (lactose) has natural sugar. Added sugar can include both natural sugars—like white sugar, brown sugar, and honey—and manufactured sugars like high-fructose corn syrup. Food labels will list total sugar, which is a combination of both added and naturally occurring sugar. Nutritionists recommend avoiding chemically manufactured sugars: high-fructose corn syrup, corn syrup, corn sweetener, etc.

Some claims made on food labels regarding sugar may say:

1. *Sugar-free,* meaning the product has less than 0.5 percent or less of sugar per serving.

2. *Reduced sugar* means the product has at least 25 percent less sugar per serving than a traditional serving
3. *No added sugar* or *without added sugar* means no ingredient containing sugar, like fruit, is added during processing.
4. *Low sugar* is a term that the FDA has not defined, and manufacturers are not allowed to make this claim on food labels.

Protein

You may find protein listed on food labels. The FDA requires a %DV be listed if a claim of "high in protein" is made. Manufacturers must also list protein if the product is intended for infants and children under four. If the product is intended for children four years of age through adult, protein does not have to be listed on the label.

Vitamins and Minerals

The %DV of vitamin D, calcium, iron, and potassium must be listed on labels. Manufacturers may voluntarily list other vitamins and minerals.

Dual Columns

Occasionally you may find dual columns on food nutritional labels. When a food product may be consumed in one sitting or in multiple sittings, the FDA requires both single serving and whole container nutritional information. In addition, you may find two separate columns for foods where additional ingredients are added in its preparation. You will find a column for nutritional information as packaged and as prepared.

Ingredients

Manufacturers are required by law to list all the ingredients in each product you purchase, with the exception of water if it is less than five percent of the total weight. Ingredients on food labels are listed by weight in descending order. Food labels must also list any FDA-certified food color additives. The FDA allows manufacturers to list some ingredients collectively — flavors, spices, and artificial flavorings. Artificial colorings which are exempt from FDA certification can also be grouped together. These include pigments obtained from natural sources such as dehydrated beets or beta carotene.

Storage

Storage instructions are another requirement. Manufacturers *must provide* instructions on how to safely store their products both before and after opening the package. For example, "Store in a cool dry place." "Refrigerate unused portions in a non-metallic container."

Cooking Instructions

If needed, instructions for how to prepare the product must be stated on the label. This includes any cooking equipment needed, like a microwave or oven, temperature, and cooking time.

Contact Information

Manufacturers must list their contact information on the label so you can contact them with questions about their product.

Country of Origin

All food manufacturers in the United States must indicate the country of origin of ingredients used in their products. According to the USDA, "Country of Origin Labeling (COOL) is a labeling law that requires retailers—such as full-line grocery stores, supermarkets, and club warehouse stores—to notify their customers with information regarding the source of certain foods. Food products covered by the law include "muscle-cut" and ground meats from lamb, goat, and chicken; wild and farm-raised fish and shellfish; fresh and frozen fruits and vegetables; peanuts, pecans, and macadamia nuts; and ginseng."

Miscellaneous Nutritional Terms

Some miscellaneous terms you may find on food labels:

1. *Low calorie* means 40 calories or less per serving.
2. *Low cholesterol* means 20 milligrams or less of cholesterol and 2 grams or less of saturated fat per serving.
3. *Reduced* means the item has at least 25 percent less of the specified nutrient or calories than the traditional product.
4. *Good source of* means the food product provides at least 10 to 19 percent of the daily value of a particular vitamin or nutrient per serving.
5. *Excellent source of* means this product provides at least 20 percent or more of the daily value of a particular vitamin or nutrient per serving.
6. *Calorie free* means the food product has less than 5 calories per serving.
7. *High in* means the food product provides 20 percent or more of the daily value of a specified nutrient per serving.

Labeling on Prepared Foods

The FDA requires supermarkets to provide nutritional information for all prepackaged food. In addition, they require nutritional information to be available for food that is intended to be "eaten on the premises, while walking away, or soon after arriving at another location." For example, if you purchase macaroni and cheese from the deli case or a piece of pizza, nutritional information for that item may be displayed on the case. If it is not, the deli clerk should be able to provide that information to you.

Food Labels Based on Dietary Restrictions

Dairy Free

Dairy-free products do not contain any milk or milk products from cows, sheep, or goats. You may find the letters *DF* on dairy-free products.

Lactose Free

Lactose-free products contain milk but are free of lactose, a type of sugar found in milk that is difficult to digest. You may find the letters *LF* on lactose-free products.

Gluten Free

People with celiac disease follow a gluten-free diet, which eliminates any foods that contain gluten, a protein found in wheat, oats, rye, and barley. Some dairy products, which have had flavorings or ingredients added, may also contain gluten. You may find the letters *GF* on gluten-free products.

Keto

Keto is short for ketogenic, a diet that is high in fat and low in carbohydrates (sugars). Carbohydrates cause the body to break down fat into molecules called ketones. Ketones circulate in the blood stream and are the main source of energy for many cells. Most of the calories in this diet come from proteins and fats.

Certified Keto

If eating a keto diet is important to you, look for the Certified Keto logo. The Paleo Foundation trademarked the term Keto Certified® to identify foods that meet the ketogenic diet standards.

Paleo Diet

The paleo diet, sometimes called the caveman or Stone-Age diet, consists of lean meats, fish, low-glycemic fruits and vegetables, seeds, and nuts.

Certified Paleo

If eating a paleo diet is important to you, look for the Certified Paleo® label. It was developed by the Paleo Foundation to identify food products that meet the standards of a paleo diet. Paleo foods are grain free, legume free, and dairy free and do not contain any artificial colorings, preservatives, or flavor enhancers. A paleo diet is also gluten free.

Vegan

The term vegan has a clear meaning in the vegan community. A vegan product does not contain any ingredients of animal origin, including milk, eggs, honey, and gelatin; and none of its ingredients are tested on animals. The USDA, FDA, and FTC do not have any formal definition or standards for this term. Some states have attempted to pass their own laws standardizing its meaning, which only further complicates its definition. You may find the letters *VG* on vegan products.

Certified Vegan

If eating a vegan diet is important to you, look for the Certified Vegan® logo label. Food bearing this label has been certified to be dairy-free/non-dairy, egg free, and vegan by the Vegan Awareness Foundation.

Vegetarian

A vegetarian does not eat meat, poultry, or any meat products, like bone broth, but will eat dairy and eggs. You might find the letter *V* on food products that are vegetarians.

Engine 2

The Engine 2® diet was created by Rip Esselstyn, a former athlete and firefighter. This style of eating focuses on unprocessed, plant-based foods, is low in fat, and free of vegetable oils. An Engine 2 diet consists of whole foods like legumes, grains, fruits, vegetables, nuts, and seeds.

Sugar Conscious

Many people are choosing to limit their sugar intake. Sugar-conscious foods do not have added sugar and contain less than 4 grams of sugar per serving. You can find the words "sugar conscious" on products and recipes that meet this criteria.

Whole Foods Diet

Supermarkets today carry a wider range of unprocessed and unrefined foods. A Whole Foods Diet® was created by Whole Foods Market cofounder, John Mackey. It avoids processed and refined foods and includes grains, nuts, seeds, fruits, and vegetables. Whole foods have little to no preservatives or additives; while organic food is grown or raised without the use of pesticides, growth hormones, or bio-engineering.

Whole Grain

The Whole Grain Council created the Whole Grain Stamp® to help consumers identiy real whole-grain food products. The 100% stamp guarantees that each "serving contains a full serving or more of whole grains." The 50% stamp means each serving contains 50 percent of a whole-grain serving. Some companies may sell whole-grain products but are not using the stamp. If a product does not bear the stamp, its label should list the number of grams of whole grain in each serving or say "100% whole wheat". You can trust those terms. If you see the terms "whole grain" (name of grain), "whole wheat", "whole" (other grain), "stoneground whole" (grain), "brown rice", "oats", "oatmeal" (including old-fashioned and instant), or "wheat berries" you can feel confident you are eating whole grain.

KOSHER

Kosher® certification on fresh meats means the animals are raised and processed following strict guidelines and under rabbinical supervision. Animal products labeled kosher are free range, fed only grain, and never given any antibiotics.

Halal

Food with a Halal® or Zabiah Halah® label must be handled according to Islamic law and under Islamic authority.

Labeling Based on Production of Foods

Following are general definitions of the most prevalent food labeling terms. These terms can vary for different animals, like chicken and beef. Variations in the application of specific terminology will be addressed in respective chapters.

Certified Organic

To be certified organic by the USDA, crops cannot be grown using synthetic fertilizers, pesticides, herbicides, or sewage sludge. They also cannot be genetically engineered or irradiated.

Certified organic animals must be fed only organically grown feed, and this feed must not contain any animal byproducts. In addition, the animals can't be treated with synthetic hormones or antibiotics. Animals must have access to the outdoors, and ruminants—cattle, sheep, bison, deer, elk, goats—must have access to pasture. Organic animals cannot be cloned.

For products bearing the USDA Organic seal, both the growing and processing facilities must be inspected and approved by a USDA-accredited certifying agent.

Country of Origin

Country of Origin Labeling (COOL) is a labeling law that requires grocery stores, supermarkets, and warehouse stores to inform their customers about the county of origin of chicken, lamb, goat, farm-raised and wild-caught fish and seafood, perishable agriculture commodities, peanuts, pecans, macadamia nuts, and ginseng. Congress passed the Consolidated Appropriations Act in 2016, which ended requirements for retailers to inform customers about the country of origin for beef and pork.

Irradiation

Food irradiation is a technology that applies ionizing radiation to food to extend its shelf life and to improve the safety of food by eliminating microorganisms and insets. The FDA regulates the sources used for irradiation and only approves those sources that are safe. To know if the food you are buying has been irradiated, look for a statement "Treated with radiation" or "Treated with irradiation" or a radura symbol.

The FDA approved a variety of foods for irradiation in the United States: beef and pork; crustaceans, like lobster and crab; fresh fruits and vegetables, including lettuce and spinach; poultry; seeds and sprouts; shell eggs; shellfish, like oysters and mussels; and spices and seasonings.

Proponents of irradiation believe it prevents foodborne illnesses like salmonella, extends the shelf life of food by destroying organisms that cause spoilage, controls insects, delays sprouting and ripening, and sterilizes food. Opponents believe the irradiation of food increases the risk of cancer and diminishes and destroys its nutrients.

USDA Inspected

Food products bearing a USDA inspection seal have been inspected by USDA employees or company employees under USDA supervision and must meet certain size or quality standards.

USDA Process Certified

This is a newer certification program offered by the USDA to provide farmers and producers a unique way to market their products. Farmers and producers can select one or more agricultural processes or practices, like free range or antibiotic free, and have that term certified by the USDA to be accurate. To receive this certification, the claim must be supported by a documented management system and be indepentently verified by quality USDA American Marketing Service auditors.

Fresh

This label on food means the internal temperature of food was never below 26 degrees F.

Natural or All Natural

These terms indicate that the meat had limited processing, which means the raw product was not altered during processing. In addition, no artifical ingredients, colorings, or chemical preservatives have been added. The animal may or may not be free range and may have been given antibiotics if it was ill.

Free Range

A free-range existence is important for animal welfare. The USDA approves the labeling of meat and poultry products as free range. In order for their products to be labeled free range, producers must provide a description of the housing conditions when they submit their application. This label is approved if there is continuous, free access to the outdoors for over 51 percent of the animals' lives. Feedlot-raised livestock do not qualify.

This is a potentially misleading label. No farm inspection is required to determine that the animals do, in fact, have access to the outdoors or how much time they spend outside; and there is no common standard that producers are required to follow for eggs and dairy products.

Cage Free

The USDA states that eggs labeled as cage free "must be produced by hens housed in a building, room, or enclosed area that allows for unlimited access to food, water, and provides the freedom to roam within the area during the laying cycle."

Pasture Raised

Pasture raised—also called pastured, meadow raised, or pasture grown—means animals spent at least some time outdoors on pasture, feeding on grass or forage. Unless it is third-party verified, this label can be misleading.

Food Alliance Certified

If buying free range, cage free, or pasture raised food products is important to you, look for a Food Alliance® certification. This label indicates that food products come from animals fed grass, corn, and grains. Access to pasture is required, and this label indicates that products come from animals who spend the majority of their life outside on pasture. Antibiotics are only given to sick animals, and they receive no growth hormones. This certification must meet specific requirements on health, shelter, and handling.

Animal Welfare Approved (AWA)

This is the only US label that guarantees that animals were raised outdoors on pasture or range for their entire life. In addition, the animals must be raised on a farm that follows sustainable, high-welfare farming practices. It is also the only label in the US that requires auditing of the production, transportation, and slaughter of animals.

Grassfed

Grassfed means that, after it is weaned, its source of food comes from grass or forage and not from grains like corn or soy. The animals must have continuous access to pasture until slaughter. Mineral and vitamin supplements can be given. Some cattle raised as organic will eat grass and be finished on organic grain.

American Grassfed®

Beef bearing this label was produced from animals that were grassfed throughout their entire lives. The label also certifies and verifies that the animals had continuous access to pasture and were not raised in confinement.

Animal Welfare Certified by Global Animal Partners

The Global Animal Partnership uses independent, third-party auditors to inspect farms and verify the level at which farms meet standards in raising free-range, pasture-raised, and cage-free animals. Look for this symbol if buying these products is important to you. More information is available on their website.

Certified Grassfed

This certification by A Greener World guarantees that food products bearing this label come from animals fed a 100-percent grass and forage diet, raised outdoors on pasture or range, and managed according to the highest welfare and environmental standards.

Vegetarian Fed

This label states animals were never fed any animal products. It does not guarantee that animals spend time outdoors or on pasture.

Humanely Raised

There is no legal definition or federal standard for this claim on a label. If buying meat from animals that are humanely raised is important to you, look for third party verification.

Certified Humane Raised and Handled®

The Certified Humane label on food means producers meet specific, humane care standards for animals from birth to slaughter. Animals are never kept in cages or stalls and are free to roam. Products so labeled come from animals fed quality feed and are never given antibiotics or growth hormones. In addition, farmers and ranchers must comply with the North American Meat Institute Standards for slaughtering. Annual inspections are conducted to ensure that the Certified Humane practices are followed.

No Antibiotics

This label means the animal did not receive any antibiotics during its lifetime. It does not provide any other information about conditions under which the animal was raised.

No Hormones

The label "raised without added hormones" or "no hormones" means the animal received no snythetic hormones during its life time. Federal law prohibits the administration of hormones to poultry, veal, and bison. Federal regulation does permit the use of hormones in beef and dairy cattle. rBGH or rBST is a synthetic growth hormone injected into dairy cattle to increase milk production. For more explanation, see the chapter on dairy.

No Animal By-Products

This term means the animals' diet did not contain any animal byproducts. This is required in order to be certified organic.

GMOs

Genetically modified foods are derived from organisms whose DNA has been modified. This technology is called "modern biotechnology" or "gene technology," "recombinant DNA technology," or "genetic engineering." Currently, only plants are genetically modified to improve crop yields, resist diseases, and increase tolerance of herbicides. The FDA, USDA, and EPA regulate GMO foods to ensure they are safe for human consumption. Many consumers want to avoid eating genetically modified foods.

Non-GMO Project Certified®

If avoiding GMO products is important to you, look for the Non-GMO Project label. This certifiction means the product was produced without genetic engineering and its ingredients are not derived from genetically modified organisms. The Non-GMO Project Seal certifies that products are compliant with Non-GMO Project standards, which includes strict provisions for testing, traceability, and segregation. If this seal appears on animal products, like meat or dairy, it certifies that the animals were fed only a non-GMO diet.

Fair Trade®

When products bear this label, it means its producers commit to practices like long-term working relationships; workplace nondiscrimination; fair prices and wages; no child or forced labor; safe working conditions; and environmental sustainability.

THREE

How To Select Fresh Produce

Most of the produce sold
by your supermarket is considered hybrid.

Buying fresh produce is not like shopping for a can of beans, where the contents differ very little from one brand to another. Everyday, most supermarkets will sell some fruits and vegetables that are fresh and delicious and some that can be classified as "garbage". My father was a taskmaster about fresh produce. His department stood tall every day. He trained me to select only the best and to love fresh fruits and vegetables. In addition, I learned my most valuable lesson about cooking from a grocer .... "Garbage in. Garbage out." The quality of the produce you use will affect the quality of the meal you prepare and serve your family. Using fresh ingredients is just as important as the recipe you follow.

Produce has a limited shelf life. It's best to shop often for fruits and vegetables. If you are concerned about your budget, buy only what you will use within the next few days. This eliminates waste. Your supermarket brings in fresh produce every few days. Why should it be any different at home?

Shop with your eyes and your nose. Look for produce with good shape, texture, and color and an appetizing aroma. If it smells like garbage, it probably is. Avoid produce that is moldy, bruised, or injured or has signs of insect damage.

Since produce is perishable, it should be handled gently to avoid bruising. Bruises or cuts can allow bacteria to enter, causing the produce to spoil sooner.

When you are buying pre-cut or prepackaged items, make sure they are cold to the touch and are either refrigerated or surrounded by ice. Never buy damaged, opened, or torn packages. Some prepackaged products, like lettuce, will have "Best-If-Used-By" dates. Always check dates when shopping and use items by the recommended date.

Selecting a Produce Market

When selecting a market to patronize, you might want to consider certain factors. Chain supermarkets decide at the corporate level what produce to purchase, giving the individual departments little control over what they sell. They are price oriented, so their quality will be hit-or-miss. Gourmet produce markets or small specialty food stores often personally select their produce. Their quality is normally good, but prices can sometimes be higher. Farmers' markets normally have exceptional produce, but their prices can, also, be more expensive.

If you like to shop at farmer's markets and purchasing organic produce is important to you, get to know your local farmers. Becoming a certified organic farmer is a costly and complicated process. Some farmers follow organic farming practices but are not certified.

When I purchase my produce at a supermarket, I prefer a high-volume market that sells product before it overstays its welcome and begins to spoil. I avoid markets that smell or ones where flies hover over displays. The presence of flies is a good indication that some produce has begun to rot.

What about buying organic produce? Certified organic produce is grown under strict USDA guidelines. Organic means that chemicals, herbicides, and pesticides have not been added to the soil. In addition, farmers are prohibited from using sewage-sludge–based or pesticide-based fertilizers. Organic produce cannot be genetically engineered or irradiated. Irradiation is the process of applying ionizing radiation to produce. Large-scale food manufacturers like irradiation because it extends the shelf life of food and eliminates micro-organisms and insects.

Organic produce usually costs more. When food costs are rising, this may not fit into your budget. There are some fruits and vegetables that are more important to purchase “organically. Scientists have found that some foods retain higher residue levels of pesticide after they have been harvested. These fruits and vegetables make "*The Dirty Dozen List*." This list changes from year to year, and the 2023 list follows:

The 2023 Dirty Dozen

Apples
Strawberries
Grapes
Peaches
Spinach
Green beans
Nectarines
Sweet bell and hot peppers
Blueberries
Cherries
Pears
Kale and collard and mustard greens

In addition, some sweet corn, papaya, and summer squash sold in the United States is produced from genetically modified seeds. If you are concerned about genetically modified produce, then buy organic varieties of crops.

Scientists have also found that some fruits and vegetables have low levels of pesticides after harvest. This produce is considered safer to purchase in a non-organic form and is called "*The Clean 15.*" This list changes from year to year, and the 2023 list follows:

The 2023 Clean 15

Avocados	Frozen sweet peas	Grapfruit
Sweet corn	Asparagus	Cantaloupe
Pineapples	Eggplant	Mangos
Onions	Kiwis	Cauliflower
Papayas	Cabbage	Sweet potatoes

Most supermarkets claim to have superior produce, but there are few brand names on fruits and vegetables that guarantee consistency. In addition, produce does not carry any quality assurance labeling like meat or pork, so it's important to learn to distinguish the good from the bad and the ugly.

What about heirloom fruits and vegetables? You can find heirloom varieties at your local farmer's markets, specialty food stores, and sometimes even at the supermarket. They are usually pricier than hybrids. Are they worth the extra money?

Most produce sold by your supermarket is considered hybrid. Over the years, plant breeders have manipulated the genes of fruits and vegetables by breeding them to withstand disease and pests, putting texture and flavor on the back burner. These hybrids are hardy and beautiful but lack a truly delicious taste.

Heirlooms are bred for flavor. Several years ago, growers began saving open-pollinated seed varieties, which are called heirloom seeds. These seeds have not been manipulated, meaning they reproduce without human intervention. Heirlooms are open-pollinated, meaning their flower is pollinated with pollen from another plant to create a fruit whose seeds can reproduce. Hybrids have viable seeds, but their seeds don't reproduce. To create a hybrid, growers cross-pollinate two different seed varieties and grow the seeds the mix produces.

Heirloom seeds have been selected, nurtured, and handed down from one generation to another. There are differing opinions on how old seeds must be to be classified "heirloom". Some think the seeds must be over 100 years old, others believe 50 is the magic number, while another school of thought prefers the seeds predate 1945—which marks the end of World War II and the beginning of the widespread use of hybrid seeds.

When you can find heirloom fruits or vegetables and your pocketbook can afford the extra cost, they are worth every penny. Your taste buds will be grateful.

FOUR

How to Select and Store Fresh Fruit

I am lucky my father taught me how to select ripe, delicious fruit, not only to eat out of hand but also to serve my family. Too many times, shoppers don't know how to select the "perfect fruit" … instead, putting bruised or overripe fruit or fruit that will never ripen into their shopping carts.

No more. The following are tips on what to look for when buying fruit and general guidelines on shelf life and storage once you bring them home. For fruit that should be stored in a bag, a reusable, eco-friendly storage bag is preferable. Preparation tips are included for only the more unusual varieties of fruits.

Apples

Did you know there are 2,500 varieties of apples grown in the United States and more than 7,500 grown worldwide? Apples can be grouped into four categories based upon their usage: eating (snacks and desserts), cooking (baking), crabapples (jelly), and those used for cider.

The most common apples found in supermarkets are:

Braeburn This New Zealand apple has a mottled red and yellow skin. It is aromatic, crisp, and juicy and is good for eating or baking.

Fuji The Fuji apple came to the United States from Japan. It has a tart-edged sweetness, a green to yellow under color blushed with reds and, a firm, crisp texture, with outstanding flavor. The Fuji apple holds its texture well when baked.

Gala This apple is red mottled over a yellow background. It is sweet and slightly spicy, and good for eating or using in salads.

Golden Delicious The Golden Delicious apple, with its sweet, mellow flavor, is a versatile apple. It holds its shape well when baked yet is the perfect eating apple with a tart, crisp, and juicy taste.

Granny Smith The Granny Smith apple is the number one choice for pies. It is also my favorite apple for snacking and salads. It has a freckled green skin.

Honeycrisp This apple is crisp and juicy with a balanced sweetness and acidity. It has a light green/yellow skin that is covered with a red-orange blush. The Honeycrisp is delicious to eat but also good for baking.

Jonagold This juicy, apple has a tangy, sweet flavor and is perfect for eating, cooking, or using in pies. It has a mottled red and yellow skin.

Jonathan This is a crimson apple. It has a spicy tang and is often used in making cider.

McIntosh Red The McIntosh Red has juicy, white flesh, and its skin is a mixture of both red and green coloring. It is a mainstay in making cider but is also great for eating or using in salads. It doesn't hold up well to lengthy cooking.

Minneiska SweeTango This apple, bred for eating, is a cross between the Honeycrisp and Zestar! apple. It has the crispness of a Honeycrisp apple and the juiciness of a Zestar!. Its skin is a deep red color over a yellow background.

Mutsu (also known as **Crispin**) The Mutsu apple has a sweet, honey flavor with sharp, tangy notes. Its skin is yellow green with brown tones near the stem. It is good for eating but is considered a superior baking apple.

Pink Lady (also called **Cripps Pink**) The skin of this apple has a pink blush overlayed on greenish-yellow undertones. Its flesh is firm and crisp with a tangy, sweet flavor. Pink Lady apples are good for baking as well as eating.

Red Delicious This is the number one eating apple in the United States. This heart-shaped apple is bright red with a crunchy, mildly sweet flavor.

Rome Beauty This apple was discovered in Rome, Ohio (not Italy), in 1816. The Rome Beauty is a nearly solid red apple with firm flesh and a tough, smooth skin. It is best suited for baking as it keeps its shape along with its sweet flavor.

Winesap The Winesap apple has a deep red skin, against a slightly yellow background and is somewhat oblong in shape. It is used for both eating and cooking, as it has a firm, crisp flesh and a sweet aromatic flavor. The Winesap is also used in making cider.

Zestar! This apple has a sprightly sweet-tart taste and is juicy with a light crisp texture. The Zestar! is normally red in color but, depending upon the amount of sun it receives, can have a rosy-red blush or be creamy yellow.

Selecting: When buying apples, press the skin gently. Apples should feel firm to the touch. Avoid apples that are soft or mushy or indent easily when their skin is pressed.

Never buy apples with dull skin, bruises, or punctures. Apples should have a smooth, clean, shiny skin and possess a color that is consistent with their variety. Color is the best indicator of taste. Overripe apples will be soft and lack a firm crunch.

Storing: Apples can be stored safely in the refrigerator for up to 2 weeks. Apples left at room temperature for more than 48 hours will turn soft.

Availability: Most varieties of apples are available year-round. Jonathan apples are usually available only in the fall and winter. Winesaps are available September through April or May, and Rome Beauties are available October through June or July.

Apricots

Selecting: Buy plump apricots with a golden, orange color and velvety skin. Unless blemishes break the skin, they will not affect the quality of apricots. When ripe, apricots will give to gentle pressure and smell fragrant. Soft, ripe fruit has the best flavor but needs to be eaten immediately. Avoid buying apricots that are pale yellow or greenish yellow in color or ones that are hard, shriveled, or bruised.

Storing: Ripe apricots should be stored in a reusable, paper, or plastic bag and refrigerated for 3 to 5 days. To ripen apricots, place them in a closed paper bag at room temperature. Allow them to soften for a few days.

Availability: Apricots are harvested in the spring and summer and are best in June and July.

Asian Pear

The Asian pear is firm, crunchy, and very juicy, with a lightly sweet, yet tart, taste. This fruit resembles a cross between an apple and a pear. Grown mostly in Japan, there are over 100 varieties of Asian pears. Skin colors range from greenish-russet brown, greenish yellow, to golden bronze.

Selecting: When selecting Asian pears, shop with your nose. Asian pears should have a mild pear fragrance and are best hard. Do not buy this fruit if it is wrinkled or soft. Asian pears are best eaten when their flesh is firm.

Storing: When placed in a reusable, paper, or plastic bag and refrigerated, Asian pears will keep up to 4 weeks. They will keep up to 2 weeks at room temperature.

Availability: The season for Asian pears varies according to the variety, but they are generally available from July through late October.

Bananas and Plantains

There are two kinds of bananas—the sweet banana, which we eat, and the cooking banana, also known as the plantain.

Selecting: Select plump bananas that do not feel mushy or show signs of damage. Avoid bananas with green tips; instead select fruit with yellow skin that is flecked with tiny brown spots. When buying plantains, select plump fruit. Color of skin may range from green to black at any stage in the ripening process. When ripe, plantains will be soft and have dark-brown or black skins that are transparent, rather than opaque.

Storing: Bananas should not be refrigerated. This will cause them to turn black. Store them at room temperature. Once home, this fruit will continue to ripen, turning brown when overripe. Bananas should last 4 to 5 days at home. If bananas are too green to eat, you can place them in a paper bag to accelerate the ripening process.

Availability: Both bananas and plantains can be purchased year-round.

Cooking tip: Once they have been cut, dipping bananas in a mixture of lemon juice and water will retard browning.

Blackberries

Selecting: Select berries that are plump with a blue to purplish-black color and bright, clean appearance. Blackberries should have a firm, but not hard, texture. Always check the bottom of the container for mold. Overripe berries are soft. If their hulls are still attached, this indicates they were picked too early, and they will have a tart flavor.

Storing: Blackberries should be refrigerated and used within 1 to 2 days. Do not wash berries until right before using.

Availability: The peak season for blackberries is May through August; therefore, you'll find more competitive pricing during these months. Due to the increased importation of fruit, blackberries can usually be purchased year-round.

Blueberries

Selecting: Look for deep, purple-blue to blue-black berries with a slight silver frost. Blueberries should be plump and free of moisture. The best indicator of maturity is color. Reddish berries are not ripe and therefore not as palatable, but they can still be used in cooking. Avoid green, dull, lifeless, or mushy berries. Always check for mold, especially on the bottom of the container.

Storing: Blueberries are the least fragile berry and can be stored in the refrigerator for 5 to 6 days. For best results, keep the berries dry during storage.

Availability: Blueberries grown in North America are in season spring and summer. Imported fruit is available year-round.

Cactus Pears

This pear comes from the prickly pear cactus, native to the Americas. It is sometimes called *prickly pear* or *cactus fruit.* It has a stiff, spine-covered rind and is normally eaten raw. Its flavor and color vary according to the plant's blossom. The cactus pear can taste like a strawberry, watermelon, honeydew melon, fig, or banana.

Selecting: Cactus pears should be firm, not hard. Do not purchase shriveled, soggy, or overly hard fruit. To determine if cactus pears are ripe, place them in a bowl of water. If they sink, they are ready to eat. If they float, let them ripen a few more days.

Storing: When placed in a reusable, paper, or plastic bag and refrigerated, this fruit will keep one week.

Availability: Early spring through late fall.

To eat this spiny creature: It is important to wear gloves when prepping cactus pears. Pass the pears through an open flame, then pull out the spines or simply cut them out with a knife. Once the spines have been removed, slice off both ends of the pear, cut it in half lengthwise, and peel back the skin. Try sprinkling the fruit with lemon or lime juice before eating.

Cherimoya

Sometimes called the custard apple, the cherimoya has an irregular oval shape, leathery green skin, and is covered with scales. The flesh is a creamy white color and is speckled with large, shiny black seeds. Its flesh has a soft texture, almost custard like, and a sweet mild flavor.

Selecting: Purchase this fruit when it is somewhat firm and ripen it at home. Cherimoya should feel heavy for its size. Its skin should be pale green. Avoid this fruit if it has blemishes, broken skin, brown splotches, or a fermented smell.

Storing: Store this fruit at room temperature until ripe. When ripe, the skin of a cherimoya will give to gentle pressure. When it is overripe, its skin will start to blacken.

Availability: Late November through May.

To eat cherimoya: Cut this fruit in half lengthwise and spoon out the flesh. Discard any seeds. Dipping it in lemon juice will prevent cherimoya from turning dark. It is best when served chilled.

Cherries

There are three types of cherries: sweet, sour, and sweet-sour, a cross between the sweet and sour varieties. Sweet varieties are best for eating. The *Bing* cherry, a sweet variety, is most typically found in supermarkets. *Rainier* cherries, another sweet variety, are my husband's favorite. They are delicious, although they can be a bit expensive. This cherry has a golden skin with a pinkish-red blush and a very delicate, sweet flavor. Occasionally, markets run specials on *Rainier* cherries. Sour cherries are normally used for pies, preserves, and cooking and are rarely sold in supermarkets.

Selecting: When purchasing sweet red cherries, select fruit that is plump, bright, and glossy with a deep red to purple color. Bright green stems are a sign of freshness. Cherries have past their prime if they are soft, dull, or shriveled. Avoid buying fruit that has brown bruised spots.

Rainier cherries are best when they are firm and lack blemishes. Sour cherries should be firm, not hard, and have even color.

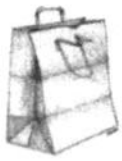

Storing: Cherries are perishable and should be refrigerated immediately when you get home from the market. This fruit is best when eaten within 1 to 2 days of purchase. Always wash your cherries just before eating. Typically, cherries are sold in plastic bags. I keep them in the same packaging and refrigerate them once I arrive home.

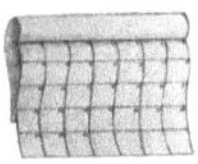

Availability: Cherry season runs May through August.

Clementines

Clementines, often sold under the brand names *Cuties*® or *Halos*®, are a hybrid of the mandarin orange. Like the mandarin, they are smaller than navel oranges, have few to no seeds, and a sweet flavor. Their thin, soft skin is easy to peel.

Selecting: Clementines are sold in crates or mesh bags. Select the smaller fruit (2 to 3-inches in diameter). Smaller clementines will have more flavor. Select clementines with a uniform bright orange color. Feel inside the mesh bag. Clementines should feel heavy for their size and firm, not hard. Their skin should feel loose. Avoid this fruit if it has blemishes, dull spots, or green near the stem end. Shop with your nose. Ripe clementines will have a lovely citrus aroma.

Storing: When stored in the refrigerator, clementines should last 2 to 3 weeks.

Availability: November to February.

Coconuts

Coconuts are normally shipped by boat. Although they have a 4-month shelf life, it can take several months for them to reach the supermarket. Therefore, they should be inspected carefully before purchase. Coconuts sold in markets have their outer shell removed, exposing the inner nut, a woody-brown shell, covered with coarse brown fibers.

Selecting: When selecting a coconut, pick one that feels heavy for its size. Shop with your ears. When you shake a ripe coconut, you can hear the juice splash inside. All coconuts have three eyes. Avoid coconuts with cracks or mold around the eyes. There should be no liquid oozing from this area. Avoid coconuts with white spots around the eyes. Patchy stains on the surface of the coconut indicate it may have a fractured shell that has allowed some of its liquid to escape.

If you have a recipe calling for *young green coconut,* you may be more likely to find one in Asian markets. A young green coconut has been harvested before it has turned brown and has fully ripened. Its liquid will be very sweet and its meat very tender. To select the best green coconut, pick one that is round. Green coconuts tend to become oblong as they age.

Storing: An unopened coconut will keep up to 4 months at room temperature; however, since it can take several months to reach your supermarket, I don't like to keep a coconut more than one month. If you cut the coconut open, fresh coconut chunks or grated coconut should be stored in airtight containers in the refrigerator for no more than 4 days or frozen and kept up to 6 months.

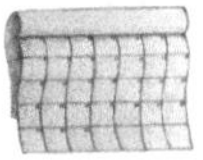

Availability: The peak season for coconuts is September through April, although they are available year-round in markets.

To open up this odd nut: The shell of the coconut has three eyes. Find the softest eye and poke it open with an ice pick or other sharp instrument. Drain out the coconut liquid into a bowl. Using a hammer, tap the coconut on its "equator" line until it cracks open, and the two halves can be pulled apart. When the shell pops away, use a flexible spatula to separate the white flesh from the shell. You can peel off the dark skin if you prefer. Cut the coconut meat into desired sizes with a sharp knife.

Cranberries

Selecting: Look for brightly colored cranberries; the deeper the color, the less bitter the berry. Supermarkets normally sell cranberries in plastic bags, but avoid packages that contain mushy, wet cranberries or bags that are ripped or damaged.

Storing: Cranberries can be stored up to 1 month when refrigerated.

Availability: Peak season for cranberries is November, but they are available September through January.

Currants and Gooseberries

Currants are small fresh berries that are red, white, gold, or black in color. Red currants are used in making jelly and glazes. White currants have a low acidity and are both eaten and used in cooking. Black currants have a harsh taste and are normally cooked before eating. Gooseberries are quite tart and resemble small, elongated green grapes covered with stripes. They are popular in Europe.

Selecting: Currants and gooseberries should be firm and brightly colored with green stems. Avoid shriveled or leaky currants with brown stems.

Storing: Currants will only keep 1 or 2 days in the refrigerator.

Availability: Currants are available in the summer. New Zealand gooseberries are in season from October through December. Oregon gooseberries are in season from July to August.

Dates

Dates are soft, semi-dry, or dry. Soft dates are moist, low in sugar, and have a soft flesh. Semi-dry dates are high in sugar, contain a moderate amount of moisture, and have firm flesh. Dry dates are high in sugar and have a hard, dry flesh.

Selecting: Do not buy shriveled dates or ones with mold or sugar crystals on their skin. Look for plump, soft fruit with smooth, shiny skin.

Storing: When placed in a reusable, paper, or plastic bag and refrigerated, fresh dates will keep up to 2 weeks. Store dates in an airtight container in a cool, dry place. They should keep for about 6 months.

Availability: Year-round, but peak season is late fall.

Figs

Figs are a very delicate fruit with protruding stems. This fruit must be harvested at its peak because it will not ripen after it is picked. Figs bruise and damage easily, have a short season, and are difficult to transport, making them a bit pricey.

Selecting: Buy only firm fruit whose stems are intact. The quality of this fruit will not be compromised if the skin around the stem is slightly shriveled or if its base is slightly torn or moist. Do not buy bruised figs. Overly green figs are not ripe.

Storing: This fruit will keep in the refrigerator for 2 days. Figs should be brought to room temperature before eating.

Availability: Black Mission: May through November. Brown Turkey: May through December. Calimyrna: July and August. Kadota: May through October.

Grapes

Grapes are green, red, or blue-black in color and can either contain seeds or be seedless. Supermarkets normally carry the *Thompson* seedless green grapes. This grape has a delicate, sweet flavor with tart undertones. Red grapes are sweet, with a spicy edge. Varieties include the *Flame seedless, Cardinal, Emperor, Red Globe,* and *Tokay.* Blue-black grapes have a richer flavor and a sweet tartness.

Selecting: Color is the best measure of flavor. Select full-colored fruit. Grapes should be plump, fragrant, and firmly attached to their stems. Avoid packages with shriveled grapes that have fallen off their stems. Check the point where the grape attaches to its stem and avoid grapes that are soft or brown around the stem.

Storing: Supermarkets normally package grapes in vented plastic bags. Grapes will keep up to 1 week when refrigerated in this type of packaging.

Availability: Your market will carry grapes year-round, although different varieties of grapes peak at different times.

Grapefruit

Grapefruits either have a thick or thin peel. This variation is caused by differences in the climate where the fruit is produced and is a measure of taste. A low-humidity climate like Arizona will produce grapefruits with a thick peel, a blemish-free skin, and a more acidic flavor. Grapefruits grown in a tropical climate, including Florida, will have a thin peel, a slightly blemished skin, and a sweeter taste. There are two main varieties of grapefruit—the *Duncan* and *Marsh*. The Duncan has a light yellow rind and pale, yellow, juicy flesh. Marsh grapefruits are sweeter and less acidic. The *Marsh Ruby* is the ancestor of all pink grapefruit grown today. The *Star Ruby* has a deep rosy flesh and a tangy, sweet flavor.

Selecting: Select grapefruit that are shiny and seem heavy for their size: the heavier the fruit, the juicier it will be. This fruit should be firm. Rough skin or skin that does not "give" when pressed is an indication of dry fruit. Skin color is a gauge of flesh color: the more blush of pink or red to the skin, the deeper the color of the fruit.

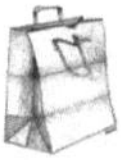

Storing: Grapefruits can be stored for up to 2 weeks in the refrigerator.

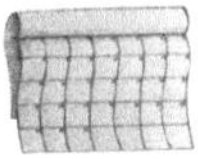

Availability: Year-round.

Guava

Guavas vary in appearance. This fruit can be round or pear-shaped and will have either a bumpy or smooth green or yellowish rind. Its flesh is pink to red, white, or yellow. Pear-shaped, white fruits are considered superior.

Selecting: Fruit should feel tender and "give" to gentle pressure when pressed. Never buy spotted, mushy, or very green guavas. Look for skins that have some yellow color but are without spots. Shop with your nose. Guavas should smell sweet and flowery, yet slightly musky.

Storing: Store at room temperature until soft, then transfer to a reusable, paper, or plastic bag and refrigerate. Guavas will last 2 days once ripe.

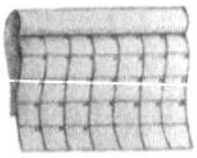

Availability: June to August and November to March.

To eat: Cut guavas in half crosswise and scoop out the flesh with a spoon.

Jackfruit

Jackfruit is the largest fruit in the world, weighing as much as 100 pounds, so you may not find it whole in the produce department. Jackfruit has a hard, bumpy skin that is green or yellow in color. Its interior contains edible, fleshy, yellow bulbs. When ripe, the bulbs have a sweet, tropical, fruit flavor and a texture and color similar to pineapple. Ripe jackfruit can be eaten raw or used in desserts. When unripe, jackfruit has a neutral taste and a stringy, meaty texture. It absorbs flavors well and is a good meat substitute. It is popular as a vegan option for barbecued pulled pork. You can purchase ripe jackfruit in bite-size pieces or bulbs in plastic-wrapped styrofoam trays. You will find raw jackfruit packed in brine, water, or syrup in cans or pouches in the canned fruit section of the supermarket and often in the frozen foods section. If you are buying jackfruit as a meat substitute, look for the words "young" or "packed in brine" on the label.

Selecting: When buying whole jackfruit, look for ones with yellowish green skin, brown patches, and a fragrant scent. Avoid dark green fruit. If buying bulbs packed in styrofoam trays, select fruit that looks tender and soft with a vibrant yellow color and no dark patches.

Storing: Ripen jackfruit at room temperature. When ripe, it will yield slightly to gentle pressure. When wrapped tightly in plastic wrap or placed in an airtight container and refrigerated, cut jackfruit will keep up to 7 days. Frozen jackfruit will keep for up to 1 month.

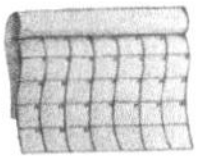

Availability: Year-round, peaking August to September.

To cut open a jackfruit: Place newspaper on the counter for an easier clean up. Oil a large chef's knife. Slice the fruit in half. Using a paper towel, clean up any sap that oozes out. Using the sharp knife, cut each half into halves and remove the thick middle stem. Oil your hands and pull out the yellow colored fruit pods and remove the white fibers and tip. Using a small paring knife, split pods lengthwise and remove the seed and rubbery seed skin.

Kiwifruit

Kiwifruit is a small, oblong fruit with thin, hairy brown skin. Its flesh is green or yellow and dotted with tiny black seeds. The taste of kiwifruit is a mixture of strawberry and melon. Gold kiwifruit has thin, smooth-brown skin and bright yellow flesh. Although the hairy, brown skin of a kiwifruit is edible, it is normally peeled away before eating.

Selecting: Kiwifruit should feel firm to the touch, not soft or mushy. Avoid fruit with soft spots or bruises. Test for ripeness by pressing gently on the skin. It will yield slightly to pressure when ripe.

Storing: Kiwifruit can be stored in the refrigerator for a few days. To ripen it, place in a paper bag and leave it at room temperature.

Availability: If imported, kiwifruit is available year-round.

To eat: Peel the hairy skin off with a sharp paring knife and cut the fruit into slices, wedges, or cubes.

Kumquats

Kumquats are a tiny orange citrus fruit with an oblong or round shape. Because of their thin skin, kumquats are normally eaten whole, rind and all.

Selecting: Buy firm, glossy fruit, with leaves still attached to the stem. Pass up fruit that is bruised, wet, or shriveled.

Storing: Kumquats will last a few days stored at room temperature. If they are placed in a reusable, paper, or plastic bag, they will keep for 2 weeks in the refrigerator.

Availability: December through June.

Hint for eating: Gently squeeze and massage the skin to blend the flavors of the rind and the flesh before eating.

Lemons

The most common variety of lemon sold in the United States is the *Eureka*. It has few seeds, juicy pulp, and a high acid content. We often see Meyer lemons in specialty food stores. *Meyer* lemons are a cross between a regular lemon and a tangerine. They are rounder than other lemons and have yellow-orange rinds when ripe.

Selecting: Lemons should be plump and feel heavy for their size. Select bright, shiny fruit. If the rind is an orange-yellow color, it means the lemon was picked when fully ripe. Pass up shriveled, hard-skinned, soft, or spongy fruit. Lemons with a greenish rind are not as juicy. Lemons that do not give when pressed gently will not be as juicy.

Storing: Lemons will keep up to 2 weeks if placed in a reusable, paper, or plastic bag and refrigerated.

Availability: Year-round. The peak season is April through July. Meyer lemons: November through January.

Limes

There are three varieties of limes—the *Key* lime, the *Persian* lime, and the *sweet* lime. The Key lime is small and full of seeds with a thin, splotchy, yellow-green rind. It is aromatic and juicy, with a strong acidic taste. The Persian lime is larger and almost always seedless. It has a thicker "lime-green" rind. The sweet lime has little acidity and is popular in the Middle East and India.

Selecting: Persian limes should feel heavy for their size but not hard when squeezed. Select smooth-skinned, brightly colored fruit that is not shriveled. Brown spots on the rind of Persian limes will not affect the flavor. Key limes should be light yellow with a fine-grained skin. Pass up fruit that is moldy or blotchy. Brown spots on the rind of Key limes will affect their quality. Limes that do not give when pressed gently will not be as juicy.

Storing: Place limes in a reusable, paper, or plastic bag. Persian limes will keep in the refrigerator for 10 days, Key limes for 5 days.

Availability: Persian limes—year-round. Key limes —June through August.

Lychee Nuts

The lychee nut is a most interesting creature. It is a small, round fruit with a tough, knobby shell and a perfume-like fragrance of roses and musk. It is a deep–red when picked but turns a rosy brown within a few days. It has clear or white pulp, and its jelly-like flesh will pop out of its shell much like a hard-boiled egg.

Selecting: Do not buy lychee nuts that are dried out. Look for nuts with a deep rose color and a thin skin.

Storing: Unshelled, they will keep for several weeks in the refrigerator.

Availability: June to August.

To eat this interesting fruit: Slice open the shell with a paring knife. Gently squeeze the skin until it opens, slide the inner flesh out, and remove its hard seed by cutting the fruit open.

Mangoes

Throughout the year you will find different varieties of mangoes in your supermarket. This is because their peak seasons vary. The *Honey* mango has a yellow peel. The *Francis* has bright yellow skin with green overtones. *Haden* mangoes have bright red skin with green and yellow overtones with small white dots. The *Keitt* has dark to medium green skin and will sometimes possess a pink blush. *Kent* mangoes have a dark green skin and will often possess a dark red blush. A dark red blush covers most of the skin of a *Tommy Atkins*, but it will have green and orange-yellow accents. The flesh of mangoes is golden in color; however, the flesh of the Francis mango will be more orange, and the Kent will be more yellow.

Selecting: Mangoes should feel heavy for their size and have firm, unblemished skin. Shop with your sense of smell. Hold the mango to your nose, stem end up, and smell the fruit. If it smells sweet and feels slightly soft to the touch, it is ready to eat. If it smells sour or a bit like alcohol, it has fermented and is not palatable. Also, check the area surrounding the stem. It should be plump and round. A few brown speckles are normal but avoid spotted or shriveled fruit.

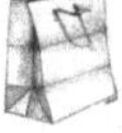

Storing: Most supermarkets sell hard mangoes, and you must ripen them before eating. Therefore, it is a good idea to plan ahead when buying mangoes to allow the fruit time to properly ripen. Leave the fruit at room temperature until the skin yields to pressure but does not feel mushy. Once ripened, mangoes will keep in the refrigerator for 4 days.

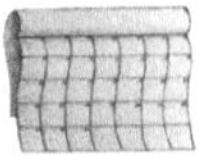

Availability: In season, May to September, but available year-round.

To eat: The mango is a pitted fruit. Slice off the top and bottom of the mango, exposing the pit, which is large. Place the mango upright on a cutting board and slice the skin off in a downward motion, parallel with the pit. Remove sections of the flesh by cutting the fruit into desired sizes. The pit is a real draw back in this fruit and must be carefully carved out with a sharp knife.

Melons

Selecting: As a general rule, select melons that give when pressed gently on the blossom end. Ripe melons should have a sweet smell and feel heavy for their size. Melons with lumps or soft spots are past their prime. Do not buy melons that are rock-hard or lopsided. Lopsided melons were picked too early. When buying hard melons, shop with your ears. Knock on melons with your knuckle. If they are ripe, hard melons will sound hollow. When buying specialty melon varieties, follow these general rules. To determine ripeness, some melons have specific criteria that I've identified below.

Cantaloupe When selecting a cantaloupe, look for one that is completely covered with a thick straw-colored netting. There should be no trace of the stem. Use your sense of smell. When ripe, cantaloupes will emit a slight cantaloupe fragrance. They will, also, yield to slight pressure on the blossom end, which is the end opposite the stem.

Honeydew A good honeydew melon should weigh at least 5 pounds and have a waxy, cream-colored rind. Honeydew melons smell like honey.

The rind of a ripe honeydew melon will become smooth and waxy, and it should have a creamy yellow color. If you press on the bottom (the end opposite to the stem) of a ripe honeydew melon, it should feel soft or slightly springy.

Watermelon My father taught me to thump a watermelon with my knuckle. If it sounds hollow, it's ripe. Characteristics to look for are a symmetrical, dull-colored body, and a slightly flat, yellowish, almost butter-colored underbelly. If the underbelly is white, the watermelon will likely be underripe. If it is bright yellow, it will be overripe. It should not have flat sides.

Crenshaw Crenshaw melons should have a golden-yellow rind. When ripe, they give off a spicy fragrance and have springy, but not mushy skin. A Crenshaw melon is softer than other melons, and, therefore, requires gentler handling.

Hami and **Canary** Ripe Hami and Canary melons should have a bright yellow-colored rind with no green remaining. A Canary melon should weigh 4 to 5 pounds.

Galia The skin of a Galia melon should have a sweet aroma and it should feel firm all over when pressed gently.

Santa Claus The Santa Claus melon has thick skin, so it won't have a melon aroma when ripe. When pressed gently, the end of the melon should be slightly soft. The riper the melon, the yellower the skin.

Persian When ripe, the rind on a Persian melon should be pale green with a delicate netting.

Storing: Melons should be stored at room temperature until fully ripe. Once the fruit has matured, it can be stored in the refrigerator for up to 5 days. Once you cut your melon, it should be placed in an airtight container or wrapped tightly with plastic, as it can absorb odors from other foods. Cut melon will keep 3 days in the refrigerator.

Availability: Cantaloupes: Year-round, with peak season June through November. Crenshaws: July through October. Watermelons: May through September. Honeydew: Year-round, with peak season June through October. Hami: Late June to November. Canary: Summer through mid-Fall. Galia: May through August. Santa Claus: Late Spring through Fall. Persian: Late June to November.

Oranges

The *Valencia* orange is very sweet with low acidity and is good for juicing. In the US the *Navel* orange is considered the best orange for eating. It is more bitter than the Valencia and has a thicker peel. The *Cara Cara,* often called "pink navel" or "red navel", is an extremely sweet orange with a touch of berry flavor. The *Blood Orange* has a deep red flesh, with a touch of raspberry flavor and is less sweet than the Cara Cara.

Selecting: Buy oranges that feel heavy for their size and have an even shape. Oranges with a thinner skin will be juicier than ones with a thick skin, and small- to medium-sized fruit will be sweeter than larger specimens. Avoid oranges with large bruises or soft spots or ones that feel spongy. Sometimes oranges will turn green. This occurs when there are blossoms on the tree when the fruit is picked and is called regreening. Sometimes these "green" oranges are sweeter because they have overripened.

Storing: Oranges can be stored in the refrigerator or at room temperature but will be juicier when stored at room temperature.

Availability: Year-round.

Papayas

There are two types of papayas, *Hawaiian* and *Mexican*. The Hawaiian variety weighs about one pound, is shaped like a pear, and has yellow skin when ripe. Its fruit is bright orange or pink, and its center is filled with black, edible seeds. The Mexican variety can weigh up to 10 pounds, has green skin, and salmon-red to bright orange flesh.

Selecting: Hawaiian papayas should have a warm, yellow color with smooth, unblemished skin. Shop with your nose. Papayas will have little aroma. When ripe, the neck of the fruit will be somewhat green. Mexican papayas stay green even when ripe. Select fruit that has "give" when pressed. Do not buy hard or shriveled papayas or ones that are overly soft or smell fermented. Dark spots on the skin of papayas often penetrate the fruit and spoil the flavor. If your supermarket sells already-cut papayas, choose one with a deep-salmon or red flesh. Pale red or pinkish pulp indicates under-ripe fruit.

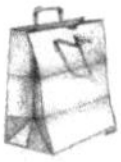

Storing: To ripen a papaya quickly, place it in a paper bag with a banana and let it sit at room temperature. Once ripe, this fruit should be placed in either a reusable, paper, or plastic bag before refrigerating. It will keep 3 days.

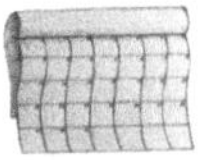

Availability: Year-round.

To eat: Cut the papaya in half, lengthwise, scoop out the small black seeds, and eat the flesh with a spoon. Papaya can be peeled with a vegetable peeler. Although the seeds are edible, they are usually discarded.

Passion Fruit

Similar in size to an egg, passion fruit has a hard shell that is smooth and waxy. It is either purple or yellow and has a yellowish, jelly-like pulp. Its flavor is slightly musky with a sweet-tart to very tart taste.

Selecting: Look for fruit that is large, plump, fragrant, and feels heavy for its size. Ripe passion fruit will have a deep purple, dimpled shell. If you find mold on the shell, simply wipe it off. Mold will not affect the quality of this fruit. Very hard passion fruit is not ripe.

Storing: If your passion fruit has smooth skin, it needs to ripen at room temperature. Turn the fruit over occasionally as it ripens. Once ripe, it will keep 5 days in the refrigerator.

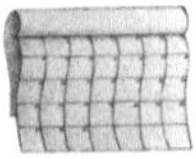

Availability: Florida fruit: year-round. New Zealand fruit: February to July. California fruit: July to March.

To eat: Slice the fruit in half and spoon out the pulp.

Peaches and Nectarines

Peaches and nectarines are very similar. Peaches have a fuzzy skin, and the skin of nectarines is smooth. They are classified as either *clingstone, freestone,* or *semi-freestone,* (also known as *semi-clingstone*).

Clingstone varieties have flesh that is firmly attached to the stone or pit. Their yellow and bright red flesh is sweeter and juicier than freestones. The flesh of freestone varieties separates easily from the stone. Freestone peaches can have a white or yellow flesh, are larger than clingstones, and not as sweet. The semi-freestone is a hybrid of the clingstone and freestone. Although not as juicy as a clingstone, its flesh is easier to remove from the pit. Peaches with yellow or orange flesh have a tangy, sweet flavor. White fleshed peached are higher in sugar content and less tart.

The best eating peach is considered the *Elberta. Cresthaven, Glohaven,* or *Red Haven.* Freestone peaches are good for baking. If you are going to can peaches, use a freestone variety.

Nectarines are peaches without the fuzz. They are classified as either freestone or clingstone, can have white or yellow flesh, and a sweet or tart taste. Popular nectarine varieties are: *Arctic Rose, Flaming Red, Diamond Ray, Fantasia, Karla Rose.*

Selecting: Peaches should have a well-defined crease, a sweet fragrance, and be soft to the touch, not mushy. Do not buy peaches that have "green shoulders" around the stem end. This is an indication the peach was picked prematurely. Peaches with large, flattened bruises will not ripen well. If the skin of the fruit is shriveled at the stem end or has turned a red-brown color, the peach is over ripe. Nectarines should be plump, have a smooth, unblemished skin, and a slight softening along the crease. Do not buy hard, dull, or shriveled nectarines.

Storing: To ripen peaches, place them in a cool place, with their stem end down. If the peaches give slightly when pressed and are becoming fragrant, they are ready to eat. If you place nectarines in a paper bag, they will ripen in about a day. Handle peaches and nectarines gently as any bruising will show. Once ripe, these fruits will keep in the refrigerator for 3 to 5 days.

Availability: North American fruit is available spring and summer. Imported fruit is available year-round.

Pears

There are two types of pears—the granular, hard winter pears used for poaching and the buttery, soft pears that we eat. Pears come in nearly 1,000 varieties. This fruit does not ripen well on trees and is, therefore, picked in a fully mature state, but unripened condition.

Anjou This pear is egg-shaped with pale-green or red skin. It has firm, juicy flesh and a sweet, mellow flavor. Anjou pears do not change colors as they ripen. They can be used for both cooking and eating.

Bartlett The majority of pears grown in the United States are Bartlett pears. The Bartlett is considered to be one of the better eating pears. It has a smooth texture and juicy flesh, and its green skin turns yellow as it ripens. A majority of the Bartlett harvest is canned.

Bosc The Bosc pear has yellow-brown skin. It has crisp, creamy white flesh that tastes sweet, yet spicy. Bosc pears have fat bottoms and long, tapering necks that come to a point. They do not change colors as they ripen and are ideal for both baking and cooking.

Comice Known as the "Queen of Pears," the Comice is considered the best eating pear. This French variety is a fat pear with yellowish-green skin and a russet to red blush. Its flesh has a buttery, sweet taste and a fruity fragrance.

Selecting: Pears should be firm and have good color for their variety. Do not buy pears that have bruises or blemishes. At time of purchase, the skin on pears should be bright, shiny, and tight.

Storing: To ripen, place them end down in a cool place. To speed up the ripening process, place pears along with an apple or banana, in a paper bag that has a few punctures. Pears will be fragrant when ripe, and the flesh near the stem will yield to gentle pressure. Also, as a pear ripens, its flesh will become matte and may contain a few brown spots. Once ripe, pears can be stored for 2 to 3 days in the refrigerator.

Availability: Anjou and Bosc: fall, winter, and spring. Bartlett and Comice: fall and winter.

Persimmons

The persimmon is grown in America, Japan, and Israel. All varieties have an orangish skin and four papery leaves called the calyx that sit on its top. As the national fruit of Japan, persimmons are traditionally eaten on Japanese New Year. Its name in Latin means "food of the gods".

Common Japanese varieties are the *Hachiya* and the *Fuyu.* Hachiya persimmons are heart-shaped with a creamy, sweet flavor and apricot-like flesh. They have a sharper taste than other varieties. Because it is quite fragile, Hachiya fruit is wrapped in tissue and packed in wooden boxes when shipped. The Fuyu fruit is shaped like a tomato and eaten like an apple. It has a sweet, slightly spicy taste. The persimmon fruit grown in Israel is called the *Sharon fruit*. It has a square shape and an orange-tan color. The Sharon fruit is both seedless and coreless with sweet flesh.

Selecting: Look for bright red-orange fruit that is plump and glossy. Yellow patches on persimmons are an indication they are not ripe. Because Hachiya persimmons are so delicate, they are shipped hard and should be ripened at home. Fuyu persimmons should be purchased firm and may need only a bit of ripening.

Storing: Hachiya fruit can be stored up to 1 month at home before ripening. To ripen, place at room temperature until soft. This could take up to 1 week. Fuyu fruit may need only a bit of ripening or may be ready to eat when purchased. Once ripe, persimmons have a short shelf life, so eat immediately. To ripen Sharon fruit, place at room temperature for 48 hours. Once ripe, the Sharon fruit may last up to 10 days refrigerated.

Availability: California fruit – October to December, with peak season in mid-October. Sharon fruit – late November to mid-February.

To eat: Wash the fruit and cut it in half with a knife. Remove the core and discard the seeds and the calyx. The skin is edible.

Pineapples

The pineapple is a large fruit with a crown of spiny leaves. It has a tough, waxy rind that is either dark-green, yellow, orange-yellow, or reddish when the fruit ripens. The flesh of pineapples ranges from white to yellow depending upon their variety. Pineapples are picked ripe because once they are off the tree, their starch will not turn to sugar.

Selecting: Select pineapples that are plump. This fruit should seem heavy for its size, and its outer skin should feel slightly soft to the touch. Leaves on the crown should be fresh, with a deep green color. Pineapples with dry, brown leaves or a dull, yellow appearance will be more acidic to the palate. My father taught me to pull gently on the leaves. If the leaves can be removed easily with gentle pressure, the pineapple is ripe.

Shop with your nose. The stem end of fresh pineapples will have a sweet aroma. Highly colored pineapples will have a sweeter taste because they were picked ripe. Avoid bruised, discolored pineapples with soft spots, an unpleasant odor, or dark, watery eyes. The eyes of a pineapple should be flat and almost hollow.

Storing: If you buy your pineapple chilled, keep it refrigerated. If it was at room temperature at the time of purchase, keep it at room temperature. Pineapples ferment quickly, so they should be kept in a cool place out of direct sunlight. Once you cut your pineapple, place the pieces in an airtight container or wrap them tightly in plastic wrap. Cut pineapple stored in an airtight container will keep 3 days in the refrigerator.

Availability: Year-round. Peak season is March to June.

To eat: Cut off the top and bottom with a large, sharp knife. Slice off the skin from the top downward. I prefer to remove the eyes of the pineapple with a small paring knife. Cut in a circular motion around the eye and pry it out. Cut the fruit into four wedges and remove the core.

Plums

Plums can be as small as a cherry or as large as a baseball with a round, elongated, or heart shape. A good ripe plum has a sweet-tart taste. The skin of this fruit can be green, yellow, red, blue, purple, or almost black depending upon its variety. Most varieties of plums have a yellow, golden, or amber flesh, although a few have a red tone.

Selecting: Plums should have good color and feel firm to the touch. Do not buy fruit that is too soft or too hard and avoid plums with cracks or blemishes.

Storing: Ripen at room temperature. The skin of a plum will lose its shine when it is ready to eat. Once ripened, plums will keep 4 to 5 days in the refrigerator.

Availability: California plums: June through September. Chilean plums: January through March.

Pomegranates

A pomegranate is a round fruit, 2½ to 5 inches in diameter. It has a hard, pink, or crimson skin and is topped with a calyx. Just inside this unusual fruit is a white, spongy pith that surrounds a thin membrane. Inside the membrane are pods of ruby-red kernels that contain translucent, edible, crimson seeds. The pomegranate's many tiny seeds have made it the symbol of fertility legends all around the world.

Selecting: Pomegranates should be firm to the touch and feel heavy for their size. Shop with your ears. To determine ripeness, tap the fruit. If it makes a metallic sound, it is ripe. Fruit that is overripe will have cracks in its skin. Do not buy bruised, shriveled, dull, or overly hard pomegranates. Plan to buy this fruit ahead as pomegranates become juicier and have more flavor over time.

Storing: Unopened, this fruit will keep at room temperature for 2 to 3 weeks or up to 1 month in the refrigerator.

Availability: August to December.

To eat: Cut off the crown and scoop out some of the white core with a spoon. With a knife, cut the outer rind, dividing the fruit into quarters. Place your thumb down the center of the core and pull the four sections apart. Remove the white pith and discard. Turn the skin of the pomegranate inside out and pop the seeds out. To remove any remaining white pith from the seeds, place the quartered sections into a bowl of cold water. The pith will float to the top, and the seeds will sink to the bottom.

Pomelo

The pomelo is an Asian citrus fruit and considered to be the ancestor of the grapefruit. Shaped like a tear drop, it has a thick pale rind and green or yellow flesh. Pomelos can be quite large—sometimes as big as a basketball. The pomelo is firmer and less juicy than grapefruit.

Selecting: Select pomelos that feel heavy for their size. Shop with your nose. Rub the skin with your finger. A ripe pomelo will emit a grassy, floral fragrance. Avoid this fruit if its skin is blemished or puckered.

Storing: When refrigerated, pomelos will keep up to 2 weeks.

Availability: December to February.

Raspberries

A raspberry consists of a cluster of cells called drupelets that look like tiny beads. There are three main types of raspberries: *red, golden,* and *black*. Red raspberries thrive in cool, marine climates. Golden raspberries taste a bit like apricot. Black raspberries are purplish black and have small seeds and a hollow core.

Selecting: Select berries that are full and round with a soft, hazy gloss. Always look at the bottom of the container when buying raspberries. A stained, moldy bottom is a sign of decay. Avoid raspberries that have dents or bruises or ones that have broken apart. Raspberries will turn quickly, so it is best to use them the day of purchase.

Storing: Raspberries are very delicate and must be refrigerated. Wash raspberries just before serving, as water speeds their decay. This fruit will keep for 1 to 2 days refrigerated.

Availability: Red raspberries – Year-round, peaking June to early September; Golden raspberries – June to October; Black raspberries – season in July.

Star Fruit

The star fruit is an oval fruit with five prominent ribs. It has a yellow, waxy skin and yellow, translucent flesh. It gets its name from the five-pointed star that is exposed when it is cut open. This greenish-yellow fruit is about 2½ to 5 inches in length, turns a dark-yellow color when ripe, and its ribs will have brownish edges. There are two types of star fruit: sweet and tart. The tart fruit is smaller and has a lemony taste. It is mainly used in cooking. The sweet fruit is larger with thicker, fleshier ribs. Star fruit may or may not contain seeds.

Selecting: Star fruit should be large, plump, and firm with shiny skin. A general rule of thumb to follow when selecting this fruit is that the more yellow its color, the sweeter its flesh. Avoid fruits with green skin or brown spots.

Storing: Place star fruit in a covered container and keep at room temperature for 2 days to ripen. When the fruit is a solid golden yellow, it will be ready to eat. Star fruit will keep 1 week in the refrigerator.

Availability: Sweet star fruits: summer to late winter. Tart star fruits: late summer to midwinter.

To eat: Slice off the ends of the fruit and discard. If the outer edges of the ribs are too brown, they will be tough and bitter. Cut any overly brown edges off the ribs. Slice the star fruit crosswise and pick out any seeds.

Strawberries

Selecting: Strawberries should be plump with a bright red color. Their caps should be green and look fresh. Avoid fruit with limp or spoiled caps. The size of a strawberry is not an indication of flavor. Small or large strawberries can be sweet and juicy. Do not buy strawberries with white or green splotches or mold. Moisture speeds decay so don't buy fruit with excess moisture. Always check the quality of the fruit from the bottom of the container as well.

Storing: When you bring this fruit home, it is a good idea to pick through the strawberries and discard any bruised or damaged berries. Cover and refrigerate the strawberries by placing them in a reusable, paper, or plastic bag or by lightly wrapping them in plastic. Do not wash them until just before eating.

Availability: Year-round. Peak season for strawberries is spring through summer.

Tangerines, Tangelos, and Tangors

Tangerines are orange-colored citrus fruits with a loose skin that can be easily separated from the fruit. Tangerines contain more water and less sugar than oranges and are less acidic and darker in color. Tangelos are a hybrid of grapefruits and tangerines and are known for their juiciness and mildly sweet flavor. Tangors are a cross between tangerines and oranges with a flavor more like oranges.

Selecting: Tangerines should fill their skin. You can count on a high-quality fruit when tangerines are sold with their stems and leaves on. Do not buy fruit with soft or dented spots or fruit that feels hollow. Tangelos should feel heavy for their size. A ripe tangelo has smooth skin and feels firm or slightly soft.

Storing: When placed in a reusable, paper, or plastic bag and stored in the refrigerator, these fruit will keep for 1 week.

Availability: Tangerines: winter through early spring. Tangelos: winter. Tangor: January through March.

Freezing Fruits

Most fruits can be frozen, though the texture of some fruits may be softer and mushier when thawed than when they are fresh. These fruits are good in smoothies or used in cooking. Follow my guidelines on selecting the freshest fruit at its peak, and freeze only ripe fruit. Freezing does not sterilize food, but the cold will retard the growth of microorganisms.

Buy high-quality freezer bags that seal tightly. Choose the size of bag that is appropriate for the amount of fruit you wish to freeze. If you are freezing individual portions, consider placing smaller bags into a larger bag. This will help prevent freezer burn.

When you freeze fruit, think about how you will use it. Portion the fruit into serving sizes and package it accordingly. If you plan to freeze strawberries for a pie, core, hull, and slice the strawberries according to the recipe you will follow. If you plan to freeze fruit for smoothies, make the slices or chunks about 1-inch thick.

1. *Wash fruit and discard any part that is poor quality.* After washing, lay the fruit out in a single layer, pat gently with paper or kitchen towels, and let it dry thoroughly before freezing.

2. *Prep the fruit.* Preparations for specific fruits follow.

Apples: Peel, core, and slice.

Apricots: Halve and pit. Peel and slice if desired. If you leave the skin on, place whole apricots in boiling water for ½ minute. This keeps the skin from becoming tough when it has been frozen.

Asian pears: Core, peel if desired, and slice.

Bananas: Peel and slice bananas into ½-inch thick pieces.

Blackberries: Freeze whole.

Blueberries: Freeze whole.

Cactus pear: Remove the spikes and peel. Freeze whole.

Cherimoya: Purée before freezing.

Cherries, sweet or sour: Pit cherries. Freeze whole.

Citrus (grapefruit, pomelos, tangerines, oranges): Peel fruits and divide the fruit into sections, removing the membrane and seeds.

Citrus (clementines, tangelos, and tangors): Peel and section into quarters.

Citrus (lemons and limes): Cut into wedges no larger than one fourth of the fruit or into ¼-inch slices.

Coconuts: Remove the brown husk, drain out the liquid, and cut the flesh into 1-inch chunks or slices.

Cranberries: Freeze whole.

Currants and **Gooseberries:** Remove the stem and freeze whole.

Figs: Freeze whole. Peel if desired.

Grapes: Stem grapes. Leave seedless grapes whole. Table grapes should be cut in half and seeded.

Guavas: Peel and remove the seeds. Cut into chunks or slices. Best frozen in syrup.

Jackfruit: Freeze bite-size bulbs.

Kiwifruit: Peel and slice.

Kumquats: Best frozen whole in syrup.

Lychee nuts: Freeze whole, unpeeled.

Mangoes: Peel, remove the seed, and cut into slices.

Melons (cantaloupe, honeydew, or watermelon): Remove the rind and seeds of cantaloupe and melons and cut them into slices, cubes, or balls.

Papayas: Peel, remove the seed, and slice or cut into chunks.

Passion fruit: Cut passion fruit in half and scoop out the flesh into a bowl. Transfer the flesh to ice cube trays and freeze. Once cubes are solid, transfer to freezer bags.

Peaches and **nectarines:** Pit, peel, and slice.

Pears: Peel, core, and slice.

Persimmons: Cut into slices or chunks.

Pineapple: Peel and cut into slices or chunks.

Plums: Leave whole or pit and cut into halves or quarters.

Pomegranate: Freeze the seeds only.

Raspberries: Freeze whole.

Starfruit: Slice into ¼-inch slices.

Strawberries: Hull, core, and slice or cut strawberries in half.

3. *For a dry pack*: Lay fruit in a single layer on a baking sheet lined with parchment paper so that the fruit won't stick to the sheet. Freeze for a few hours until the fruit is solid, then transfer it to an airtight container or a freezer bag. Press as much air out of the bag as possible. This helps prevent freezer burn.

4. *For a syrup pack:* You can freeze fruit in a sugar syrup, but this adds sugar. I prefer the dry pack. If you choose to freeze your fruit in syrup, use the following ratios of sugar to water:

Type of Syrup	**Sugar**	**Water**	**Yield**
Light	1 cup	4 cups	4¾ cups
Medium	1¾ cup	4 cups	5 cups
Heavy	2¾ cups	4 cups	5⅓ cups

To make the syrup, place water in a saucepan over a low heat and add the sugar. Stir until the sugar is dissolved, and the solution is clear. Chill the syrup before using. If you are freezing fruit in syrup, you will want to use a freezer-safe container. Place the fruit in the container and add enough syrup to just cover the fruit. To keep the fruit submerged in the syrup, place a crumpled up piece of parchment paper on top of the fruit and press the fruit down into the syrup.

5. *Use a black marker to label* the freezing date as well as the contents on the bag and return immediately to the freezer. Frozen fruit can be stored for up to 3 months.

Tips on retarding browning: Certain fruits—like apples, pears, and apricots—will turn brown when exposed to air and during freezing. You can use ascorbic acid, lemon juice, citric acid, or Fruit Fresh® to retard discoloration. Lemon juice and citric acid can mask the natural flavor of some fruits. If using ascorbic acid or citric acid, follow the manufacturer's directions. Fruit Fresh® is a combination of both ascorbic and citric acids. If you use this product, follow the directions on the label.

FIVE

How To Select and Store Fresh Vegetables

When stored at temperatures below 40 degrees F, potatoes become sweeter.

Just what is the difference between fruits and vegetables and why are some fruits considered vegetables?

Botanically, fruits come from the flower of a plant and contain seeds or pits. If that plant produces any other edible parts, like roots, leaves, stems, or bulbs, those foods are considered vegetables.

From a culinary standpoint, foods that are sweet or sour are considered fruits, while foods with a mild, savory flavor are vegetables. Technically, the avocado, tomato, cucumber, pepper, eggplant, olive, pumpkin, peas, zucchini, squash, okra, and beans are fruits, but they are classified as vegetables, because of their flavor profile and how they are used in the kitchen. I have included these foods as vegetables.

The dispute over whether the tomato was a fruit or vegetable made its way to the United States Supreme Court in 1893. This challenge arose because at that time vegetables were taxed at a higher rate than fruits. In Nix v. Hedden, the Court ruled unanimously that the tomato was a vegetable, acknowledging that botanically it was a fruit, but it was used like a vegetable in the kitchen.

Aloe Vera Leaves

The Aloe vera plant has been used for centuries for its medicinal properties. There are over 420 species of this succulent. The leaf has three sections: the outer rind, an inner clear gel, and found between the outer rind and inner gel, a middle layer of bitter, yellow latex. The aloe latex, a laxative, can be used to treat constipation.

Selecting: Look for leaves that are firm and full and have few blemishes.

Storing: Aloe leaves will keep for 1 to 2 weeks in the refrigerator. Its gel is very perishable. When placed in an opaque, airtight container and refrigerated, the gel will keep 5 to 7 days.

Availability: Year-round.

To prep the leaf: Wash the leaf to remove any surface bacteria. Using a sharp knife, slice off the spiky top, sides, and any jagged edges. Slide the knife under the top layer of skin and remove it. Using a spoon, gently scoop out the gel.

Amaranth Greens

Amaranth is grown all around the globe. Once considered a weed in the US, amaranth greens are edible and taste much like spinach. When young, amaranth can be eaten raw, but as it ages, it must be braised as it becomes bitter and fibrous.

Some amaranth leaves are green, while others are variegated green-and-red or streaked with purple.

Selecting: Look for amaranth with crisp, perky leaves. Avoid specimens that are wilted or have black spots or yellow discoloration.

Storing: When wrapped in damp paper towels and refrigerated, amaranth greens will keep 3 to 4 days.

Availability: Year-round.

Cleaning: If you buy bunches of fresh amaranth greens, it is important to clean them thoroughly to remove any sandy grit. Place the leaves in a large bowl of cold water and gently swirl them to release the sand. Remove them from the water and transfer to paper towels to dry or spin them in a salad spinner.

Artichokes

Selecting: A good artichoke will have tightly packed, crisp leaves. As artichokes age, their leaves spread apart. Look at the cut end. A black end means the artichoke has been stored too long. Do not buy this vegetable if it is wilting, dried out, or moldy. Fall and winter artichokes may have bronze tips or a whitish, blistered appearance. This is caused by exposure to a light frost. Some artichoke connoisseurs believe this vegetable is more tender and intensely flavored after a frost.

Storing: If refrigerated in a reusable, paper, or plastic bag, an artichoke will keep up to 1 week.

Availability: Year-round, with a peak season March through May and again in October.

To prepare for boiling: Place the artichoke on a cutting board. Using a sharp knife, cut off the stem so that the artichoke will stand upright and then slice an inch off its top. Remove any tough, outer leaves around the stem. Using your cooking shears, snip off the sharp tips of the leaves. Hold the artichoke upright and place it under a solid stream of running water to wash out any debris.

To remove the heart when eating: The inside of an artichoke has three parts—the stem, the heart, and the hairy choke, which is not edible. Gently open up the leaves to expose the hairy choke inside. Put your hand over the stem end and gently separate the heart from the body of the artichoke. Using a spoon, separate the hairy choke from the artichoke heart. Cut off the stem end and discard the hairy choke, which starts at the heart and ends at the stem.

Arugula

Arugula that is grown in hothouses has a milder taste. It is often added to mesclun or spring mix prepackaged salads. When grown in fields with a lot of exposure to sunlight, arugula will have a peppery taste and can be extremely sandy.

Selecting: Arugula should have crisp, emerald-green leaves. Do not buy this vegetable if it is yellow or if its leaves are limp or its stems are withered or slimy. If your supermarket sells arugula in bunches, check the area where the stems have been rubber-banded together. This is the first place rot may develop.

Storing: If you buy arugula in bunches, loosely wrap it in damp paper towels and place it in a reusable, paper, or plastic bag before refrigerating it. This vegetable will keep up to 3 days when refrigerated.

Availability: Year-round, but it is more plentiful in late summer.

Tips on cleaning: If you buy bunches of fresh arugula, it is important to clean them thoroughly to remove any sandy grit. Place the leaves in a large bowl of cold water and gently swirl them about to release the sand. Remove from the water and transfer to paper towels to dry or spin them in a salad spinner.

Asparagus

Selecting: The skin of asparagus is a medium green with purple highlights. The cut ends are white or light colored. Take note of the ends. Spears with large white-woody stalks and only a few inches of green at the tips were harvested late and will be tough. The white, woody bottoms of asparagus should be less than 15 percent of the total length of the spear. Look for firm, plump, round spears. The tips of asparagus should be tight and compact. Do not buy asparagus that has wet, slimy, or smelly tips. Shop with your ears when buying asparagus. If you give the bunch a squeeze and it squeaks, it is fresh. Also, its spears should snap easily when bent.

Storing: Asparagus will keep 2 to 3 days if refrigerated. When shopping in your supermarket, you may find asparagus standing upright with its cut ends in ice or water. This procedure prolongs its shelf life. You can do this at home as well, but it's important to change the ice or water several times a day. To pamper asparagus for a special dinner party, cut an inch off the bottoms, wrap the ends with wet paper towels, place the spears in a reusable, paper, or plastic bag, and store them in the vegetable crisper of your refrigerator.

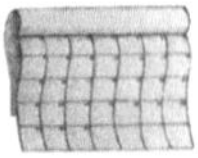

Availability: Year-round, with a peak season March through June. Prices on asparagus will be better between November and early July.

Tips on prepping: If a bundle of asparagus includes both thick and thin spears, separate them by size. Fat spears are best eaten whole. Cut thin spears on the diagonal for a sauté or stir-fry. Use a vegetable peeler or paring knife to remove the tough outer flesh on the lower part of fat spears. Peeling makes for faster cooking and a smoother, more elegant taste.

Avocado

Eighty percent of the avocados grown in California are *Hass*. This vegetable has a green, pebbly skin that turns black as it ripens. The skin is pliable and peels off easily.

Selecting: If you want to use your avocado immediately, select one that yields to gentle pressure. If you are shopping ahead and plan to use the avocado in a few days, pick one that is firm to the touch. Pass up avocados that are bright green and feel rock-hard. They are difficult to ripen. Also, don't buy this vegetable if it is sunken, shriveled, or feels mushy.

Storing: Avocados should be stored at room temperature until they are ready to eat. To speed up the ripening process, place them in a paper bag with an apple. Once ripe, avocados will keep up to 2 days in the refrigerator. If you only use half of an avocado, leave the pit in, brush the flesh with lemon juice, place it in a reusable or plastic bag or wrap it tightly with plastic wrap, and refrigerate.

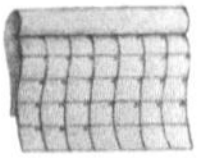

Availability: Year-round.

Beans

Although shell beans are a member of the legume family, your supermarket will sell them in the produce department. Unlike dried legumes, shell beans are sold fresh in their pods, ready to be shelled, or pre-shucked. They can be purple, yellow, creamy white, or deep green and can have a round or flat shape.

Green beans The green bean has many names, among them are the flat green bean, pole bean, and string bean. My mother always called them string beans. They got this name because older varieties had fibrous side strings.

To use: Cut off the stem ends but leave the curved tips if they are in good condition. If the beans have side strings, pull these off.

Wax beans Wax beans (also known as yellow beans) are similar to green beans, but they don't contain chlorophyll, which gives beans their green color.

Haricot vert French green beans, also known as haricot vert, are longer and skinnier than the flat green bean. They are harvested earlier and, therefore, thought to be more tender and flavorful.

Cranberry Cranberry beans, an Italian favorite, are round and plump and speckled with pink and wine-colored splotches. When cooked, shelled cranberry beans turn the same color as cooked pinto beans. In fact, they are a good substitute for pinto beans.

Fava The fava bean, also known as the broad bean, grows in big, bumpy green pods. Inside the pods are large flat bright green beans that are covered with a tough, clear skin that is removed before eating.

To shell fava beans: Snap off the stem end of the fava pod towards the "string" side of the pod. Pull down and remove the "string" that runs along the inner curve of the pod.

Open the pods and remove beans from the pod. Bring a large pot of water to a boil. Add enough salt so the water tastes as salty as the sea. This helps the beans stay green. Add fava beans to boiling water and blanch for 1 minute and drain. Prepare a large bowl of ice water. Plunge blanched fava beans into ice water and let sit until completely cool, 3 to 5 minutes. Shell the beans again. Using your thumb nail, break through the shell at the dimpled point and pull up to remove the "cap" at the top of the bean. After you remove the top of the shell, pop out the fava beans. Fully shelled fava beans are bright, emerald, green with an amazingly tender texture.

Lima Lima beans are plump, large, pale green beans that have a kidney-like shape. As lima beans age, they turn a creamy yellow color.

Selecting: Don't just grab a handful of beans. Sort through them and select tender, crisp, well-formed beans. If freshly picked, green beans will have a smooth, velvety skin. Do not buy beans that have white mold on their tips or beans that are dried or shriveled. If the beans inside the pods are visible, the beans were overgrown. If fava beans are bulging in the pod, that means they are probably old.

Storing: When you get home from the supermarket, wash the beans before storing them in a reusable, paper, or plastic bag. This extra moisture helps them stay fresh and crisp. Beans will keep 4 to 5 days in the refrigerator.

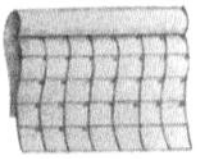

Availability: Year-round, with a peak in summer months. Yellow wax beans are not generally available during the hot summer months.

Beets

While beets are normally red, many varieties are now available including the *golden beet, baby beet, white beet, striped beet* (like the *Chioggia beet*, which has red and white candy-cane like stripes) the *Cylindra*, which looks like a carrot, and the *mangelwurzel* beet, which looks like a top-heavy fat beet.

Selecting: The greens on beets should be bright, dark green, and fresh. Select smooth, hard, round beets with deep color. Beets with a diameter of 3 inches are fine for cooking, but small, younger beets with a diameter of approximately ½ inches cook faster. Avoid large beets with unpalatable, woody cores, as they take the longest time to cook. Do not buy beets that have soft, moist spots or shriveled, wrinkly skin. Beets with wilted greens may be acceptable to purchase because the leaves deteriorate faster than the roots.

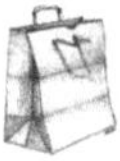

Storing: Cut the greens off the beets, leaving at least 1 inch of the stem attached, before refrigerating. Pick through the leaves, discarding the ones that are damaged. Greens stored in reusable, paper, or plastic bags will keep for 2 days in the refrigerator. Unwashed roots will keep up to 3 weeks in the refrigerator.

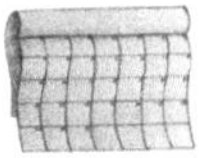

Availability: Year-round, with a peak season June through October.

Black-Eyed Peas

Technically beans, black-eyed peas are cream colored with a kidney shape. Their name reflects the distinctive black eye on their curved, inner side.

Selecting: Black-eyed peas should be firm and plump. Most supermarkets sell fresh, shelled black-eyed peas in 1-pint containers.

Storing: Refrigerate and keep no more than 1 week.

Availability: Year-round, but most supermarkets stock fresh black-eyed peas around the holidays for New Years.

Bok Choy

Also called *pak choi, pok choi, pichay/petsay*, bok choy is one of two green leafy Chinese cabbages. Bok choy has thick, clustered, light-green or pearly-white stalks and dark green leaves. It has a mild, grassy flavor with a bit of a spicy kick. Less common varieties of boy choy include *Shanghai choy, choy sum*, or *tat soi*. Shanghai choy is a baby bok choy with dark green, spooned-shaped leaves and pale green stalks. Choy sum has long, pale stalks, light green leaves, and tiny yellow flowers, which is why it is often called *Chinese flowering cabbage. Tat soi,* often referred to as the new spinach, has spoon-shaped round leaves and a buttery texture and a mustard-like flavor.

Selecting: Good quality bok choy should be thick, firm, and fleshy. Its leaves should be crisp and green, and its stalks should be plump and firm. Poor quality bok choy will have wilted or spotted leaves with limp, discolored stalks. If

Choy sum has smaller stalks, it will be more tender and milder in flavor. Tat soi with flower heads may be tougher and more bitter.

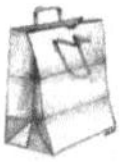

Storing: Bok choy will wilt in a few days. Refrigerate it in reusable, paper, or perforated plastic bags.

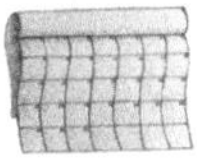

Availability: Year-round.

To prep: Using a sharp knife, trim off the end of the bok choy stem. Place bok choy under cold running water and scrub away any dirt with a vegetable brush.

Broccoli and Broccoli Rabe

Calabrese The most common type of broccoli found in the supermarket is Calabrese broccoli. It normally has a deep emerald-green color, although broccoli with purple and white flower heads is growing in popularity.

Broccoflower This vegetable is a hybrid of broccoli and cauliflower. It is shaped like a cauliflower but has lime green florets. Its flavor is somewhere between broccoli and cauliflower.

Broccoli rabe Broccoli rabe is a green cruciferous vegetable. Broccoli rabe is the common name for rapini, a member of the turnip family. It has long light-green stems with dark-green spiky leaves, which surround small broccoli-like buds and occasional yellow flowers. It has a bitter, but zesty flavor and is a popular vegetable in Italian cuisine.

Broccolini Broccolini, a hybrid of broccoli and Chinese broccoli —sometimes called baby broccoli—has long, thin, slender stems and smaller flowering heads. Its taste is sweeter than Calabrese broccoli.

Chinese broccoli Chinese broccoli is a leafy, green vegetable with long, thick stems and broad leaves. Its flavor, though similar to Calabrese broccoli, is more pungent.

Romanesco Romanesco is chartreuse in color and has distinctive pointed spiral cones.

Selecting: When buying *Calabrese broccoli,* look for buds that are tightly closed and crisp leaves. The buds should be an even, deep green color, and the stems should be a lighter green than the buds. Avoid broccoli with large, thick, whitish stalks.

Select *broccoli rabe* with small, firm, green stems, tightly closed buds, and an abundance of florets. Shop with your nose. Smell the stalks of broccoli rabe where they are tied together and avoid any with a mustard-like smell. Pass up broccoli rabe that has yellowed flowers or stalks that are split at the bottom. This is a sign of age.

Select *broccoflower* with tightly compact florets and bright green leaves. Avoid ones with brown spots, soft spots, or bruises.

Look for *broccolini* with tight heads, firm stems, and moist ends. Do not buy broccolini with flowers.

Chinese broccoli should have firm, crisp stems. If the end of the stem is brown, it is past its prime. Look for Chinese broccoli with thinner stems as it will be more tender.

Romanesco should have a firm head and feel heavy for its size. Avoid specimens that are discolored.

Storing: Broccoli, broccolini, Chinese broccoli, and Romanesco will keep in the refrigerator up to 4 days. Broccoli rabe should be wrapped in a wet paper towel and placed in a reusable, paper, or plastic bag before refrigerating.

Availability: Broccoli—Year-round, with a peak season from October through April. Broccoli rabe—Year-round, but best in late fall to early spring. Broccolini—Year-round. Chinese broccoli—Year-round. Romanesco—early fall.

Burdock Root

Burdock root is a popular ingredient in Japanese cuisine and is valued for its healing properties. There are two types of burdock root—*wild* and *Japanese*, which is cultivated. The average length of a burdock root is 2 feet, but it can grow up to 4 feet long. The skin of burdock root can be beige to brown to nearly black. Its fibrous flesh is grayish white, and it is about as thick as a carrot. When cooked, this root will turn either a shiny gray or brown.

Selecting: Select unwashed roots that are straight, firm, and crisp with few fibrous roots attached. Thinner roots will be less stringy.

Storing: Store at room temperature in an airtight container away from heat, light, and moisture.

Availability: Year-round.

Cabbage

Members of the cabbage family include common *green cabbage*, *red cabbage*, *white cabbage*, *Savoy cabbage*, and *Brussels sprouts*. The Savoy cabbage is considered to have the best flavor. Brussels sprouts are miniature heads of cabbage that grow around a central stem.

Selecting: Cabbage will normally feel very heavy for its size. When buying green or Savoy cabbage, select heads with dark green leaves. As cabbage ages, its outer leaves wilt and are removed, exposing the lighter colored underneath leaves. The leaves on cabbage should be thick and crisp, not limp. A fresh cabbage will show no signs of browning. Do not buy cabbage that has a strong odor. If it smells like garbage, it probably is. Avoid purchasing this vegetable if its core is woody or split.

Brussels sprouts should be firm with a good green color, have compact leaves, and clean ends. Do not buy puffy, yellow, or wilted Brussels sprouts.

Storing: This vegetable keeps up to 1 week in the refrigerator when placed in a reusable, paper, or plastic bag or tightly wrapped in plastic.

Availability: Red, green, and white cabbage: Year-round, Savoy cabbage: fall, Brussels sprouts: Year-round, peaking in November and December.

Carrots

Carrots have evolved over the years, resulting in purple, white, gold, black, red, and round varieties. Most of us only find the typical orange carrots in our supermarkets. "*Mini-peeled carrots*" are also now available in most markets. If you get confused when you buy mini carrots, read the label. A *baby carrot* is harvested before it reaches maturity. Baby-cut carrots are cut and shaped from larger carrots.

Selecting: Select well-shaped carrots with smooth exteriors and closely trimmed tops. My father taught me the brighter the color, the sweeter the flavor. Do not buy soft, wilted, or split carrots. Dark, slimy, yellowed tops that are beginning to sprout are an indication of decay. Mini-peeled carrots should be plump, not slimy, broken, or whitish. For the freshest carrots, buy bunches with bright green, leafy tops. The tops deteriorate quickly once the carrots are harvested, so if the tops are green, it means they were recently picked.

Storing: Carrots should be stored in reusable bags or in their original plastic bag and will keep in the refrigerator for up to 10 days. If you buy carrots with green tops, remove the leaves before storing. Do not store carrots with fruit, like apples or pears. These fruits emit ethylene gas, which causes carrots to turn bitter. When buying mini carrots, check the "Best-If-Used-By" date.

Availability: Year-round. Fresh, young bunch carrots that have their tops are found in the spring.

Cauliflower

About ten years ago, colored cauliflower began popping up in farmers' markets and grocery stores. Cauliflower can be found in white, purple, orange, and green colors. Anthocyanin—which is also found in red, blue, or purple fruits and vegetables—gives cauliflower its purple color. Carotenoids—also found in carrots, squash, and other yellow vegetables and fruits—gives cauliflower an orange color. Green cauliflower, a hybrid of broccoli and cauliflower, is sometimes called broccoflower. Green cauliflower contains more beta carotene than white cauliflower, but not as much as broccoli. The four different colors have a similar taste and texture—sweet and nutty—but vary slightly in nutritional value.

Selecting: A good quality head of cauliflower will have uniform color and densely-packed, compact curls with bright green leaves that are firmly attached to its core. White cauliflower should have a creamy, white color. Pass up this vegetable when it has tiny, black mold spots, blemishes, or yellow, wilted leaves. This is an indication of an old cauliflower. Its leaves should look fresh and vibrant.

Storing: Cauliflower will keep up to 1 week in the refrigerator when placed in a reusable, paper, or plastic bag.

Availability: Year-round, though you'll find the best quality during colder months.

Tips on prepping: I have found it more and more difficult to purchase cauliflower that is free of black spots. If this is the only product available, cut the black mold spots off with a sharp paring knife.

Celery and Celeriac

Most supermarkets sell *Pascal* celery. You will often find packages of celery hearts, which are the inner, mildly flavored, and sometimes stringless stalks of Pascal celery. Supermarkets may sell *celeriac*, sometimes called celery root.

Selecting: Good quality celery will have straight stalks and rigid ribs that snap crisply when bent. The leafy tops should look fresh with good green color. Do not buy celery with slimy leaves. When celery is overly large with dark green stalks, it may be bitter or stringy. Celeriac should feel firm and heavy for its size. Avoid specimens with soft spots.

Storing: Keep celery in its original perforated bag in the vegetable crisper of your refrigerator or transfer it to a reusable, paper, or plastic bag. It will keep for up to 1 week.

Availability: Celery—year-round. Celeriac—November through April.

Tips on prepping celery: My mother taught me to remove the strings from celery by snapping the rib at the point where the stalk changes in color from green to white. This exposes the strings. Using a small paring knife, gently pull the strings from the stalk.

Tips on prepping celeriac: Scrub the root with a vegetable brush to remove any excess dirt. Use a sharp knife to peel off the outer skin. Celeriac will turn brown after it is peeled. Soak it in lemon water to avoid discoloration.

Chayote

The chayote, a member of the Cucurbita family, is a large, edible, pear-shaped seed cultivated in Mesoamerica. Chayotes sold in the US are normally light green in color with fairly smooth skin. The chayote has a mild taste with a balance between apple and cucumber and a jicama-like crispness.

Selecting: Choose firm chayote. Smaller chayotes will be more tender, and their skin is normally edible. Larger chayotes will have tougher skin.

Storing: When wrapped in a paper towel, chayotes will keep 3 weeks in the refrigerator.

Availability: Year-round, but more available September through May.

Chestnuts

Although the chestnut is technically a nut, your supermarket may stock chestnuts in the produce department. Most fresh chestnuts are imported from Europe or Asia. Chestnuts can be roasted, boiled, puréed, preserved, or candied. They are used in desserts or in savory dishes. Chestnuts are also available dried, and these dried nuts can be ground into flour.

Selecting: It is difficult to select good chestnuts because it is hard to judge their inner quality by their outer shells. Your best bet is to buy chestnuts at a high-volume market that moves product quickly. Once the shells are cracked open, a good quality chestnut will be light tan in color and plump and meaty. Chestnuts with greenish mold between the nut and its outer skin or hard, darkened areas should be discarded.

Storing: Chestnuts will keep up to 1 week in the refrigerator.

Availability: October through March, peaking in December.

To remove the shell: Using a sharp paring knife, make an X on the domed side of the chestnut. Roast in an oven at 400 degrees F for 20 minutes. It is easier to remove the shells when the chestnuts are warm, so remove only a few at a time from the oven. Cool slightly and break away the shell. Remove the brown inner skin.

Corn

Selecting: Examine the husks first. Husks should be bright green and fit snugly. My father taught me to pull back enough of the husk to expose the kernels. To judge the quality of corn by its kernels, look for evenly spaced rows that are plump and milky all the way to the ear. The silks should be dry and deep gold in color. Avoid corn with soggy silks. Occasionally, you will find that your supermarket sells corn packed in trays. Examine these ears carefully as they may be old. Corn with flattened, tightly packed kernels will be starchy.

Storing: Place the ears in a reusable, paper, or plastic bag before refrigerating. They will keep for 1 to 2 days.

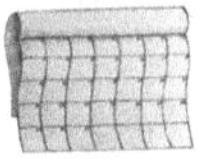

Availability: Florida corn—October to June, peaking in April to June. California corn—May to October, peaking in June and July. Ohio corn—peaking from August to October. Colorado Olathe corn—peaking late July and early August.

Cucumber

This vegetable has a crisp texture and mild flavor. The American *common* cucumber is about 8 inches in length with smooth, dark green skin that is often waxed. *Pickling cucumbers*—known as *gherkins, American dills,* and *French cornichons*—are small. Gherkins and cornichons are about 2 inches in length, while American dills are about 4 inches. American pickling cucumbers have knobby warts and pale stripes, and their skin ranges in color from dark to light green. Supermarkets often carry the *English* cucumber, which is narrow and thin-skinned. It has a mild flavor, fewer seeds, and firmer flesh. The *Persian* cucumber has a thin, smooth, slightly ridged skin and is slimmer and smaller than the common cucumber. Although technically a muskmelon, the *Armenian* cucumber is a long, light chartreuse colored fruit that looks and tastes like a cucumber.

Selecting: Look for cucumbers that are firm and well-shaped with deep green color. Do not buy yellowing, puffy, or shriveled cucumbers. Check for soft spots or soft ends, which is an indication of spoilage. The flesh of cucumbers should be pale green. Yellow flesh indicates they have started to decay.

Storing: Placed in reusable, paper, or plastic bags or wrapped in plastic, cucumbers should keep 1 week in the refrigerator.

Availability: American common cucumbers—year-round. Pickling cucumbers—summer.

Edamame

Although a member of the legume family, the edamame is a shell bean. You may find edamame fresh in the produce department of your supermarket. Unlike dried legumes, shell beans are sold fresh in their pods, ready to be shelled, or pre-shucked. Edamame are fresh soybeans. They are as bright in color and as sweet to the taste as green peas. Inside their small, flattened pods are smooth-skinned, plump beans that resemble lima beans.

Selecting: Select brightly colored, even-sized, plump pods. Avoid shriveled or discolored edamame.

Storing: This vegetable should be placed in an open container and will keep for 1 week in the refrigerator.

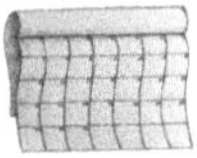
Availability: Year-round.

To prepare: Place the pods in a bowl and sprinkle them with salt. Rub the salt over their skin, coating evenly. Allow the beans to sit for 15 minutes, then boil 1 pound of edamame in 1 gallon of water over a high heat for 7 to 10 minutes.

To eat: To remove the beans inside the pod, place the pod to your lips and squeeze the beans out into your mouth.

Eggplant

Although there are several varieties of eggplants, the most common type found in supermarkets is the deep purple *Black Beauty*, also called the *American* or *globe* eggplant. The *Italian* eggplant is similar in appearance to the Black Beauty; but it is smaller, and its flesh is more tender. The *Chinese* eggplant has a long, narrow body with a light purple skin and white flesh. The *Japanese* eggplant also has a long, slender body, but its flesh is deep purple. *Fairy Tale* eggplants will have a purple and white striped skin and sweet, tender flesh. The *Graffiti* eggplant is distinguished by blotchy purple and white stripes. *White* eggplants have a white skin, but inside they are similar to the American eggplant. Most white eggplants are grown from heirloom seeds.

Selecting: Eggplants should be firm and hard and feel heavy for their size. Choose eggplants with a smooth, glossy, skin with no signs of green. Pass up soft or spotted eggplants or ones that have wrinkly skin. Shriveling is a sign of aging. Eggplants become bitter with age.

Storing: Eggplants keep about 4 days in the refrigerator.

Availability: Year-round.

Endive and Escarole

Belgian endive is a torpedo-shaped member of the chicory family. Its leaves range in color from white to yellow green. *Red endive* is burgundy in color and is similar to Belgian endive but is more bitter. *Curly endive*s grow in bunches of long, deep green, curly-edged leaves with thin white ribs. *Frisée*, its French name, or *riccia*, in Italian, is a variety of curly endive. It has smaller leaves with delicate, ragged edges and a more tender texture. Its center leaves are a creamy yellow color, and the edges turn light apple green. *Escarole* has broad, lightly ruffled leaves that form an open, flattened head. It is light-yellow to deep green in color.

Selecting: Curly endive or escarole should be brightly colored and have perky leaves. Do not buy endive that has brown discoloration, excessive dirt, or dry, yellowing leaves. Endive with lighter colored leaves will be less bitter.

Storing: When placed in reusable, paper, or plastic bags and refrigerated, endive, curly endive, frisée, and escarole will keep up to 5 days.

Availability: Year-round—peaking in December through April.

Fennel

This odd-looking vegetable has become a popular ingredient in recipes. It can be eaten raw or cooked. Its enlarged bulb bottom, composed of onion-like layers, culminates in stringy, celery-like stalks. The bulb bottom and stalks enclose a sweet-tasting, dense heart. Fennel tastes like licorice or anise and has the crisp, crunchy texture of an apple.

Selecting: Pick fennel that has large, squatty, white bulbs, a pale green color, and fluffy green fronds. Do not buy split, shriveled, dried-out bulbs with brown or soft spots. If the stalks have been cut away, that means the fennel has been on the shelf too long.

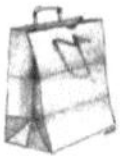

Storing: If placed in reusable, paper, or plastic bags or wrapped in plastic and stored in your vegetable crisper, fennel will last up to 3 days.

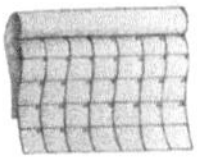

Availability: Year-round.

To prep: Cut off the stalks at the top of the bulb and trim a thin slice off the darkened end of the bulb. Gently pull away the outer layer and discard it. This part of the fennel tends to be stringy and tough. Separate and discard the dark green, outer stalks from the pale, tender inner portions. Immediately place the bulb into a bowl filled with cold water and 1 tablespoon lemon juice until ready to use.

Garlic

There are two main types of garlic—softneck and hardneck. The *softneck* garlic has a fibrous stem that dries into a grass-like top. *Hardneck* garlic has an intense flavor and a long, hard stem, surrounded by firm cloves that are easy to peel. *Elephant* garlic looks like a large garlic bulb but is more closely related to the leek. It has a mild flavor and a potato-like flesh. *Garlic scapes* are the long, deep green, curly stems and flower buds of the hardneck garlic plant. They taste like a unique blend of onion, scallion, and garlic. *Green garlic* is harvested before the bulb matures. It has an herb-like, mild, fresh, sharp flavor.

Selecting: Look for large, plump, and firm bulbs with a tight, unbroken covering. As it ages, garlic shrivels, loses its plumpness, and begins to sprout. Age turns the flavor bitter. Do not buy soft or spongy bulbs. Some specialty food stores sell peeled garlic. If you are buying garlic that has already been peeled, look for pearly white, firm cloves with no shriveling, mold, or soft stickiness. Look for garlic scapes with firm green stalks. Avoid scapes with bruises or damage. Scapes with yellow or papery tips on the flower bud are old and will be tough. Select green garlic with white or purple, long tops and dark green leaves. Shop with your nose. Green garlic should smell like garlic.

Storing: Store garlic bulbs in a cool, dimly lit place with good circulation. Moisture will make garlic spoil, so be sure to keep it dry. Peeled garlic will keep in the refrigerator for up to 2 weeks. You'll be sorry if you don't store it in a covered container. Store garlic scapes like you would cut flowers—in a vase filled with water. They will keep 2 to 3 days.

Green garlic will keep for 2 to 3 days when placed in a reusable, paper, or plastic bag and refrigerated.

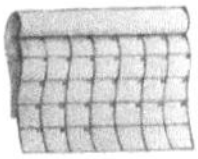

Availability: Year-round. Green garlic and garlic scapes are available late spring to early summer.

To extract the cloves: Rub or cut off the loose outer skin to expose the cloves. Gently pull the cloves away from the core of the bulb. Using the side of a large knife, smash each individual clove to break its skin. Peel the skin from each clove.

Ginger

Selecting: The skin of this root should be firm and smooth, with a light sheen. Shop with your nose. Fresh ginger will have a spicy fragrance. Do not buy knobby, shriveled, or moldy ginger.

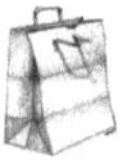

Storing: To store ginger in your refrigerator, wrap it in dry paper towels and place it in a reusable, paper, or plastic bag. Ginger will keep up to 2 weeks.

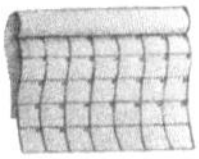

Availability: Year-round, peaking March through September.

To use: Cut off only as much ginger as you need. Using the back of a spoon or a vegetable peeler, remove the outer skin. Grate, slice across the grain, or chop as needed.

Greens

Collard greens These greens are popular in the American South. Collards are vegetables that have large green leaves and tough stems. Collard greens are the edible leaves from this plant.

Dandelion greens When young, these leaves add a bitter, tangy flavor to salads. When old, they should be cooked.

Kale Curly kale has dark green, curly leaves and fibrous stems. Tuscan kale, an heirloom green from Italy, also has fibrous stems, but its leaves are flatter and puckered.

Flowering kale Flowering kale has ruffled pink, purple, and red leaves. While it is edible, it is most often used as a garnish.

Mustard greens Mustard greens are dark green in color and have a sharp mustard flavor.

Turnip greens Turnip greens are similar to mustard greens but have a purplish tint and a mellow, turnip flavor.

Selecting: Greens should have a vibrant deep green color and fresh plump, crisp leaves. Do not buy greens with yellow, bruised, or pitted leaves or thick fibrous stems. Shop with your nose. Greens with a strong odor have deteriorating leaves.

Storing: Place in a reusable, paper, or plastic bag and refrigerate. Greens will keep up to 5 days.

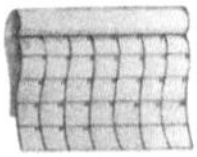

Availability: Collard greens—Year-round, peaking December through April. Dandelion greens—Year-round, peaking in April and May. Kale—Year-round, peaking in December through February. Mustard greens—Year-round, peaking December through April. Turnip greens—Year-round, peaking in October through March.

Horseradish

Selecting: Buy horseradish that is hard and free of spongy or soft spots. Overly large horseradish may be fibrous. Sprouting, green-tinged roots may be bitter.

Storing: When you arrive home, wrap horseradish in a slightly dampened dishtowel, then a dry one, and refrigerate. This root will keep up to 2 weeks in the refrigerator.

Availability: Harvested early spring and late fall.

To use: Cut off only as much as you need. Using a vegetable peeler, remove the outer skin. It is best to wear gloves when handling horseradish and to use a blender or food processor to grind it.

Jicama

Raw jicama is crunchy with an apple-like, nutty flavor similar to a water chestnut. It is sometimes referred to as a Mexican potato because when cooked it has a potato-like texture.

Selecting: Select medium-sized jicamas with smooth, unblemished skin. Scratch the skin with your nail. It should be thin, and the flesh underneath should be juicy. Do not buy jicamas with cracks or bruises or ones that are shriveled or sticky.

Storing: When stored uncovered in a cool, dry place, jicama will keep up to 3 weeks. Once you cut into it, a jicama will keep 1 week when refrigerated and placed in a reusable, paper, or plastic bag or wrapped in plastic.

Availability: Year-round, imported from Mexico and South America.

To peel: A vegetable peeler may not work well on jicama. Using a sharp knife, slice one end of the jicama off to create a flat base. Run the knife under the skin, trying to keep as much of the flesh as possible. Because the skin is quite papery, you can make a 1-inch slice into the skin and pull it off. Use a vegetable peeler or paring knife to remove any remaining skin.

Kale (See Greens)

Kohlrabi

Kohlrabi has two parts—a root and leaves. The root is spicy like a radish and somewhat sweet like a turnip. Its leaves are similar to turnip greens.

Selecting: Do not buy extremely large kohlrabi. They are tough and have a strong taste. Choose small to medium specimens with small, smooth bulb-stems and firm, green leaves.

Storing: The leaves will only keep for a few days. Remove the leaves and store them separately. The root, however, will keep for several weeks in the refrigerator.

Availability: Year-round, peaking in early summer.

To use: The leaves should be removed. Discard the stems and any tough center ribs. The leaves can be cooked like greens. Steam the bulb to loosen its skin. Then pare away the tough outer skin before cooking.

Leeks

Selecting: Good quality leeks are firm and smooth with crisp, brightly colored leaves and flexible stems. Do not buy leeks with blemishes or ones that have withered, yellowed, or slimy leaves. Leeks with a rounded rather than a flat bottom are old.

Storing: Remove and discard the tough, dark green tops. To refrigerate, wrap leeks in damp paper towels and place them in a reusable, paper, or plastic bag. They should last up to 1 week. Do not store leeks with soft fruit because leeks produce odors soft fruits will absorb.

Availability: Year-round, peaking in October through May.

To use: Place cut slices of leek into a large bowl filled with warm water. Using your fingers, whirl the pieces of leek vigorously to remove any sandy grit. The sand should sink to the bottom of the bowl. Scoop out the leeks and transfer them to a colander. Rinse and drain thoroughly. If the bottom of the bowl has a lot of grit, repeat the process.

Lettuce

Butterhead lettuce (Boston, Bibb) This type of lettuce has small, round, loosely formed heads with soft, buttery-textured leaves. Its outer leaves are pale green in color, and its inner leaves are pale, yellow green. It has a sweet and succulent flavor.

Iceberg This lettuce, also known as *crisphead,* was dubbed iceberg during the 1920s when California growers shipped it covered with crushed ice. This lettuce has a solid head of tightly wrapped leaves. It is crisp, succulent, and wilt-resistant with a neutral, watery flavor.

Looseleaf Supermarkets typically carry green and red looseleaf lettuce. This variety is crisper and more fully flavored than iceberg lettuce, although more perishable. Its leaves branch from a single stalk rather than forming a tight head.

Romaine Romaine has an elongated head of dark green, narrow, stiff leaves with a distinctive rib that reaches almost to the tip of the leaf.

Spring Mix Also called *mesclun* or *field greens,* spring mix contains a variety of lettuces, which can include spinach, red and green leaf, red and green oak leaf, lollo rosso, frisée, radicchio, chard, red and green romaine, endive, and other heirloom lettuces. It has a mild to slightly bitter taste. The lettuces in spring mix are harvested at a young age.

Selecting: Any type of lettuce should be free of blemishes. Its leaves should be an even green in color with little browning on the outside edges. When buying looseleaf lettuce, look for whole, unbroken leaves with no wilting or spoilage at either the tip or base of the leaves. Do not buy iceberg lettuce that lacks green color or is irregular in shape. Romaine with rust, oversized butts, or large, strong, milky ribs is not good quality. Select romaine that is cut close to the leaf stems and is free of browning. Good romaine lettuce will have deep green leaves all the way down to its center. If you are buying boxed or bagged lettuce, check the date. Buy boxed or bagged lettuces with at least 5 days remaining before the "Sell-By" date. Check the packaging and avoid ones that contain lettuce that is wilted or shows signs of spoilage. Avoid packages that contain lettuce with yellowing leaves or brown edges.

Storing: Do not wash lettuce until ready to use. Store whole heads in reusable, paper, or plastic bags. This helps them retain their natural moisture and stay crisp.

Romaine and iceberg lettuce will keep up to 1 week in the refrigerator. Butterhead varieties and leaf lettuce will keep 3 to 4 days. Do not store lettuce with apples, bananas, or pears, as these fruits emit ethylene gas that will turn lettuce brown.

Availability: Year-round.

To prepare: Lettuce must be washed thoroughly, particularly bibb lettuce which can be quite sandy. Do not soak lettuce in water. This only softens the leaves. One of the greatest conveniences invented for the kitchen is the salad spinner. It gives freshly washed leaves a little spin and dries them in no time. If you don't have one, consider purchasing one. It's a real time saver.

Lotus Root

Lotus root is the edible stem of the lotus plant. It is brownish pink and cylindrical, with a length of 6 to 8 inches and a diameter of 3 inches. When the lotus root is cut open, the white insides have a lace-like design with pea-shaped holes.

Selecting: Lotus roots should be firm with smooth, unblemished skin. Avoid roots with dark or soft spots. If you cut the root open and its channels are ringed with a brown or black lining, discard the root as it is old.

Storing: Whole lotus roots will keep in the refrigerator for 2 to 3 weeks. To store cut lotus root, place it in a mixture of lemon juice and water in an airtight container. It will keep for 4 to 5 days.

Availability: Year-round.

To prep: Rinse under cold running water, gently scrubbing away any mud or dirt on the root. Using a paring knife, remove any mold or dark spots. Slice off both ends and discard. Using a vegetable peeler, remove the tough outer skin. To prevent browning, soak in a mixture of lemon juice and water.

Mâche

Mâche, also called corn salad, field salad, or lamb's lettuce, is a non-lettuce salad green. Mâche leaves have an elongated spoon shape and look like low-growing green rosettes. This green has a sweet, nutty flavor.

Selecting: Select bright, lively greens. Most mâche sold in the United States is grown in greenhouses, so its root ball is still attached.

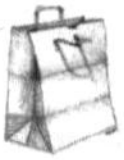

Storing: Mâche is very perishable. It will stay fresh only 1 or 2 days. To store, wrap it in paper towels and seal it in a reusable or plastic storage food bag.

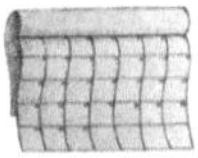

Availability: Mâche grown is greenhouses is available year-round.

Microgreens

Microgreens are the tender, young seedlings of vegetables or herbs and are usually less than 14 days old. Thin and delicate, these plants are the smallest possible manifestation of greens. Microgreens are smaller and more tender than baby lettuces, which are usually picked at about 35 days, but are more flavorful than sprouts. Microgreens have a surprisingly intense flavor for their size, packing a punch in both flavor and nutrition. Types of microgreens are *sorrel, pea greens, kohlrabi, broccoli, radish, cress, kale, wheatgrass, mustard, orach,* and *arugula.*

Selecting: Select greens that look fresh and crisp, are bright green, and have no damage.

Storing: Microgreens should be stored in their original container in the refrigerator, where they will remain dormant for 5 to 6 days until ready to use. If purchased in containers, keep pea shoots fresh by immersing their roots in water. If purchased loose, wrap shoots in paper towels and place in a reusable, paper, or plastic bag in the vegetable bin of the refrigerator.

Availability: Year-round.

Mushrooms

Mushrooms are most mysterious. They can be delicious, deadly poisonous, or have hallucinogenic properties. There are over 300 types of cultivated mushrooms, not including the many edible varieties that grow in the wild. Every year, more varieties of mushrooms are introduced. The following varieties are commonly found in supermarkets:

Chanterelle Depending upon the variety, the cap of a chanterelle can be yellow, orange, white, brown-gray, or black. Its caps are cup-shaped, wavy, and firm. Its under-side has wrinkles, not gills. This mushroom has soft flesh and an apricot-like fragrance. It grows in the wild and is also cultivated.

Cremini The cremini is quite similar to the common white mushroom; however, has a deeper flavor. Cremini mushrooms have naturally light tan to rich brown caps, are firm, and reasonably priced with a good shelf life.

Enoki This variety is a cultivated Japanese mushroom that grows in small, fragile clusters. It has white stems topped by tiny caps. Enoki mushrooms have a mild, light flavor with a slight crunch. This mushroom is normally eaten raw in salads or used as a garnish.

Hen of the Woods Also known as maitake, this mushroom has fan-shaped, feathery tendrils, which crisp up nicely when roasted, grilled, fried, or seared.

Lion's Mane This large, white, shaggy mushroom looks like a lion's mane. It has a seafood-like flavor.

Lobster This mushroom gets its name from its brightly colored, pimply surface and knobby appearance. Lobster mushrooms have a fishy aroma and crisp, white flesh.

Morels This mushroom may be tan, yellow, or black. It has short, thick, hollow stems topped with honeycomb-like, pointed caps. Morels have a rich, nutty flavor and a woodsy fragrance.

Oyster Oyster mushrooms have fluted soft brown caps. They have a velvety texture and a mild, delicate flavor. Their stems are tough and should be discarded.

Porcini The porcini mushroom has fat, firm, curved, white stalks and broad, dark brown caps. Porcini mushrooms have a spongy layer of long, tiny tubes underneath the caps. With a rich, meaty flavor, porcinis are delicate enough for sauces yet perfect with grilled steaks.

Portobello Portobello mushrooms are large, fully mature cremini mushrooms with caps that span 6 inches. This mushroom has a long growing cycle, which gives it a solid, meat-like texture and flavor. Supermarkets sell these whole, caps only, or already sliced.

Shiitakes This mushroom originated in Japan and is the most widely used mushroom in Japanese and Chinese cuisine. Shiitakes have wide, umbrella-shaped caps with open veils and tan gills. They range in color from tan to dark brown. The caps of shiitake mushrooms are soft and spongy with a meaty, chewy texture. Shiitakes have a smoky aroma. Their stems are too woody to eat.

Truffles Prized by gourmets, the truffle is round and wrinkly, with an irregular shape and rough skin. Unlike other mushrooms, it does not have a stem. Truffles range in color from very dark brown to off white.

White This is the most common mushroom found in American supermarkets. White mushrooms range in color from creamy white to beige and can be eaten raw or cooked. The caps of freshly picked white mushrooms fit closely to the stem. Mature white mushrooms have open veils and darkened caps. Fresh whites have a delicate flavor and are good in salads. Mature whites have a richer, deeper flavor and are more suitable for cooking.

Selecting: Mushrooms should have spongy, firm, and fleshy caps. Do not buy mushrooms if they have black spots or worms. Avoid mushrooms with a discolored, shriveled appearance. Wet or slimy mushrooms have past their prime.

Storing: Most mushrooms will remain fresh for 3 to 5 days. Slicing mushrooms decreases their shelf life. Store them whole. If your supermarket sells mushrooms prepacked in 1-pint containers, remove the plastic wrap when you get home and put the mushrooms in a paper bag or wrap them in paper towels. Vacuum-sealed mushrooms should keep for 7 days if refrigerated.

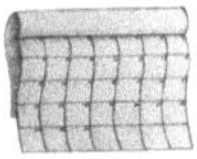

Availability: Most varieties of mushrooms are available year-round. Some exceptions: Chanterelles: season in the spring, summer, and fall. Hen of the Woods: fall. Lion's Mane: fall. Lobster mushrooms: peak in August through October. Porcini mushrooms: peak in May and June and again in October. Black truffles: December to March. White truffles: September to December. Wild morels: season in the spring.

To clean mushrooms: Either brush them with a mushroom brush or rub off any unsightly flesh. Rinse under cold, running water. While some people peel mushrooms, this is not necessary. Before using chanterelles, rinse them carefully, especially inside the wrinkles and dry them with paper towels. Before using fresh porcini, scrape any dirt off the stalks and wipe them clean with damp paper towels. Porcini mushrooms should be used as soon as possible. If you keep them for a few days, it is a good idea to stand them on their caps to prevent the tiny worms that sometimes inhabit their stalks from traveling into the caps.

If you find porcini mushrooms have worms, place the mushrooms in a Ziploc® bag and remove as much air as possible. Lack of oxygen will cause the worms to leave the mushroom.

Napa Cabbage

This Chinese cabbage, also called *celery cabbage*, has an oblong shape and crinkly, thick-veined, fibrous leaves. Its thin, crisp, delicate leaves are cream-colored, and it has celadon green tips. Napa cabbage has a mild, sweet taste.

Selecting: Select napa cabbage that has a compact head and tightly closed, crisp, green-tipped leaves. Do not buy heads with wilted, yellowed, or brown leaves.

Storing: Place napa cabbage in a reusable, paper, or plastic bag and refrigerate. It should keep for 1 week. Do not store with ethylene-producing fruits like apples.

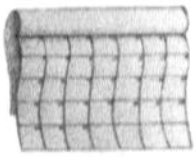

Availability: Year-round.

Nopales and Nopalitos

Nopales are the pads or paddles of the prickly pear cactus. They have a thick, meaty texture and taste like a cross between asparagus, green peppers, and string beans. Some supermarkets carry prepped and chopped nopales. When ready to use, they are called nopalitos. The spines and thorns of nopales must be removed before cooking. When cooked, nopales release a slime much like okra does. This can be removed by rinsing it under cold water and rubbing it vigorously.

Selecting: Color is the best indicator of freshness. Look for brightly colored green paddles that are about 5 to 6 inches long. The paddle should be flexible but not soft. Avoid paddles that are floppy or limp.

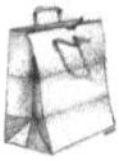

Storing: When placed in a reusable, paper, or plastic bag and refrigerated, nopales will keep 1 week.

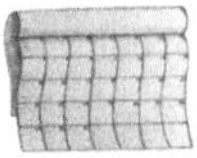

Availability: Year-round, peaking summer through fall.

Tips for prepping: Wear gloves. Place the paddle on a cutting board. Run a sharp knife back and forth across the paddle to scrape off its spines and any brown bumps, being careful not to remove of the skin. Cut off the woody stem. Rinse well.

Okra

Okra pods are fuzzy, deeply ridged, and usually olive-green in color. Some specialty food markets will sell red, white, and purple varieties.

Selecting: This vegetable is highly perishable, so it is important to select the freshest possible specimens. Choose pods that are free of bruises, uniform in color, tender but not soft, and no more than 4 inches long. Okra that is soft, shriveled, or large will be tough and fibrous. Avoid dried-out or stringy okra.

Storing: To store okra, place it in a paper bag or wrap it in paper towels, then place it in a reusable or plastic bag before refrigerating. It should keep for 2 to 3 days.

Availability: Year-round in the South. May to October in other areas. Peak season is June through August.

Onion

Onions can be classified into two different categories: spring/summer fresh bulb onions and storage onions. Fresh onions are yellow, white, or red with varied shapes—flat, top-shaped, round, or long. They have a mild, juicy taste, a thin, light-colored skin and are often used raw. Storage onions are always round.

Bermuda This onion is mild and red, white, or yellow in color.

Boiling These are small, thin-skinned onions meant for cooking whole.

Cipollini About the size of a golf ball, these onions resemble small flat shaped spears. Their name in Italian means "little onion". They are very sweet, which makes them perfect for caramelizing.

Green onions (scallions) These onions are pulled while their tops are still green and before a large bulb has formed.

Egyptian walking onion This variety resembles a clump of perennial green scallions. The plant has a bunch of bulblets where a normal onion would have flowers. As the weight of the bulbs increases, the plant stalks fall to the ground, sometimes as far as two feet from the parent plant. The bulbs waste no time in putting down roots—thus the name "walking onion". This onion has a very mild flavor.

Italian red This onion is flat with thick layers. Its inner skin layers are deep purple. The Italian red has a sweeter flavor and a crunchier texture than other red onions.

Maui A sweet, mild onion which grows in Maui, Hawaii.

Pearl onions These onions are small because they are planted close together and picked early. Pearl onions are as pungent as storage onions and have just as good a shelf life.

Spanish This is the most common onion found in supermarkets. It is a mild, globe onion.

Texas Supersweet This onion is quite large with a globe shape, growing as large as a softball. It is yellow skinned with a very mild, delicate taste.

Vidalia These onions are grown in Georgia and are known for their sweet, mild flavor.

Walla Walla This sweet, jumbo, round variety is a French onion that is grown in Walla Walla, Washington.

Welsh Native to China, Welsh onions look very similar to scallions, although they are larger. Welsh onions are moderately pungent and used in stir fries.

White White onions have a mild flavor and papery, white skin. They are good either raw or cooked.

Selecting: Onions should be dry, firm, and shiny with a thin outer skin. Do not buy onions that have sprouts. They will taste bitter. The neck of an onion should be tightly closed.

Do not buy onions that have dark patches, soft spots, or black mold. Examine the sprout end of Italian red onions. It often times is sunken. This is the first place spoilage will begin. Do not buy the Italian red onion if it has a soft, deeply sunken, yellow top. Good quality pearl onions will be uniform in size and have firm, clear skin. Do not buy pearl onions that have bruises or blemishes, soft or moldy spots, or that are too big. Look for scallions with medium-sized necks and white blanching that extends 2 to 3 inches above the root.

Storing: Onions should be stored in a cool, dark, dry, well-ventilated place. Do not store onions and potatoes together. Potatoes give off moisture that can cause onions to spoil. Fluorescent lighting will turn pearl onions green.

Availability: Most onions are available year-round. Italian red onions: in season April through August. Pearl onions: July through March. Vidalia onions: April through mid-July. Walla Walla onions: best in June and July. Cipollini: fall. Egyptian walking onion: spring. Welsh: July through December.

Orach

Considered the new kale because of its nutritional benefits, orach has a chard-like flavor but a saltier taste than most greens. Also known as saltbrush, mountain spinach, or French spinach, it can be used like chard or spinach and eaten raw or cooked.

Selecting: Orach should have crisp, perky leaves. Do not buy orach if it has yellow, wilted, or broken leaves. Shop with your nose. If you smell an unpleasant odor, pass.

Storing: When placed in reusable, paper, or plastic bags and refrigerated, orach will keep for 2 to 3 days.

Availability: Year-round, but more plentiful in spring and fall.

Parsnips

Parsnips look much like carrots except their skin is an off-white color. I just recently started cooking with parsnips. They are amazingly sweet and tasty. If you haven't used them in soups or stews, you should really give them a try.

Selecting: Parsnips should be small to medium, well-shaped, and free of pitting. It is the age rather than the size of parsnips that determines tenderness. Old specimens that have been stored too long may be tough and woody. Do not buy shriveled or spotted parsnips. When thin and long, this vegetable tends to be stringy.

Storing: To store parsnips, wrap them in dry paper towels, place them inside a reusable, paper, or plastic bag and refrigerate in the coldest part of the refrigerator. When stored in this manner, parsnips will keep up to 1 month.

Availability: Parsnips are harvested after the first frost.

Peas

Garden or **English** This is the name given to the familiar "peas in a pod." Peas are removed from the pod before eating since the pod is too stringy to eat. This type of pea is best when it's as small as possible.

Sugar snap peas Sugar snap peas have large, plump pods which contain large peas. They can be eaten raw or cooked.

Snow peas These peas are tender and have edible pods. Snow peas are flatter than sugar snap peas, and their pods contain small, premature peas.

Selecting: Select garden peas with bright green, velvety pods. Discernible pearl-shaped peas should barely fill the pod. Avoid overgrown peas that are flattened against each other like teeth. Do not buy immature peas that are flat, dark green, and wilted, or overgrown peas that are swollen and freckled with gray spots. A yellow color indicates age or damage.

When buying snow pea pods, the miniature peas should be barely visible. Snow peas are light green in color. When selecting snow peas, inspect them for small circles of rot. Sugar snap peas are a brilliant green. Avoid overgrown sugar snap peas where the visible peas bulge. Do not buy pods that are broken or have white patches or soft or moldy tips.

Storing: Peas are best eaten immediately after they are picked. When stored in reusable, paper, or plastic bags and refrigerated, garden peas will last 3 to 4 days. Sugar snap or snow peas are more perishable. When stored in the same manner, they will last up to 2 days.

Availability: Sweet young peas are available February through September, but peak in May. Sugar snap and snow peas—year-round.

Pepper, Chile

There are hundreds of varieties of chile peppers. Each type of chile has a unique subtle flavor and its own level of heat. As a general rule, the smaller the chile, the hotter it will be. Individual chiles from the same plant can vary in hotness, which in the US is measured by the Scoville scale. Bell peppers have a value of zero and habaneros rank 200,000 to 350,000.

To use: It is a good idea to wear gloves when handling chile peppers. Once your hands have been in contact with hot peppers, do not touch delicate parts of your body, like lips, eye, or face.

Anaheims This red or green pepper is mild with long, rounded tips. Anaheims rank 500 to 2,500 on the Scoville scale.

Banana The banana pepper got its name because of its long, curved yellowish color. It has a mild, tangy taste and rates 0 to 500 on the Scoville scale.

Carolina Reaper A cross between a ghost pepper and a red habanero, this pepper carries the 2020 title in the *Guinness Book of World Records* for the world's hottest pepper. It ranks 1,641,000 to 2,200,000 on the Scoville scale. It is red with a bumpy skin and a stinger-like tail.

Cherry Hots These peppers look like cherries. They are bright red, with a sweet, spicy taste, very meaty, and are medium hot, ranking from 2,500 to 5,000 on the Scoville scale.

Cubanelle Also called the Italian frying pepper, this sweet pepper has a bit of heat, ranking 100 to 600 on the Scoville scale. It is light greenish yellow and is long with a slightly wrinkled skin.

Fresno The Fresno pepper looks like a red jalapeño. It is a bit hotter, ranking 2,500 to 10,000 on the Scoville scale and has a fruitier, more smokey flavor.

Ghost Peppers The ghost pepper is also known as the bhut jolokia. It is about 2 to 3 inches long and 1-inch wide and can be red, yellow, orange, or chocolate in color. It ranges from 855,000 to 1,041,427 on the Scoville scale.

Habaneros This pepper is known for its intense heat and its sweet apple-tomato flavor. It ranks 100,000 to 350,000 on the Scoville scale. Habaneros are squat, 1 to 2 inches in length, orange in color, and shaped like a lantern.

Hatch To be called a Hatch green chile, a pepper must be grown in the Hatch Valley of New Mexico. There are several varieties of Hatch green chiles—thus their name indicates only the area where they are grown. The heat level of Hatch chiles ranges from 1,000 to 8,000 on the Scoville scale.

Hungarian Wax This pepper is mild to medium hot. It is waxy-yellow in color, with small, elongated, pointed tips. When mature, Hungarian wax peppers turn light red. The Hungarian pepper ranks 5,000 to 10,000 on the Scoville scale.

Jalapeños The most common hot pepper sold in the United States, jalapeños are about 2 inches long with green, blunt, oval pods. Rated medium-hot to hot, jalapeños register 2,500 to 8,000 on the Scoville scale. Most jalapeños are green, although occasionally markets carry red ones. When smoke-dried, red jalapeños are called chipotles, which register 8,000 on the Scoville scale.

New Mexico The New Mexico pepper is long and tapered and may be brown, green, red, orange, or yellow in color. When dried, New Mexico chiles are used for chili powder.

Pasillas In Mexico, the fresh version of this mild pepper is called chilaca. When dried, it is called pasilla. Pasilla peppers are incorrectly called poblanos in California. Pasillas rank 1,000 to 2,000 on the Scoville scale. The pasilla pepper is often used in mole sauce.

Poblanos This is a large, deep green chile, which is shaped like a long, pointed heart. It is moderately hot and a favorite to use when making chile relleños. When smoke-dried, it's called an ancho chile. The poblano chile ranks 1,000 to 1,500 on the Scoville scale.

Serranos This chile has a small, bullet-shaped pod. Serranos are commonly used in salsa and guacamole and are twice as hot as jalapeños. Serranos rank 10,000 to 25,000 on the Scoville scale.

Shishito Shishito peppers are a vibrant green color and turn red as they mature. They are slender and grow to be between 2 to 4 inches in length. Although mild, ranging from 50 to 200 on the Scoville scale, a shishito pepper will occasionally pack a punch.

Thai peppers The variety of Thai pepper most commonly found in the supermarket is the *Bird's Eye.* All Thai peppers are bright red and small and thin. They range from 50,000 to 100,000 on the Scoville scale.

Selecting: Select firm, plump chiles with shiny skin and a fresh smell. Do not buy wrinkled or soft chiles. Also, if the skin is mushy toward the stem end, or if the skin is soft, or brown, the chile will be inferior.

Storing: Refrigerate in reusable, paper, or plastic bags for up to 1 week.

Availability: Normally year-round. Hatch chiles are in season August through September.

Pepper, Sweet Bell

Bell Peppers The most common bell pepper is green. Bell peppers are also red, yellow, orange, purple, white, and even brown. Some are even speckled. Red, orange, and yellow bell peppers are sweeter than green but also more expensive.

Long Sweet Peppers These peppers are long and thin, have few seeds and thick walls. They can be red, yellow, orange, or green in color.

Mini Sweet Peppers These small, crunchy, peppers are red, yellow, and orange in color, have few seeds, and are often times sweeter than bell peppers.

Selecting: Look for fresh, firm peppers that are bright and thick-fleshed with a firm green calyx and stem. Bell peppers should feel heavy for their size and have a crisp, shiny skin. Immature green bell peppers are soft, pliable, thin-fleshed, and pale green in color. Do not buy bell peppers with wrinkled skin or any soft or brown spots. Bell peppers have lobes on the top. The number of lobes can help you determine which pepper to buy. Bell peppers with four or more lobes are better for eating raw. Peppers with three lobes are better for roasting, sautéing, or grilling. Mini sweet peppers are packaged in plastic bags. Check the bag carefully. Do not purchase if the peppers inside have a wrinkled skin or any soft or brown spots are visible.

Storing: Sweet bell peppers will keep in the refrigerator for 3 to 4 days. It is best not to wash bell peppers until you are ready to use them.

Availability: Year-round, with peak season May through August.

Potato

There are numerous varieties of potatoes and three categories of potatoes: starchy, waxy, and all-purpose.

Starchy potatoes, like russets, are high in starch and low in moisture. The cells in starchy potatoes separate easily during the cooking process. When cooked, they have a glistening appearance and a dry, fluffy texture. They are good to use when baking or mashing potatoes or for French fries. Starchy potatoes also have a low-sugar content, so they do not brown excessively if deep-fried.

Russet Russets grown in Idaho are called Idaho potatoes, but are called russets outside of Idaho. This is the most widely used potato in the United States. This variety has thick, netted, brown skin and white flesh. It is light to dark brown in color with a large, oval shape. Russet potatoes are good for baking, mashing, frying, or boiling. They are the preferred potato to use when making mashed potatoes or French fries.

Waxy potatoes are low in starch and high in moisture. They are smooth, creamy, and moist when cooked. The cells in these potatoes adhere during the cooking process, helping them hold their shape. Use waxy potatoes when you want the potato to stay intact. Waxy potatoes can be boiled, roasted, baked, or steamed.

Adirondack Red The Adirondack Red potato has delicate, purplish-red skin and pinkish-red flesh. It has an earthy, sweet flavor.

Creamers Also known as baby potatoes, these marble-sized potatoes are less than ½ inch in diameter.

Fingerlings Fingerlings are small, thin-skinned potatoes that are shaped like a fat finger. Normally, these potatoes have a rich, buttery texture and are excellent for baking, roasting, grilling, and steaming. The Russian Banana is one of the most popular fingerling varieties. This potato is about 3 to 4 inches long with thin skin and firm, dense buttercream flesh. Peewee potatoes are a fingerling potato measuring less than 1 inch in diameter.

New potatoes New potatoes, sometimes called baby potatoes, are immature, freshly dug potatoes that have never been kept in storage. They have thin, delicate skins and fine textured flesh. The skin of a true new potato will come off when scratched with your fingernail.

Round reds Also known as the new potato, Red Bliss, or boiling potato, this variety has rosy, red skin with dense, waxy white flesh.

German Butterball The German Butterball is a medium-sized round potato with smooth, yellow skin, which is lightly netted with shallow eyes, dark brown spots, and brown patches. Its flesh is yellower than butter.

All-purpose potatoes have a medium starch and moisture content. They are given this designation because they can be used in a variety of ways.

Blue and **purple** These potatoes originated in South America. They have a nutty flavor, and their flesh colors range from dark blue to lavender to white.

Long whites This potato is long and shaped like a russet. It has thin, light tan, silky smooth skin and a firm creamy texture. When exposed to light, tend to turn green.

Round whites Shaped like a baseball, this variety has smooth, light tan skin with white flesh. Round whites have a creamy texture and hold their shape well after cooking.

Yukon Gold A cross between the North American white potato and the wild South American, yellow-fleshed potato, the Yukon Gold potato has thin, smooth, eye-free skin. Its golden flesh has a dense, creamy texture and a buttery flavor. They are the best mashing potato.

Selecting: Select firm, smooth, clean potatoes that have few eyes and good color. Potatoes should be blemish-free. Russets should have a net-like textured skin, oval shape, and brown color. Irregularly-shaped potatoes produce more waste when peeled. Do not buy potatoes with wrinkled or wilted skin, sprouts, or cut surfaces. Avoid potatoes with soft, dark spots.

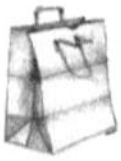

Storing: Potatoes will keep up to 2 weeks when stored in a cool, dark, well-ventilated place. Prolonged exposure to light will turn potatoes green. Green potatoes contain solanine, which has a bitter flavor and can be toxic if eaten in large quantities. When stored at temperatures below 40 degrees F, potatoes become sweeter.

Availability: Year-round. Blue and purple potatoes are more available in the fall. Fingerlings: October through April. Long whites: spring through summer. New potatoes: late winter through midsummer. Round red potatoes: late summer and early fall. Russets: year-round.

Cooking tip: Peeled, uncooked potatoes will discolor. To prevent this, immerse peeled potatoes in cold water for no more than 2 hours until ready to use.

Radicchio

Radicchio looks like a small head of wine-red, white-veined lettuce. It has a distinctive, spicy bitter flavor, which mellows when it is roasted, grilled, or sautéed. When it is cooked, radicchio turns a rich brown color. The most common variety sold in supermarkets is the *Chioggia*.

Selecting: Select heads that have crisp, full-colored leaves, with no blemishes or bruises. Larger heads will be more bitter. This product is expensive and, therefore, is a slow mover. Buy from a high-volume store. Do not buy radicchio if the leaves are brown or wilted.

Storing: When placed in reusable, paper, or plastic bags and refrigerated, radicchio should keep 1 week.

Availability: Year-round, with a peak season from mid-winter to early spring.

Radish

Radishes are root vegetables that are round, oval, or tapered. There are several varieties of radishes, all with some degree of peppery bite. Although normally eaten raw, radishes can be steamed, sautéed, or stir-fried. Their green tops are edible and add a peppery taste to salads.

Red globe Most supermarkets carry only red globes. This radish is small, round or oval in shape, with solid, crisp flesh. Red globe radishes are sold in bunches with their greens still attached or in bags with their tops removed.

Black radish This radish has a dark brown to black skin, which is thick, tough, and coarse. It is turnip-like in shape, and its white flesh has an earthy, spicy, bitter taste, which mellows when cooked.

Daikon Native to Asia, the daikon radish is shaped like a cucumber and has white skin. Its white flesh is juicier and spicier than the red globe. A staple in Asian cuisine, the daikon radish is often used in stir-fry or pickles.

French Breakfast The French Breakfast radish has an elongated shape. Its red skin tapers to white at the root end. The French Breakfast radish has a crisp texture and mild flavor. The French like to eat them raw on a buttered baguette sprinkled with salt.

Korean A varietal of the daikon, the Korean radish is jade green in color and stouter, fatter, and heavier than the daikon. Its white flesh is dense and crisp.

Watermelon An heirloom of the daikon radish, the watermelon radish has white and green skin and pink flesh. Its flavor packs a slight kick.

White Icicle With a white skin and tube-like shape measuring about 4 to 5 inches in length, this heirloom radish has white, crisp flesh and a mild flavor.

Selecting: Select fresh, bright radishes that are firm, well formed, tender, and crisp. Skin should be smooth and unblemished. If the tops are attached, the greens should be firm and perky. When gently squeezed, radishes should feel firm. Do not buy radishes with cracks, cuts, or yellowing. If you are buying prepackaged radishes, check the bag to be sure the radishes are free of mold and excessive cracking. Black radishes should be free of cracks and feel heavy for their size. Daikon and Korean radishes should be firm, and their skin should have a glossy sheen and no scratches.

Storing: If you buy radishes with their leaves attached, remove the greens before storing. The tops deteriorate first and can hasten spoilage. If the radishes are not already packaged in plastic, place in a reusable, paper, or plastic bag before storing. They will keep up to 2 weeks in the refrigerator.

Availability: Year-round, peaking during the spring.

Rhubarb

Rhubarb looks somewhat like celery but its stalks range in color from pale green to dark red. There are two types of rhubarb—*strawberry* rhubarb grown in hothouses and *cherry* rhubarb grown in fields. Rhubarb grown in fields has deeper color and more juice but is, also, more acidic. The stalks of rhubarb are edible, but the leaves are toxic if eaten in large quantities because they contain oxalic acid. The leaves are normally removed before sale.

Selecting: Select firm, crisp rhubarb with brightly colored stalks. Look at the ends of the stalks. Do not buy rhubarb with bruises or blemishes. The redder the stalks, the more flavorful rhubarb will be.

Storing: Place in a reusable, paper, or a plastic bag and refrigerate for up to 1 week.

Availability: Seasons in spring and summer. Hothouse rhubarb is available mid-January through mid-April.

Shallots

Shallots have a garlic-like head that is composed of many cloves. Their skin color varies from golden brown to gray to rose-red, and their off-white flesh is tinted with magenta. Shallots have a firm texture and a sweet, aromatic, yet pungent, flavor.

Selecting: Look for large, plump, firm, well-shaped shallots. Do not buy this vegetable if it is wrinkled, or sprouting, or shows any signs of black mold.

Storing: Shallots, when stored in a cool, dry, well-ventilated place, will keep up to 1 month.

Availability: Fresh green shallots are available in the spring. Dry shallots are available year-round.

Spinach

There are three categories of spinach—flat-leafed, curly (also called savoy), and semi-savoy. Within those three categories, there are several different varieties.

Flat-leafed spinach is more tender with a milder flavor, especially in the baby variety. It has broad, flat-shaped leaves.

The leaves of **curly spinach (savoy)** are firm, dark, and crinkly, have a slightly crunchy, crisp texture, and a bitter taste. Savoy spinach is normally sold in bunches and has a strong iron flavor with a slightly bitter aftertaste.

Semi-savoy spinach has lightly crinkled leaves and the same crisp texture and flavor as savoy.

Selecting: Spinach should be deep green with crisp, perky leaves. Do not buy spinach if it has yellow or broken leaves. Shop with your nose. If you smell an unpleasant odor, pass. If you are buying bagged spinach, inspect the bag carefully. Spinach deteriorates quickly. Also, check the "Best-If-Used-By-Date" to be sure it hasn't past its freshness date.

Storing: Place in reusable, paper, or plastic bags and store for 2 to 3 days in the refrigerator.

Availability: Year-round.

Sprouts

Sprouts are grown from the seeds of vegetables like broccoli and radishes, from grains like alfalfa, or from beans like soybeans. They are the first phase of a plant's life cycle and are grown in water for 2 to 5 days. Sprouts vary in taste and texture. *Radish* and *onion sprouts* are spicy. *Soybean* and *mung* sprouts are hardy and will hold up nicely when cooked. *Alfalfa* and *pea sprouts* are delicate and used in salads and sandwiches.

One of the most common sprouts found in a grocery store is the *alfalfa* sprout. Alfalfa sprouts are thread-thin and white with tiny green tops, a subtle nutty flavor, and crisp texture. Another common variety is *mung*. These bean sprouts are 2 inches long with small, light-yellow leaves and silvery white shoots. They have a high-water content and a subtle nutty flavor.

Other sprouts that are occasionally available are *beet, broccoli, clover, fenugreek, dill, lentil, mustard, onion, pea, pumpkin, radish, soybean, spelt, sunflower*, and *wheat*.

Selecting: Look for crisp sprouts with firm, moist, white roots. Do not buy slimy, dark, or musty-smelling sprouts.

Storing: Hardy sprouts will keep in the vegetable crisper for up to 3 days. Delicate sprouts generally last about 2 days.

Availability: Year-round.

Sunchoke

The sunchoke, also known as the *Jerusalem artichoke, sunroot, earth apple*, or *topinambour*, is the tuber of a type of sunflower, or the underground part of its stem. It looks like gingerroot, with a light brown skin. Sunchokes are about 1 to 2 inches in diameter and about 3 to 4 inches long. Their flesh is ivory-colored and has a nutty, slightly sweet taste, much like jicama. Sunchokes can be eaten raw or cooked.

Selecting: Select firm, clean tubers with few bumps and no blemishes. Sunchokes with soft spots, wrinkled skin, sprouts, or blotchy green areas have past their prime.

Storing: Sunchokes bruise easily so they should be handled with care. Store them in a dry, cool, well-ventilated area away from light. When wrapped in paper towels and placed in a reusable, paper, or plastic bag, sunchokes will keep in the refrigerator for up to 1 week.

Availability: Year-round, although they are at their peak from October to April.

To prepare: Scrub sunchokes with a vegetable brush. Using a sharp knife, remove any bumps, then peel with a vegetable peeler. To prevent sunchokes from turning brown, place them in a bowl of cold water with lemon juice.

Sweet Potato

There are three common varieties of sweet potato, also called the Beauregard, Garnets, and Jewels. The most popular variety, the *Beauregard*, is uniform in size and shape with smooth skin and deep orange flesh. *Garnets*, more popular with organic farmers, have garnet-colored skin, orange-yellow flesh, and excellent flavor. *Jewels* have a more orangey skin and deep orange flesh.

Selecting: Look for firm sweet potatoes, with smooth skins that are free of bruises and cracks. Avoid wrinkled or sticky sweet potatoes or ones that have sprouts.

Storing: Do not refrigerate sweet potatoes, but keep them in a cool, dark place. They will keep for 1 to 2 weeks.

Availability: Year-round.

Swiss Chard

The leaves of Swiss chard are similar to beet greens but are larger, flatter, and wider with a mild flavor and texture similar to spinach.

Selecting: Select Swiss chard that has fresh, green leaves that are moist and crisp. Do not buy this vegetable if its leaves are yellowed, wilted, or browned. If the leaves have tiny holes, this is an indication of insect damage.

Storing: Do not wash Swiss chard until ready to use. Wrap it in damp paper towels, place it in a reusable, paper, or plastic bag, and store it in the refrigerator. It will keep for 3 to 5 days.

Availability: April through November.

Tomatillo

The tomatillo is native to Mexico. It is greenish yellow in color, 1 to 2 inches in diameter, and encased in papery husks.

Selecting: Choose firm, dry tomatillos that fit tightly into their husks. Check to be sure the husks are dry to the touch. Underneath the husk, a tomatillo should be green, which is an indication it is not totally ripe—its preferred state. Do not buy sticky or yellow tomatillos.

Storing: If kept in their husks, placed in a paper bag, and refrigerated, tomatillos will keep up to 1 month.

Availability: Year-round.

Tomato

Supermarkets sell a variety of tomatoes: *hothouse, cherry, grape, beefsteak, Roma, Campari, Kumato*, and *vine-ripened.* Over the years, plant breeders have manipulated the genes of tomatoes by breeding them to withstand disease and pests, putting texture and flavor on the back burner. These hybrid tomatoes, which are always stocked at the supermarket, are hardy but lack a truly delicious taste.

Some supermarkets will also sell *heirloom* tomatoes, which are open-pollinated; this means their flower is pollinated with pollen from another plant to create a fruit whose seeds can reproduce. Hybrid tomatoes have viable seeds, but their seeds don't reproduce themselves. Unlike hybrids, bred to be disease and pest resistant, heirlooms are bred for flavor and possess a rich, sweet taste and a fine acid balance.

Most importantly, heirloom tomatoes are cultivars that have been selected, nurtured, and handed down from one generation to another. There are differing opinions on how old seeds must be to be classified "heirloom". Some think the seeds must be over 100 years old, others believe 50 is the magic number, while another school of thought prefers the seeds predate 1945—which marks the end of World War II and the beginning of the widespread use of hybrid seeds.

Selecting: Select firm and plump tomatoes that feel heavy for their size. Do not buy pale, spotted, or mushy specimens. Avoid tomatoes with blemishes or cracks. Color is the best indicator of quality. Pick brightly colored tomatoes. My father taught me to shop with my nose. Smell the stem end of the tomato. If it's ripe, it will smell like a tomato. Ripe tomatoes should give slightly when pressed but not feel rock hard.

Storing: Tomatoes must be treated gently. Place only ripened tomatoes in the refrigerator. Cool temperatures slow the ripening process. To ripen, place tomatoes at room temperature stem side down. To hasten the ripening process, place tomatoes in a paper bag and keep at room temperature.

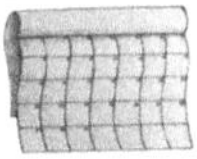

Availability: Year-round.

Turmeric Root

Turmeric is a flowering plant that is part of the ginger family and native to India and Southeast Asia. Also known as "Indian saffron," turmeric is a popular ingredient in Asian, Middle Eastern, and Indian cuisine. Both fresh turmeric root and dried or powdered turmeric are used in cooking.

Selecting: While some supermarkets stock fresh turmeric root, it will more likely be available at gourmet or health stores or Indian or Asian markets. Select firm roots. Avoid roots that are soft or shriveled.

Storing: When placed in an airtight container and stored in a cool, dark place away from light, fresh turmeric root will keep up to 6 months.

Availability: Year-round.

Turnip and Rutabaga

Turnips have a smooth, white, purple-tinged skin with several circles of ridges at the base of their leaves. Their flesh is normally white. Young turnips have a delicate, slightly sweet flavor. As they age, their taste becomes stronger, and their texture becomes woody. Rutabagas are larger and rounder than turnips and their flavor is sweeter.

Selecting: Turnips should feel heavy for their size. Look for smooth, firm, unblemished skin and fresh green leaves. Do not buy turnips that are larger than 3 inches in diameter because they may be woody. When buying rutabaga, select specimens with smooth skin that feel heavy for their size. When a rutabaga is bruised or cut, that means it has been in storage too long.

Storing: Place turnips in a reusable, paper, or plastic bag and refrigerate for 1 week. Place rutabaga in a reusable, paper, or plastic bag and refrigerate for 2 weeks.

Availability: Turnips—year-round, peaking in October through March. Rutabaga—in season September through June.

Wasabi

Wasabi is a perennial herb that is native to Japan. Also known as Japanese horseradish, wasabi roots are grated to make a smooth, green paste, which is used as a condiment for sashimi and sushi. Difficult to grow, wasabi roots require a special kind of soil, shade, an even temperature, and constant water, making it very expensive to purchase.

Selecting: Look for whole firm roots. Avoid roots that are slimy or deteriorating.

Storing: Place in a glass of water. Stems should not be submerged. Store in the refrigerator, changing the water every day. Wasabi lasts only a few days.

Availability: Real wasabi roots are difficult to find and may only occasionally be available in specialty food markets or from specialty producers.

To prepare: Wash wasabi and scrub it with a brush. Carefully peel and grate.

Watercress

Watercress has small, crisp dark green leaves. A member of the mustard family, it has a slightly bitter, peppery taste.

Selecting: Buy watercress that has deep green, whole leaves. Shop with your nose. Smell the watercress. If it has an unpleasant odor, do not buy it. Avoid watercress if it shows signs of yellowing or wilting.

Storing: Watercress is very perishable. It can be stored two different ways. When placed in a reusable, paper, or plastic bag and refrigerated, watercress will keep 3 to 4 days. To extend its life, remove the rubber band that holds the stems together and place the stems in a glass of water and refrigerate.

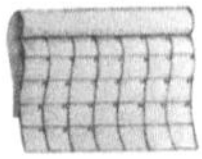

Availability: Year-round.

Winter Squash

Winter squash have thick, tough skin and stay on the vine longer than summer squash. The seeds of winter squash are only edible if they have been roasted and shelled.

Acorn squash An acorn squash is round with even groves around the entire squash. Its skin is green with patches of orange or yellow. Its flesh is a yellow orange, a bit stringy, with a sweet taste. Acorn squash weigh between 12 ounces and 2 pounds.

Buttercup squash This squash has a stocky shape and a turban-like top that enlarges as the squash matures. When baked, it tastes like roasted chestnuts and sweet potatoes.

Butternut squash The butternut squash has an elongated, pear shape with thin, tan, smooth skin, and it has a creamy texture when cooked. Butternut squash usually weigh between 2 to 3 pounds.

Delicata squash Delicata squash is small, weighing about 1 pound, and oblong in shape with bright yellow, dark green, or orange strips. Its thin skin is edible. The flesh of delicata squash has a sweet, nutty, almost corn-like taste.

Fairytale pumpkins Fairytale pumpkins are a large, flat squash with large deep ribs. Weighing in at 20 pounds, its skin turns from dark green to an orange-brown when ripe. Fairytale pumpkins are one of the only winter squashes that can be eaten raw. Its flesh is sweet and orange-yellow in color.

Hubbard Hubbard squash are quite large. Supermarkets might pre-cut them and sell them in halves. Found in a variety of colors ranging from bluish, gray, orange, dark green, and light green, the Hubbard squash has a teardrop shape.

Kabocha squash The kabocha squash is large and round with dark green, speckled, bumpy skin. Its flesh has a sweet, tender, slightly nutty flavor.

Long Island Cheese Pumpkin This winter squash is one of the oldest pumpkin varieties grown in the US. Its skin can be yellowish or tan with pinkish tones. The cheese pumpkin has sweet, firm flesh. Cheese pumpkins get their name because their shape resembles wheels of cheese.

Pumpkin This is a name given to hard-skinned squash. In the United States, it refers to a large, rounded, orange squash that is used for jack-o'-lanterns. They are often referred to as field pumpkins. This type of pumpkin has flavorless flesh and is, therefore, best for carving. Smaller pumpkins are good for eating and can be prepared the same as acorn squash. These smaller pumpkins are called "sweet" or "sugar" pumpkins. Miniature pumpkins can be cream or orange in color.

Red Kuri The Red Kuri squash is a small- to medium-sized winter squash, about 7 inches in diameter and weighing about 4 to 7 pounds. It has a hard, bright red-orange skin and golden yellow flesh. The Red Kuri, also known as the Hokkaido, has a sweet, nutty flavor.

Rouge Vif d'Etampes pumpkin Also known as the Cinderella pumpkin, this winter squash is round and squat with a brilliant red orange color.

Spaghetti squash This squash has a pale-yellow skin, a thin, hard shell, and bright yellow or orange flesh. When cooked, its flesh has a lightly sweet, mild flavor and pulls apart into noodle-like strands, resembling pasta.

Sweet dumpling squash This small squash is 4 inches in diameter and weighs less than 1 pound. Its yellow skin has bright orange or dark green stripes inside its ridges. It is difficult to peel so it is often sliced into wedges and baked with the skin on. Its flesh is pale yellow or orange, and the sweet dumpling squash has stringy pulp.

Turban squash This winter squash resembles a turban. It has a hard, bumpy skin with multi-colored patches of green, orange, yellow, and white. It grows about 10 to 15 inches in diameter and will weigh between 5 to 6 pounds. Its flesh is a pale yellow-orange with a bland flavor. Because it is so colorful and lacking in flavor, it is more often used as a decorative squash.

White pumpkins Most white pumpkins found at the supermarket are field pumpkins and are best used for decorations or carving. There are some heirloom varieties, like the lumina, that are good for eating; but these varieties are most likely found in farmers' markets.

Selecting: Buy rock-hard squash. When you press hard on squash, it should not give to pressure. Its skin should be matte, not shiny. Select squash with firm, full, cork-like stems. Avoid specimens that have skinny or green stems. When buying butternut squash, look for small bottoms and a long neck. Do not buy squash with soft spots or bruises. When buying delicata squash, avoid specimens with bruises, soft spots, or cuts.

Storing: Store squash in a cool, dry place. Thick-skinned squash like hubbard can last for months. Squash with soft, moist flesh surrounding the seedpod deteriorate more quickly.

Availability: Year-round, but September and October are prime months.

Zucchini and Summer Squash

Harvested before they reach full maturity, there are several varieties of summer squash.

Zucchini Zucchini is the most common summer squash and is normally deep green but can also be golden yellow. Yellow zucchinis retain their color when cooked. The French and British call this squash *courgette.*

Costata Romanesca The Costata Romanesca zucchini is striped with pale green ridges and darker green valleys. When young, this squash is sweet and juicy.

Cousa The cousa looks much like a spaghetti squash, but its flesh and seeds are edible. It has a thin skin and a sweeter taste than zucchini.

Round zucchini The round zucchini, also called the eight-ball zucchini, tastes like the common zucchini; but its short, flat shape makes it a good candidate for stuffing. Round zucchinis have few seeds and are heavy for their size. When cooked, their flesh has a green tint.

Yellow Yellow squash comes in two varieties—*crooknecks* and *straightnecks*. Crooknecks are harvested when they are 2 inches in diameter and about 5 to 6 inches long. They are wider at the blossom end than the stem end, and their stem is curved. Crookneck squash have thick warty skin, sweet flavor, and crunchy texture. Straightnecks look much like crooknecks, but their necks don't curve. They also have a bumpy skin and a pale-yellow flesh.

Patty pan Scalloped or pattypan squash have a flattened or bell shape and a scalloped edge. They range in color from cream, sunny yellow, pistachio, and ivy green. Their skin is smooth and edible, and their flesh has a bland taste.

Tatuma Tatuma, a Mexican heirloom squash, is firmer, sweeter, and more flavorful than other summer squash. It looks much like a pale green zucchini.

Zephyr The Zephyr squash is a hybrid of the summer yellow crookneck, the winter delicata, and yellow acorn squash. It is yellow with a defined green bottom and a tapered neck.

Squash blossoms Squash blossoms are extremely perishable. They are sometimes found in farmers' markets and specialty food markets.

Selecting: Select small to medium squash with shiny, taut skin. Smaller squashes are normally more tender and have fewer seeds. If the skin is lightly scratched or bruised, it will not compromise the quality of the squash. Do not buy overly large squash or ones with pitted skin or a spongy texture. Soft spots or wrinkled skin are signs of age or rot.

Storing: When placed in reusable, paper, or plastic bags and stored in the vegetable crisper of the refrigerator, summer squash will keep 1 week.

Availability: Year-round, but peak season is spring to summer.

Freezing Fresh Vegetables

Most fresh vegetables can be frozen, though the texture of some vegetables when thawed may be softer and mushier than when they are fresh. You may not be able to use these vegetables in salads, but they can be used for cooking in soups, casseroles, and pasta dishes. Follow my guidelines on selecting the freshest vegetables at their peak, and freeze only top-quality vegetables. Freezing does not sterilize food, but the cold will retard the growth of microorganisms.

Buy high-quality freezer bags or containers that seal tightly. Choose the size of bag that is appropriate for the amount of vegetables you wish to freeze. If you are freezing individual portions, consider placing smaller bags into a larger bag. This will help prevent freezer burn. If you use containers, leave about a ½-inch space at the top to allow for food to expand. If you use bags, press as much air out of the bag as possible before sealing.

Wash vegetables thoroughly in cold water before freezing. Discard any part that is poor quality. Pat dry with paper or kitchen towels, and allow the veggies to dry thoroughly before freezing. If you find insects present in any veggies you want to freeze, like broccoli or cauliflower, soak the veggies for 30 minutes in a solution of 4½ teaspoons of salt to 1 gallon of water.

When you freeze vegetables, **prep them the same as you would when using them fresh;** for example, if you normally peel carrots, peel them before freezing. Think about how you will use them once they are thawed. Leave veggies whole or cut them into pieces, depending upon the recipe you will use them in. If you plan to use frozen carrots in a stew, cut them into appropriately sized pieces. Portion the veggies and/or pieces into serving sizes and package accordingly.

Most vegetables need to be blanched before freezing. Blanching cleans the surface of dirt and organisms, retards the loss of vitamins, and helps retain flavor, color, and texture. There are two types of blanching—water and steam. I do not recommend using a microwave oven to blanch. Once veggies are blanched, they should be drained, cooled, and dry before they are packaged and frozen. Never freeze hot vegetables.

Water Blanching

Water blanching is the most common method used to prepare veggies for freezing. Using a blancher with a blanching basket and cover is best. If you don't have one, a wire basket and a large kettle with a lid will work. Use 1 gallon of water for every pound of veggies. Fill the blancher with water and bring the water to a rolling boil over a high heat. Place the veggies in the blanching basket or wire basket and submerge the basket into the water. Cover. When the water returns to a rolling boil, set the timer. Specific times for blanching different veggies are included in the chart that follows.

Steam Blanching

To steam blanch, use a large kettle with a cover and a basket that will hold the veggies 3 inches above the bottom of the kettle. Fill the kettle with an inch or two of water and bring the water to a rolling boil over a high heat. Place the veggies in a single layer so that the pieces will receive equal amounts of steam.

After blanching, drain vegetables and cool completely. Make sure the vegetables are completely dry before freezing.

Lay veggies in a single layer on a baking sheet lined with parchment paper so that the pieces won't stick to the pan. Freeze for a few hours until the vegetable is solid, then transfer it to an airtight container or a freezer bag. Press as much air out of the bag as possible. This helps prevent freezer burn.

Use a black marker to label packages with the contents and freezing date. Freeze at 0 degrees F or lower. Frozen veggies do not need to be thawed before they are cooked.

Blanching times vary according to the vegetable and its size. Preparation instructions for veggies that need blanching as well as times are found in the following chart. **Blanching times are for water blanching unless steam is indicated.** Information about how to freeze veggies that are not blanched can be found after the chart.

Vegetable	Preparation	Blanching Time
Asparagus	Remove woody ends. Cut into 2-inch pieces or leave in spears.	Thin stalks: 2 minutes Medium stalks: 3 minutes Large stalks: 4 minutes
Artichokes	Remove stems and any tough outer leaves. Slice ½-inch off the top. Using cooking scissors, snip off the sharp tips of leaves. Add juice of 1 lemon to blanching water. Once blanched, cut in half and remove hairy choke.	Water: 7 - 10 minutes Steam: 9 - 11 minutes
Arugula		1 minute
Beans: Green, Wax, Haricot Vert	Remove ends. Leave whole or cut into 1- to 2-inch pieces.	3 minutes
Beans: Lima, Butter, Pinto, Fava	Shell before freezing. Sort by size.	Small beans: 2 minutes Medium beans: 3 minutes Large beans: 4 minutes
Beets	Trim off the green leaves, leaving ½-inch of the stem. Cook in boiling water until tender. Remove stem and peel the beet. Cut into slices or cubes.	Cooking time Small beets: 25 - 30 minutes Medium beets: 45 - 50 minutes

Vegetable	Preparation	Blanching Time
Broccoli	Trim ends. Cut into pieces no more than 1 ½-inch across.	Water: 3 minutes Steam: 5 minutes
Brussels Sprouts	Trim ends. Remove outer leaves. Sort by size.	Small: 3 minutes Medium: 4 minutes Large: 5 minutes
Cabbage: Napa Cabbage	Remove outer leaves and core. Cut into medium to coarse shreds or thin wedg-es.	Shredded: 30 to 60 seconds Wedges: 1 to 2 minutes
Carrots	Remove tops and peel. Leave small carrots whole. Cut large carrots into strips, slices, or cubes.	Whole small: 5 minutes Slices, strips, cubes: 2 minutes
Cauliflower	Remove outer leaves and core. Cut into 1-inch pieces.	3 minutes
Celery	Cut away leaves and any white parts. Remove coarse strings and chop into desired length.	2 to 3 minutes
Celeriac	Peel and cut into disks or cubes.	4 minutes
Chayote	Cut into pieces and remove seeds.	2 minutes
Corn: Whole Kernels	Remove husks and silks and wash. Cut kernels from cob about ⅔ depth of kernel.	4 minutes
Corn: Whole Ears	Remove husks and silks and wash.	Small 1¼" or less diameter: 7 minutes Medium 1¼ to 1½" diameter: 9 minutes Large over 1½" diameter:
Edamame	Leave whole. Once blanched, edamame can be removed from pods. To freeze indi-vidual edamame, place on a parchment-lined baking sheet to freeze.	2 minutes
Eggplant	Peel and cut into ⅓-inch slices. For each gallon of water use ½ cup lemon juice to retard browning. If you plan to fry the slices, place freezer wrap between each slice.	4 minutes
Endive	Freeze whole.	3 to 4 minutes

Vegetable	Preparation	Blanching Time
Fennel	Slice bulb into quarters or 2-inch slices.	30 seconds
Greens: Amaranth, Beets, Collards, Chard, Dandelion, Flowering Kale, Kale, Mustard, Spinach, Turnip	Remove stems. Blanch leaves only.	Collards: 3 minutes Other greens: 2 minutes
Kohlrabi	Trim off roots and tops. Peel. Freeze whole or in ½-inch cubes.	Whole: 3 minutes Cubes: 1 minute
Leeks	Trim off the end. Chop or slice.	30 to 45 seconds
Lotus Root	Clean thoroughly and cut into ¼-inch slices.	3 minutes
Mushrooms	Trim off stems. For best color, soak in 1 pint water and 1 teaspoon lemon.	Whole, halved, or quartered: 3½ minutes Slices: 3 minutes
Nopales, Nopalitos	Wear gloves. Use a brush to scrub the nopales. This should remove most of the spines. Peel with a vegetable peeler to remove any stubborn spines, imperfections, or hairs. Chop the pads into strips or cubes.	1 minute
Okra	Separate by size. Remove stems at the end of the seed cell, leaving seed cells intact. Leave whole or slice crosswise. If you plan to fry, slice blanched pods crosswise and dredge with flour after blanching. Place in a single layer on a baking sheet lined with parchment paper and freeze until firm.	Small pods 4" or less: 3 minutes Large pods: 4 minutes
Parsnips	Trim off ends, peel, and slice into ¼-inch slices.	2 to 3 minutes
Peas with edible pods: Snow, Sugar, Sugar Snap, or Chinese	Remove ends and strings. Leave whole.	Small pods: 1½ minutes Medium pods: 2 minutes

VEGETABLES

Vegetable	Preparation	Blanching Time
Peas: Green, Black-Eyed Peas	Shell.	1 to 1½ minutes
Peppers: Sweet Bell	Cut in half, remove stems and seeds. Can be cut into ½-inch strips or rings.	Halves: 3 minutes Strips or rings: 2 minutes
Potatoes	Peel. Small potatoes can be left whole. Large potatoes should be cut into at least quarters. Determine use and cut potatoes into size needed. To use in mashed potatoes, cut into 1-inch chunks.	Whole, small: 10 minutes Cubes or strips: 3 to 5 minutes
Radishes	Remove ends and thinly slice.	2 to 3 minutes
Rutabaga	Cut off ends, peel, and cube.	3 minutes
Summer Squash (including Zucchini)	Cut into ½-inch slices.	1 to 2 minutes
Sunchokes	Peel. Leave whole or slice into halves, cubes, or slices.	Whole: 2 minutes Halves: 1 minute Cubes or slices: 30 seconds
Turnips	Peel and cut into ½-inch cubes.	2 minutes

Blanching is not required for the following vegetables:

Aloe Vera Leaves: Wrap fresh leaves tightly with aluminum foil or place in freezer bags. Before freezing, place in an air-tight container.

Avocados: You can freeze avocados whole, in halves, sliced, or mashed; however, freezing will alter the texture. It is preferable to use frozen avocado in recipes where it will be mixed with other ingredients, like guacamole, dressings, or smoothies. To freeze avocados in any form, wash the outer skin of the avocado and dry. To freeze whole, wrap tightly with plastic wrap, place in a freezer bag, and seal tightly. Whole avocados will keep in the freezer for 3 to 6 months. For halves, follow the directions for whole avocados, but cut in half. I prefer to leave the skin on and pit in. Use a pastry brush to coat the avocado halves with lemon juice. Wrap tightly in plastic wrap and place in freezer bags. For slices or pieces, peel and remove the pit. Slice into wedges or cubes. Sprinkle with lemon juice. Place on a baking sheet lined with parchment paper and freeze until firm. Transfer to a freezer bag. To freeze mashed avocados, peel, pit, and mash. Add lemon juice to taste. Place in a freezer container.

Bok Choy: Shred boy choy into bite-sized pieces for stir-fry or soup. Transfer to a freezer bag.

Burdock Root: Cut into julienne pieces or thin strips. Place in water to remove its high lye content. Pat dry with paper towels. Wrap tightly in plastic wrap and place in freezer bags.

Chestnuts: Chestnuts can be frozen in their shell or shelled. To freeze boiled or shelled chestnuts, place them on a baking sheet lined with parchment paper and freeze until firm. Transfer to a freezer bag. To freeze unshelled chestnuts, which are best for roasting, place them in freezer bags.

Cucumbers: Peel or leave the peel on. Slice. Place slices on a baking sheet lined with parchment paper and freeze until firm. Transfer to a freezer bag.

Garlic: To freeze whole bulbs, place in a freezer bag, seal tightly, and freeze. For cloves, separate the cloves and remove the paper skins. Place cloves on plastic wrap and wrap tightly to prevent freezer burn. Place in a freezer bag. For puréed garlic, prep the cloves as if you were freezing them separately and slice off ends. Place the garlic cloves in a food processor and chop. Add a little olive oil and purée to desired consistency. One tablespoon of olive oil for one head of garlic is a good measurement. Place garlic purée in an ice cube tray and freeze until hard, about 2 hours. Transfer frozen cubes to freezer bags.

Ginger: Peel and mince or grate. Place 1 teaspoon portions on a baking sheet lined with parchment paper and freeze until firm. Transfer portions to a freezer bag.

Green onions: Slice off the root ends and thinly slice the white and green sections. Place slices on a baking sheet lined with parchment paper and freeze until firm. Transfer to a freezer bag.

Horseradish root: Peel and grate. Place grated horseradish in 1 tablespoon portions on a baking sheet lined with parchment paper. Freeze until firm and transfer to a freezer bag.

Jicama: To freeze whole, wrap jicama with aluminum foil and place in the freezer. To freeze cubes or slices, pat dry with paper towels before placing in freezer containers. Moisture can cause decay.

Onions: Cut off the tops and root ends of onions. Peel and chop or dice into ¼- to ½-inch pieces. Place onions on a baking sheet lined with parchment paper and freeze until firm. Transfer to a freezer bag.

Peppers, Chile: Remove stems. Freeze whole. No blanching is needed.

Pumpkin and Winter Squash: Cut into small pieces and remove the seeds. Bake in a 350 degrees F oven until soft. Remove the pulp from the rind. Using a potato masher, mash the pulp, and then cool, package, and freeze.

Rhubarb: Trim the stalks and remove and discard leaves. Cut rhubarb into ½-inch thick slices. Place slices on a baking sheet lined with parchment paper and freeze until firm. Transfer to freezer bags.

Shallots: Trim off both ends and peel. Chop or slice into desired size. Place pieces on a baking sheet lined with parchment paper and freeze until firm. Transfer to freezer bags.

Sweet Potatoes: Cook until tender in boiling water, in the oven, or steam. Cool and peel. Cut into halves, mash, or slice. Cooked sweet potatoes may darken. To prevent this, dip them in a solution of ½ cup lemon juice and 1 quart of water. If you mash your potatoes, add orange or lemon juice before freezing to prevent darkening.

Tomatoes: Cut an X in the bottom of each tomato. Drop in a saucepan of boiling water for 30 seconds. Peel and core. Leave whole or cut into pieces.

Tomatillos: Remove husks. Freeze whole or cut into halves depending on the size. Place on a baking sheet lined with parchment paper and freeze until firm. Transfer to freezer bags.

Turmeric Root: Trim to remove any flaky pieces of the root. Pat dry with paper towels. Slice into pieces. Wrap each piece tightly with aluminum foil before placing in a freezer bag.

VEGETABLES

Vegetables Not Recommended for Freezing

While some experts feel that certain vegetables can be frozen, the freezing process will dramatically alter some vegetables. I do not recommend freezing the following:

Escarole
Lettuces - iceberg, looseleaf, romaine, spring mix
Mâche
Microgreens
Radicchio
Sprouts
Watercress

Please note: *Orach* and *wasabi root* are difficult to find where I live. I have no experience freezing either of these veggies, so I have not included them in the above information.

Home Made Vegetable Stock

Save peelings and trimmings from veggies like onions, tomatoes, squash, potatoes, bell peppers, mushrooms, and herbs to make stock. Place the scraps in a Ziploc® bag or airtight container and refrigerate or freeze until you have 4 to 6 cups. Place veggie scraps on a baking sheet lined with parchment paper and roast for 20 minutes at 300 degrees F. Transfer veggie to a large kettle with enough water to cover. Add 1 teaspoon salt and 10 peppercorns, bring to a boil, reduce the heat, and simmer for 1 to 1½ hours. Cool and strain out veggies. Place in airtight containers and refrigerate for up to 5 days or freeze for up to 6 months.

SIX

How to Select and Store HERBS and SPICES

Herbs are the fragrant leaves of annual or perennial plants that grow in temperate zones and are used to flavor foods. They are sold dried or fresh. Dried herbs, also called spices, are available all year-round in the spice aisle of your supermarket. They possess a stronger, more concentrated flavor than fresh, but lose their spiciness quickly. When ground or crushed, their zest diminishes even more quickly. When substituting dried for fresh, follow these guidelines: **¼ teaspoon powdered herb = 1 teaspoon dried = 1 tablespoon fresh.**

Dried herbs give off more flavor when heated, so add them at the beginning of cooking. When you buy dried herbs, keep them in tightly sealed containers in a cool, dark place. Mark the date you open the jar with a black marker and keep for up to 6 months.

When shopping for fresh herbs, select ones with even green color and no signs of wilting, yellowing, or insect damage. Fresh herbs should be washed before using. After washing, pat dry with paper towels. To help prolong the life of some herbs, place them in a glass of water, stems down, cover with a reusable, eco-friendly produce storage bag or a plastic bag, secure the glass with a rubber band, and refrigerate. Change the water every 2 days. This works nicely with basil, cilantro, mint, and parsley. Fresh herbs lose their flavor if you cook them too long, so they should be added towards the end of cooking.

Allspice Known as *Jamaica pepper*, allspice comes from the pea-size berries of evergreen pimiento trees. The dried berries are dark brown and can be purchased whole or ground. This spice tastes like cloves, cinnamon, and nutmeg.

Basil A member of the mint family, the basil's taste is a cross between licorice and cloves. Although it is a summer herb, it is available year-round in supermarkets in both a fresh and dried form. When buying fresh basil, choose evenly colored leaves that show no sign of wilting or yellowing. To store, wrap the leaves in damp paper towels, place in a reusable, paper, or plastic bag, and refrigerate.

Bay Leaves Most often used to flavor soups, stews, vegetables, and meats, bay leaves, also known as bay laurel, have a complex flavor—a combination of eucalyptus, mint, lemon, and fresh-cut grass. There are two varieties—*Turkish* and *Californian*. The Turkish variety has a more subtle flavor. Bay leaves are always available dried, although fresh leaves can sometimes be found in the produce department.

Caraway Seeds A popular spice in German cuisine, caraway seeds have a warm, nutty flavor with a delicate touch of anise.

¼ teaspoon powdered herb = 1 teaspoon dried = 1 tablespoon fresh

A member of the parsley family, these tiny brown seeds are hard, ridged, tapered, and slightly curved.

Cardamon Seeds Native to India, cardamom has a warm, spicy sweet flavor and pungent aroma. A member of the ginger family, cardamom can be purchased in the pod or ground. While ground is more convenient, it is not as flavorful. You can grind the entire pod or remove the seeds from the pod and grind them separately. A mortar and pestle work nicely for this purpose.

Chervil A member of the parsley family, chervil can be used like parsley. This aromatic herb has curly, dark green leaves that resemble ferns and an elusive anise flavor.

Chili Powder Most often used in Southwestern cuisine, chili powder is a blending of many spices—dried chiles, garlic, oregano, cumin, coriander, and cloves.

Chives Related to the onion and leek, this herb has slender, vivid green hollow stems and a mild onion flavor. It is available fresh year-round, and when stored in plastic, will keep 1 week in the refrigerator. Select chives with a uniform, green color and no signs of wilting or yellowing. Chives are also sold freeze dried.

Cilantro These leaves have a lively, pungent fragrance, which some describe as a mix of orange and sage. Cilantro is the name given to the lacy, green leaves of the coriander plant. Cilantro is best purchased fresh. Select leaves with a bright, even color with no sign of wilting or yellowing. Cilantro will

Preserve fresh herbs by drying them at the lowest setting in an oven.

keep 1 week in a reusable, paper, or plastic bag when refrigerated. For hints on storing, see *Vegetables.*

Cinnamon This spice has a pungent, slightly bittersweet flavor. When dried, it curls into long quills and is sold as cinnamon sticks; or it is ground into powder or sold as oil.

Cloves One of the world's most important spices, cloves are the dried, unopened flower bud of the tropical evergreen clove tree. Reddish brown and nail-shaped, they are sold whole or ground.

Coriander Related to the parsley family, coriander is known both for its seeds and its leaves, which are called cilantro. The tiny, yellow-tan coriander seeds are lightly ridged and have the aroma of lemon, sage, and caraway. It is sold ground or whole. When whole, it is used for pickling.

Cumin Cumin is the dried fruit of a plant from the parsley family. Its aromatic, nutty-flavored seeds can be white, black, or amber. The white and amber seeds are similar in flavor, but black cumin seeds have a more complex, peppery flavor. Cumin is also sold ground.

Curry Powder Curry is a powdered blend of up to 20 different spices, herbs, and seeds. Among those are cardamom, chiles, cinnamon, cloves, coriander, cumin, fennel seed, fenugreek, mace, nutmeg, red and black pepper, poppy and sesame seeds, saffron, tamarind, and turmeric. It comes in two varieties—*standard* and *Madras*, which is the hotter of the two. Curry powder should only be stored for up to 2 months.

¼ teaspoon powdered herb = 1 teaspoon dried = 1 tablespoon fresh

Dill Dill weed is sold fresh, dried, and as seeds. When fresh, dill will not look crisp. Select bunches with deep green leaves with no sign of rot or yellowing. When dried, it is sold as dill weed. Dill seed is the dried fruit of this plant. When heated, it has a stronger, more pungent flavor than the leaves.

Fennel Fennel seeds come from the common fennel plant. The seeds can be purchased whole or ground and taste like licorice. To use fennel in its fresh form, see *Vegetables*.

Fenugreek Fenugreek is a clove-like herb that is native to the Mediterranean, southern Europe, and western Asia. Its seeds smell and taste like maple syrup. Fenugreek is often included in spice blends and used as a flavoring.

Garam Masala Garam masala is a popular spice blend in Indian cuisine. It can include black pepper, cinnamon, cloves, coriander, cumin, cardamon, dried chiles, fennel, mace, and nutmeg as well as other spices.

Ginger Ground ginger sold in the spice section of your supermarket is quite different from fresh ginger and is not a good substitute. It is the spice used in gingerbread cookies and ginger ale. For tips on using fresh ginger, see *Vegetables*.

Lemon Grass One of the most important flavorings in Thai and Vietnamese cooking, lemon grass has long, thin, gray-green leaves and a woody, scallion-like base. Avoid ones with blemishes. Store fresh lemon grass in the refrigerator, tightly wrapped in a reusable or plastic bag, for up to 2 weeks.

Preserve fresh herbs by drying them at the lowest setting in an oven.

Mace Mace is the bright red membrane that covers the nutmeg seed. After it is removed from the seed, it is dried and ground. This turns it a yellow-orange color. It is sold ground or whole. Mace tastes and smells like a strong version of nutmeg.

Marjoram The most common type of marjoram sold in supermarkets is sweet marjoram, a member of the mint family. It is a summer herb with oval, inch-long, pale green leaves. It has an earthy, woodsy flavor with hints of sharpness and bitterness.

Mint The two most popular varieties of mint are *peppermint* and *spearmint*. Mint is sold dried, fresh, or as an extract. Peppermint has bright green leaves, purple-tinged stems, and a peppery taste. Spearmint has true green leaves and a milder flavor and aroma. It is sold year-round but is more readily available in the summer. Choose leaves with even coloring that show no signs of wilting.

Mustard Mustard greens are a member of the same family as broccoli. Its seeds are white (or yellow), brown, or black. The white seed is the main ingredient in American style mustard, while brown seeds are used for pickling, as a seasoning, and in European and Chinese mustards. The seeds are sold whole or ground into powder.

Nutmeg This herb comes from the nutmeg tree. When picked, its fruit is split to expose the seed. The membrane surrounding the seed is removed and becomes the spice mace. The seed is sold ground or whole. Nutmeg has a warm, spicy, sweet flavor and aroma.

Oregano Oregano belongs to the mint family and is related to marjoram and thyme. It is sold either fresh, ground, or dried. It has a similar taste to marjoram but is not as sweet and has a stronger, more pungent flavor and aroma. When buying this fresh, select bright green bunches with no sign of wilting or yellowing. When placed in a reusable, paper, or plastic bag and refrigerated, it will keep for 3 days.

Paprika Paprika is a powder made from sweet red pepper pods. Its color can vary from bright orange red to deep blood red and its flavor from mild to hot. Most supermarkets carry a mild paprika. More pungent varieties can be found at gourmet or ethnic shops.

Parsley Sold fresh or dried, the most popular varieties are the *curly leaf parsley* and *Italian* or *flat leaf parsley*. Curly leaf is in most supermarkets; Italian is harder to find. Select bunches with bright green leaves and no sign of wilting. Wash parsley, shake off excess moisture, wrap in paper towels, then in a reusable, paper, or plastic bag, and refrigerate for up to 1 week.

Pepper The world's most popular spice comes from berries found in grape-like clusters on the pepper plant. Peppercorns are black, white, pink, red, or green. When picked before fully ripe and dried, they shrivel and turn dark. This *black peppercorn* is the strongest—slightly hot with a hint of sweetness. The *white peppercorn* is ripened, then the skin is removed before drying, resulting in a milder flavor and a light tan color. Black or white peppercorns are available whole, cracked, or coarsely or finely ground. Whole peppercorns will keep for

Preserve fresh herbs by drying them at the lowest setting in an oven.

1 year, while ground pepper is best used within 4 months. *Green peppercorns* are normally found in the same aisle as pickles. Jars should be refrigerated once opened. If packed in brine, they will keep 1 month; if packed in water, 1 week.

Red peppercorns have been allowed to ripen fully, which causes them to turn red. If red peppercorns are harvested and dried, they become black. If their black skin is removed, they become white. *Pink peppercorns* are usually imported from Madagascar and are, therefore, expensive. They are pungent and slightly sweet but not as flavorful as either black or white pepper.

Rosemary Part of the mint family, rosemary has silver-green, needle-shaped leaves and the flavor of lemon and pine. It is available fresh, dried (whole leaf), or powdered.

Saffron The world's most expensive spice, saffron comes from the yellow-orange stigmas of the purple crocus. Each flower has only three stigmas, which are hand-picked and then dried. Saffron is sold in threads or powdered. When powdered, it loses its flavor quickly. The threads should be crushed just before using.

Sage Sage has narrow, oval, gray-green leaves and a musty mint taste and smell. It is sold fresh or dried. When buying fresh, choose sage that looks fresh and has a musty mint smell. Dried, sage comes whole, rubbed (crumbled), and ground.

¼ teaspoon powdered herb = 1 teaspoon dried = 1 tablespoon fresh

Sesame Seeds These tiny, flat seeds can be brown, red, or black. A pale grayish ivory color is the most common. Possessing a slightly sweet, nutty flavor, they can be stored airtight in a cool, dark place for up to 3 months or refrigerated for up to 6 months.

Tamarind comes from the pods of the tamarind tree. It is a popular ingredient in Indian cuisine. It is sold as a powder, paste, concentrate, or in plastic-wrapped blocks. It has a sweet, tangy flavor with notes of caramel and molasses.

Tarragon This herb has narrow, pointed, dark green leaves and an anise-like flavor. It is sold either fresh, dried, or powdered.

Thyme The most common variety of thyme is *garden*. It has gray-green leaves that give off a minty, light-lemon aroma. It is sold fresh, dried, or powdered.

Turmeric This herb comes from the root of a tropical plant related to ginger. It tastes musky, peppery, gingery, and warm and has an intense yellow-orange color. It is available in supermarkets in a powdered form. For information on using fresh turmeric, see *Vegetables*.

Vanilla The vanilla bean is a pod from an orchid flower. It is cured for several months—a labor intensive, expensive process —making the vanilla bean quite pricey. You can purchase vanilla whole, powdered, or as an extract. Vanilla extract comes pure or imitation—pure being the most expensive. Vanilla beans should be wrapped tightly in plastic wrap, placed in an airtight jar, and refrigerated for up to 6 months. Extracts can be stored indefinitely if sealed airtight and kept in a cool, dark place.

Preserve fresh herbs by drying them at the lowest setting in an oven.

SEVEN

How to Select and Store Dairy

Milk, cream, and half-and half can be frozen but may become slushy, grainy, and separate when thawed. Thawed frozen dairy can be used for baking, cooking, or smoothies.

Milk

Whole milk, or milk just as it came from the cow, contains 3 ½ percent milk fat. In *2 percent milk,* also called reduced fat milk, 98 percent of the fat has been removed. *1 percent milk,* also called *nonfat milk,* contains less than ½ percent milk fat. *Buttermilk* is the pale, yellow liquid that remains after butter is churned. When bacterial culture is added, buttermilk is called cultured buttermilk.

Cream

Light cream, also called table cream, normally contains 20 percent fat, but can contain between 18 to 30 percent. *Light whipping cream* is most often found in supermarkets. It contains 30 to 36 percent milk fat. Sometimes emulsifiers or stabilizers will be added to it.

Heavy cream, also called whipping cream, is whipping cream with a milk fat content of between 36 to 40 percent.

Half-and-Half

Half-and-half is a combination of equal parts milk and cream. It contains 12 percent milk fat. *Non-fat half-and-half* combines nonfat milk with corn syrup and thickeners. It contains twice the sodium of half-and-half but half the calories.

Clotted Cream

Clotted cream is a traditional accompaniment for English afternoon tea. It is usually sold in a jar and has a 55 percent fat content. It is made by gently baking fresh, heavy cream. It has a thick consistency and can be mistaken for butter.

Butter

Butter is made by churning cream until it reaches a semisolid state. US law requires it contains 80 percent milk fat. *Unsalted butter*—No salt is added to this butter; therefore, many prefer it over regular butter. Because it has no salt, which acts as a preservative, it is more perishable than regular butter.

Whipped butter—Air is beaten into the butter, which increases its volume and creates a softer, more spreadable consistency. *Light or reduced-calorie butter* has about half the fat of regular butter.

Yogurt

Yogurt is the result of milk that has fermented and coagulated because it has been attacked by friendly bacteria. Your supermarket will sell *plain yogurt*, *flavored yogurts*; which contain sugar, artificial flavors, or fruits; and *frozen yogurt*, which resembles soft-serve ice cream.

Sour Cream

Sour cream contains 18 to 20 percent fat. It is treated with a lactic acid culture, which gives it its tang. *Light sour cream* will contain 40 percent less fat than regular sour cream. Your supermarket may also sell a *nonfat sour cream.*

Ghee

Ghee, a traditional Indian food, is a higher fat, creamier version of butter. Ghee is clarified butter that has been cooked. It will have a nuttier flavor than clarified butter

Skyr

Skyr resembles yogurt and originated in Iceland. It is made by mixing skim milk with bacterial starters and rennet.

Kefir

Kefir originated in Russia. It is a healthy, fermented dairy food similar in taste and texture to liquid yogurt.

Ice Cream

Ice cream is made with cream and either fresh, condensed, or dry milk, a sweetening agent, like sugar or honey, and sometimes additions like chocolate or nuts. The FDA requires plain ice cream to have 10 percent milk fat, while ice cream with added ingredients like nuts must have 8 percent milk fat. Most ice creams will contain 14 to 25 percent milk fat.

Gelato

Gelato, the Italian name for ice cream, is denser and richer than ice cream. It also has less air which keeps it dense, fluid, and creamy. Gelato is made with milk but contains only 4 to 9 percent milk fat.

Sherbet

Sherbet is made from a mixture of fruit purée, sweetener, and a little milk or buttermilk. It has a fat content of 1 to 2 percent.

Selecting Dairy

Dairy products should feel cold to the touch when you put them in your cart. Like all perishables, dairy products should be one of the last items you purchase. If you have to travel a good distance from your supermarket to your home, consider putting your dairy products in an insulated bag. Keeping your dairy products at their preferred storage temperature of between 33 and 40 degrees F will help extend their shelf life.

Selecting Milk, Cream, or Half-and-Half

Choose milk, cream, or half-and-half that comes in an opaque container. If exposed to light, milk, cream, or half-and-half packaged in clear containers may lose vitamin A and riboflavin. Avoid containers that leak or have been damaged in any way.

Milk is Graded

The USDA grades milk either A or B. Grade A milk, also called fluid grade milk or market milk, is the milk your supermarket will sell as whole milk, 2 percent, 1 percent, or skim. Fluid milk is more susceptible to bacterial contamination, so it must be produced and processed under more stringent health and sanitary standards. Ninety (90) percent of the milk produced in the United States is Grade A. Fifty (50) percent of Grade A milk is used in other dairy manufactured food products. Grade B milk, also known as manufacturing grade milk, is used only for manufactured food products.

Selecting Butter

Check the label for fat content. If you want really delicious butter, the higher the fat content, the better the flavor.

European butters will have an 82 percent butter fat. Check the label for additives. Some manufacturers will add canola oil. If you want butter made in small batches, look for the terms "small batch" or "slow churn" on the label.

Butter is Graded

The USDA grades butter quality based on its flavor, texture, color, body, and salt. The grades are AA, or a score of 93; A, a score of 92; B, a score of 90; and C, a score of 89. Packages of butter will bear a shield indicating its grade. Most butter sold in supermarkets will be graded AA or A.

Selecting Ghee

When selecting ghee, check the quality of the butter it is made from. Ghee connoisseurs believe the best ghee comes from pasture-raised, grassfed, organic cows.

Selecting Yogurt

Read the label. Yogurt should contain at least 15 percent of the daily value of calcium. Select yogurt that meets your needs for fat content and added sugar. The label will also indicate if yogurt has added probiotics. This is a personal choice.

Check Dates

It is important to check dates on all dairy products to be sure they have not expired. If your market continually has close-dated product, it is a sign that items are not selling quickly enough to ensure freshness.

The "Sell-By" date is the last day the manufacturer recommends a product be sold. While most dairy products will be good a few days after this date, buy dairy products that have at least 7 days before they reach their "Sell-By" date. The "Best-If-Used-By" date means that the manufacturer does not feel the product will be at its peak after that date. Dairy products can be used past this date, but check them carefully to be sure they are still good to consume. To stretch your food dollars, never buy dairy products that are at or past this date.

Labeling on Dairy Products

Processing/Pasteurization

Most milk sold in the US has been pasteurized, meaning that microorganisms that cause disease and spoilage have been destroyed by heating. The term "ultra-pasteurized" means the milk has been thermally processed at or above 280 degrees F. This process extends the shelf life of milk. The term "aseptically processed and packaged" means milk is processed using ultra-high temperature pasteurization and then is bottled immediately in a sterile environment.

Homogenization

Homogenization means the milk fat globules have been broken down mechanically until they are evenly distributed throughout the milk. This means that the cream does not separate from the milk.

BST or BGH

BST, bovine somatotropin, is a naturally occurring hormone in cows. In 1993, the FDA approved supplementing cows with a genetically produced hormone known as rBST (recombinant bovine somatotropin) and rBGH (recombinant bovine growth hormone) to help increase their milk production. The FDA and World Health Organization find these supplements do not alter the milk and are safe for human consumption. Opponents disagree. You may find some milk labeled, "farmer certified to not come from BST-supplements cows," or "rBGH free" or "rBST free."

Get to Know the Manufacturer

Investigate the creamery that makes the brand of dairy products you purchase. Where do they source their milk? What techniques do they use to make butter? This is particularly important if you prefer buying pasture-fed, grassfed, or free-range dairy.

Organic

Organic dairy products must come from animals that eat only organically grown feed, and this feed must not contain any animal byproducts. In addition, the animals can't be treated with synthetic hormones or antibiotics and must be grown without the use of synthetic fertilizers, pesticides, or fertilizers. Animals must have access to the outdoors, and cows, sheep, and goats must have access to pasture. Organic dairy products cannot come from animals that have been cloned.

Pasture Raised

This means the dairy products come from animals that get a significant amount of their nutrition from organic grass grown in a pasture. When the cows, goats, or sheep are not producing milk or when their milk is used for other products, they may be fed hay or silage. See *Understanding Food Labels*.

Grassfed

The label "grassfed" on dairy products means that the cows, goats, or sheep that produced the milk ate only grass. These animals may receive nutritional supplement like minerals and molasses, but only in small amounts. See *Understanding Food Labels.*

Free Range

"Free-range" labels on milk products mean the animals were given free access to the outdoors for a minimum of 120 days per year. There is no requirement about how much space each animal has or what the conditions of the outdoor space are. This does not mean that the animals only grazed on range. See *Understanding Food Labels.*

Checking Out

It is usually when you reach the checkstand that you discover whether any dairy products you've selected have leaks. If you have a product that leaks, insist that the cashier get you a replacement. Ask the sacker to bag all your dairy products in the same bag. This helps product stay cooler on the ride home and makes the job of putting your groceries away easier.

Using and Storing Dairy Products at Home

Refrigerate your dairy products as soon as you get home. Shelf-stable milk can be stored in your pantry but should be refrigerated as soon as it is opened.

Containers of dairy products should be tightly closed after use and put immediately back into the refrigerator. Never leave dairy products out on your kitchen counter any longer than necessary and never more than 2 hours. Once opened, butter should be covered while stored in the refrigerator. If you've put milk or cream in a pitcher for serving, don't return unused product back to its original container.

Storing Gelato

There is such a thing as a gelato freezer, but most Americans won't have one. Gelato should be stored in the freezer. Gelato is not fond of changes in temperature and prefers to be stored at a temperature of 0 degrees F or below. Store gelato in the back of your freezer and below other frozen items if possible.

Freezing Butter

If your supermarket has a special on butter and you buy a large quantity, it can be frozen for later use. To freeze butter, wrap it tightly in aluminum foil and place it in a reusable or Ziploc® freezer bag. Frozen butter will keep up to 6 months.

Freezing Milk, Cream, and Half-and-Half

Milk, cream, and half-and-half can be frozen; however, they may become slushy, grainy, and separate when thawed. If you plan to freeze your milk, cream, or half-and-half, it will not be good for drinking or putting into your coffee but will be suitable for baking, cooking, or smoothies. To freeze, place it in an airtight, freezer-safe container or bag. Do not fill the container or bag completely full. Milk products may expand as they freeze. If you use a bag, press as much air out of the bag as possible before freezing. If you want to use the milk in smoothies, you can freeze milk in ice cube trays. Once the milk is frozen, transfer it to a freezer bag. It is best to use frozen milk, cream, or half-and-half within 1 month.

Thawing Milk, Cream, and Half-and-Half

To thaw, place it in the refrigerator overnight. Do not thaw on the counter.

Freezing Sour Cream

You can freeze sour cream, but its consistency will change. You can use frozen sour cream for baking and cooking, but it won't be suitable for garnishing baked potatoes. If you haven't opened the container, you can place it directly into the freezer. If you've opened the sour cream, stir it before freezing. Place it in an airtight, freezer-safe container. If you have a large container of sour cream, consider freezing it in smaller portions. If you are concerned about freezer burn, consider placing the container in a freezer bag. You should use frozen sour cream within 2 months.

Thawing Sour Cream

To thaw, place it in the refrigerator overnight. Do not thaw on the counter.

Freezing Yogurt

Yogurt will freeze quite well, but its consistency will change. Before you freeze it, stir it, especially yogurts with fruit, to be sure all the ingredients are well combined. Place it in an airtight, freezer-safe container. If you are concerned about freezer burn, place the container in a freezer bag. Frozen yogurt should be used in 2 months.

Thawing Yogurt

To thaw, place it in the refrigerator overnight. Do not thaw on the counter. Once yogurt has thawed, give it a good stir. Most of its original texture will return.

Safe Refrigeration Times

Dairy prices are soaring. We all want to extend our food dollars as much as possible. If stored properly, dairy products will be safe to use beyond the "Sell-By" date. Following are some general guidelines. Always check product that has past its "Sell-By" date to ensure it is safe to consume.

Milk	unopened—5 to 7 days opened—3 to 7 days
Cream	opened or unopened—1 to 3 weeks
Half-and-half	opened or unopened—10 days
Heavy cream	opened or unopened—up to 1 month
Clotted cream	opened—4 days unopened—up to 14 days
Regular butter	unopened—1 to 3 months opened—up to 2 weeks
Unsalted butter	unopened—1 to 3 months
	opened—up to 2 weeks
Yogurt, Skyr	unopened—up to 1 week opened—5 to 7 days
Sour cream	opened—2 weeks unopened—3 weeks
Ghee, unopened	several months opened—6 months
Kefir	opened or unopened—about 1 week

Safe Freezing Times

Frozen yogurt	up to 3 months
Ice cream	unopened—2 to 3 months opened—1 to 2 months
Gelato	is best when eaten 1 to 2 weeks after opening
Sherbet	unopened—3 to 4 months opened—2 to 3 months

EIGHT

How to Select and Store Cheese

Soft cheeses, like Brie and mozzarella, have the shortest shelf life of all the cheeses.

Cheese is made with four ingredients: milk from either cows, goats, or sheep; salt; cultures; and enzymes. There are six basic types of cheese:

Fresh Cheeses

Fresh cheeses are soft and rindless and have a short shelf life. After opening any fresh cheese, it is best to consume it as soon as possible. Fresh cheeses include chèvre, feta, fresh mozzarella, burrata, mascarpone, cottage cheese, cream cheese, ricotta cheese, fromage blanc, and queso fresco.

Soft-Ripened Cheeses

Soft-ripened cheeses include *Brie, Camembert, soft-ripened goat cheese*, and *washed-rind cheese*. These cheeses are fresh and creamy and have soft, fuzzy, or wrinkled rinds. As they age, the rinds of washed-rind cheeses are rubbed or washed with a solution like wine or salt water. Soft-ripened cheeses also include "smelly" cheeses like *Taleggio* and *Limburger*.

Semi-Soft and Semi-Hard Cheeses

These cheeses have a high moisture content and a smooth interior. They include *American processed cheese, Asiago, Cheddar, Cheshire, colby, Edam, Gouda, Gruyère, Monterey Jack, mozzarella, Havarti, Jarlsberg, provolone*, and *Swiss*. These cheeses are the best candidates for shredding and slicing.

Hard Cheeses

Hard cheeses have a firmer texture and a sharp taste. They are good for grating. Hard cheeses include aged *Manchego, Parmigiano-Reggiano*, and *Pecorino Romano*.

Blue Cheeses

Blue cheeses include *Gorgonzola, Maytag Blue, Stilton*, and *Roquefort*. They have distinctive blue veins created by the addition of mold during the cheese-making process.

Selecting Cheese

While many people prefer to buy specialty cheeses at a specialty cheese shop, your supermarket does sell a wide variety of cheeses. Most supermarkets will stock cheese in three different locations: the dairy section, the deli section, and a stand-alone cheese case where you will find imported cheeses in pre-cut wedges and chunks. This is the place to look if you are shopping for Brie, Gruyère, or chunks of Parmesan for grating. Some higher-end supermarkets, like Whole Foods, will also have a section where both domestic and imported cheese can be cut to order.

Selecting Cheese in the Dairy Section

The shredded and sliced cheese you find in the dairy section should feel cold to the touch. The packages should not have punctures or tears and should be free of mold. Check the "Sell-By" date. Although cheese will last several days past its "Sell-By" date, to extend your food dollars never buy cheese that is near its "Sell-By" date. Pre-sliced and shredded cheeses will deteriorate more quickly than chunks or wedges.

When buying packaged shredded cheese, you may want to consider that shredded cheese has an anti-caking agent which coats, the cheese with a dryish powder. It is cellulose, made from plants, and not at all harmful to consume but often affects the melting properties of cheese.

Selecting Cheese at the Deli

If you want to purchase freshly sliced cheese from the deli counter, observe the following to ensure your deli cheese is fresh: Deli meats and cheeses should be sliced on different slicers. Deli employees should not use the same slicer for both meat and cheese. It is preferable that slicers are cleaned after every use. Supermarkets these days have minimal staff, so this may not be the case; but slicers should be cleaned on a regular basis. The towels used to clean the slicer should be changed after every cleaning. The cheese should be returned to the deli case immediately after slicing. Deli employees should change their gloves after slicing each customer's order. If addition, they are required to change gloves during the same order if they are slicing both a meat and cheese item.

CHEESE

If you don't feel the deli employees are following these safety procedures, consider buying prepackaged sliced cheese.

Selecting Cheese from the Stand-Alone Counter

One of the advantages of purchasing cheese from the stand-alone counter is that often you can have the cheese cut to order, so you are only buying what you need. In addition, you can ask to sample the cheese to determine if it is something you like. Most of the time cheese purchased from the stand-alone cheese counter will be of higher quality but also more expensive.

The employees that staff this section are trained to be knowledgeable about cheese. Get to know them. They can answer any questions you have about purchasing cheese for a charcutier tray, or they can recommend nice accompaniments, like pairing fig jam with Brie.

The cheeses in this case are usually cut and wrapped once a week. Softer cheeses are cut twice a week. Check the label. It will often indicate both the date and time the cheese was cut and wrapped.

Avoid any packages where the cheese is over ripe or moldy, except for some blue cheese or expensive Brie that ripen with harmless molds. Softer cheeses should be soft and moist but should not have cracks or be brown in color.

Selecting Blue Cheeses

A significant amount of white mold on the rind of blue cheese is an indication of improper handling. Avoid blue cheese that smells like ammonia. It should have a nutty, smoky, herbal smell.

Cheese is Graded

Cheese is graded by the USDA either Grade AA, A, B, or Wisconsin state brand. Graded cheese is inspected by trained and experienced graders and ranked by its flavor, body and texture, color, and finish and appearance. Grade AA is the highest quality. Grade A is not as good; it has a pleasing flavor but will have variations in its texture, color, and appearance. Cheese may bear a USDA "Quality Approved" seal. To carry this shield the cheese must be manufactured in a facility that follows USDA sanitary guidelines for both the plant and equipment. Examples of "Quality Approved" cheeses are processed cheese, cheese spreads, and cottage cheese. Packages of cheese found in supermarkets will rarely bear a USDA shield, but the manufacturing process of all products sold in the US are approved by the USDA.

Labeling on Cheese Products

Organic Cheese

Organic cheese is made entirely of organic milk, which means the animals producing the milk are not fed antibiotics, and their diets must be sourced from organic pastures and feed. The cows, goats, and sheep that produce organic cheese must have access to pasture and cannot be cloned.

Pasture-Raised Cheese

This label means the cheese comes from animals that get a significant amount of their nutrition from organic grass grown in a pasture. When the cows, goats, or sheep are not producing milk or when their milk is used for other products, they may be fed hay or silage. See *Understanding Food Labels*.

Grassfed Cheese

Grassfed cheese means the milk the cheese was made from comes from cows, goats, or sheep that ate grass only. These animals may receive nutritional supplements like minerals and molasses, but only in small amounts. See *Understanding Food Labels.*

Free Range

"Free-range" labels on milk products mean the animals were given free access to the outdoors for a minimum of 120 days per year. There is no requirement about how much space each animal has or what the conditions of the outdoor space are. This does not mean that the animals only grazed on range. See *Understanding Food Labels.*

Pastureized Versus Unpastureized (or Raw Milk) Cheese

The USDA requires that cheese made from unpasteurized or raw milk must be aged 60 days or longer at 35 degrees F. It is illegal in the United States to produce and sell raw-milk cheese that is not aged.

When making cheese, cheese makers use three types of heat treatment to pasteurize milk. The *Low Temperature Long Time (LTLT)* method heats milk to 145 degrees F for at least 30 minutes. The *High Temperature Short Time (HTST)* method heats milk to 160 degrees F for at least 15 seconds. A pasteurization process that gives milk a longer shelf life is called *Ultra High Temperature (UHT).* Milk is heated to 280 degrees F for 2 to 4 seconds

Saving Money on Cheese

Unless you have a brand of cheese you are fond of, there is not a huge difference in taste and texture between various brands of prepackaged sliced and shredded cheeses. If you want to save money, purchase sliced and shredded cheeses that are on sale.

When you are purchasing imported or domestic cheeses sold in wedges or chunks, brand names vary a great deal. Shop at a big box retailer like Costco or Sam's for better pricing. They often have a nice selection of specialty cheeses.

Using and Storing Cheese

Storing Hard Cheeses

Hard cheeses like Asiago, Parmesan, and Pecorino Romano can last 4 to 6 months in the refrigerator if stored properly. Wrap the cheese in cheese cloth, parchment paper, or butcher paper. Don't smother it but give it room to breathe. If hard cheese has white or blue-green mold, cut off the mold, along with a half-inch piece surrounding it. What remains should be safe to consume. If the mold is red or brown, throw the entire chunk out.

Storing Semi-Soft to Semi-Hard Cheeses

Semi-soft to semi-hard cheeses like Gruyère, Havarti, Muenster, Gouda, Edam, and Jarlsberg contain more moisture than hard cheeses, so they won't keep as long. If they are stored properly, you may be able to extend the shelf life 2 to 4 weeks past the "Sell-By" date. Wrap semi-soft and semi-hard cheese in parchment paper and then place in a reusable food storage bag or in a Ziploc® bag. If you think the cheese has gone bad, use your sense of smell and taste. It should not smell putrid and should taste like it did when you brought it home. You can cut mold off semi-soft and semi-hard cheeses, but if the mold looks unusual, it is best to toss the cheese out.

Storing Soft and Fresh Cheeses

Soft cheeses, like Brie and mozzarella, have the shortest shelf life of all the cheeses. To extend the life of soft cheeses, wrap them with parchment or wax paper and then a layer of aluminum foil or place them in a jar or Tupperware® container. When handled in this manner and placed in the cheese drawer of your refrigerator, soft cheese can last for up to 10 days. Soft cheeses with any sign of mold should be thrown out. Treat chèvre and feta as you would soft cheeses. Fresh mozzarella and burrata should be stored in the original package and liquid they came in. They should last 1 week after the "Sell-By" date but only 3 to 4 days after opening.

Storing Deli Cheese

Deli cheese will dry out more quickly than packaged sliced cheese. Once you bring it home, deli cheese will stay fresh for about 7 days.

Storing Blue Cheeses

Firmer blue cheeses, like Stilton, should be wrapped in wax paper and placed in an airtight bag or plastic container. Softer blue cheeses, like Gorgonzola, should be placed in an airtight container with a few holes in the lid so it can breathe.

Serving Cheese

Cheese should be served at room temperature. Take it out of the fridge 1 hour before you plan to eat it. Serving cheese at room temperature helps loosen its fat and gives it better texture and flavor. Do not let cheese sit more than 4 hours out of the refrigerator. Moist, soft cheese, like cottage cheese or mozzarella, should not be left out of the refrigerator for longer than 2 hours.

Freezing Cheese

If you are pinching pennies and your supermarket has cheese on sale, some types of cheese can be frozen. Do not freeze hard cheeses like Parmesan Reggiano. If properly stored, hard cheese will keep 4 to 6 months in the refrigerator. Do not freeze soft cheeses, soft-ripened cheeses, or hand-crafted cheeses.

Although its taste won't change, the texture of cheese will change when it is frozen. Frozen cheese will yield the best results if, when thawed, you grate it, melt it, or crumble it.

The best cheeses to freeze are blocks of semi-hard cheeses like Cheddar, Monterey Jack, Colby Jack, mozzarella, or provolone. Freeze cheese in its original packaging if unopened and place it in a reusable or a Ziploc® freezer bag. Press as much air out of the bag as possible before freezing. If opened, wrap the cheese tightly with plastic wrap or aluminum foil and then place it in a reusable or a Ziploc® freezer bag. Press as much air out of the bag as possible before freezing.

You can freeze packaged shredded cheese. Again, press as much air out of the bag as possible before freezing. If you shred the cheese yourself, place it in a reusable or a Ziploc® freezer bag and press as much air out of the bag as possible before freezing. Frozen shredded cheese should be used within 2 months.

To freeze sliced cheese, if unopened in its original package, place it in a reusable or a Ziploc® freezer bag and press as much air out of the bag as possible. For deli cheese or if the package has been opened, place a piece of parchment paper between each slice of cheese or the cheese will stick together. Wrap tightly with plastic wrap or aluminum foil, then place it in a reusable or Ziploc® bag. Press as much air out of the bag as possible before freezing. Frozen sliced cheese should be used within 2 months.

Thawing Frozen Cheese

Frozen cheese will keep for about 2 months and should be thawed in the refrigerator. Allow 1 to 2 days for cheese to thaw.

Safe Refrigeration Times

Cottage cheese	opened—10 to 30 days
Cream or Neufchâtel cheese,	opened—2 weeks
Semi-soft or semi-hard cheeses like Cheddar, Edam, Gouda, or Swiss	unopened—3 to 6 months opened—2 to 4 weeks sliced—7 to 10
Ricotta cheese	opened—5 days
Processed cheese food products	3 to 4 weeks
Soft blue cheeses	1 week
Harder blue cheeses	2 to 3 weeks
Sliced deli cheese	7 days
Soft cheeses like Brie	up to 10 days
Hard cheeses like Parmesan Reggiano	4 to 6 months
Fresh mozzarella or burrata	unopened—1 week after the "Sell-By" date opened—3 to 4 days

NINE

How to Select and Store Eggs

Nutritionally, there is no difference between white and brown eggs, unless the chickens have been fed an enhanced diet like flaxseed.

Selecting Eggs

Only purchase eggs that are in a refrigerated case. Eggs are shipped to your supermarket in refrigerated trucks at a temperature of 45 degrees F. This helps prevent foodborne illnesses.

Before you put eggs in your cart, open the egg carton to make sure the eggshells are clean and not cracked. Don't buy eggs with cracks. Salmonella could seep into the inside of the egg.

Expiration Dates

Check the expiration date to avoid buying out-of-date eggs. Always purchase eggs that have at least two weeks before their "Sell-By" date expires. Eggs cartons with a USDA shield must bear a "pack date" (the day the eggs were washed, graded, and placed in their carton). This date is a three-digit code which represents the consecutive day of the year—so January 1 is 001, January 31 is 031, February 1 is 032, December 31 is 365.

If you are purchasing egg products or egg substitutes, be sure the containers are tightly sealed. Also check the date.

Color

Chicken eggs can have white, brown, or even blue-green shells. Genetics is the main factor that affects egg color. The color of the egg is determined by the breed of the hen that lays it. White Leghorn chickens lay white eggs; Plymouth Rocks and Rhode Island Reds lay brown eggs. Araucana and Lushi chickens are among the breeds of chickens that lay blue or blue-green eggs. As hens that lay brown eggs age, their eggs may become larger and lighter in color. Nutritionally, there is no difference between white and brown eggs, unless the chickens have been fed an enhanced diet like flaxseed.

Sizing

Select the appropriate size for your intended use. Sizing on eggs is determined by weight, not size; therefore, some eggs in the same carton may look larger or smaller than the rest. Some recipes will specify a certain size of egg, particularly when you are baking. The best all-purpose size is large.

Jumbo—30 ounces (minimum net weight per dozen)
Extra Large—27 ounces
Large—24 ounces
Medium—21 ounces
Small—18 ounces
Peewee—15 ounces

Grading

USDA grading of eggs is voluntary. Egg packers must pay to be inspected by the USDA. If your egg carton has a USDA shield, it means the eggs were checked for quality standards, grades, and size under the supervision of a trained USDA grader. State agencies also monitor quality standards for egg packers. These cartons will bear terms like "Grade A" on their cartons and will not have a USDA shield.

Eggs have three grades: US Grade AA, A, or B. The grade is established by the interior quality of the egg and the condition of its shell.

GRADE AA eggs have thick, firm whites. Their yolks are high, round, and nearly free of defects. Their shells are clean and unbroken. Grade AA eggs are best for poaching or frying when appearance is important.

GRADE A eggs are similar to Grade AA eggs, but their whites are "reasonably" firm. Grade A eggs are the grade most commonly sold in supermarkets.

GRADE B eggs have thinner whites, and their yolks may be wider and flatter. Shells on Grade B eggs must be unbroken, but they may have slight stains. Grade B eggs are normally made into liquid, frozen, or dried egg products.

Labeling on Egg Products

If buying free-range, cage-free, or pasture-raised eggs is important to you, it is best to investigate the producer and confirm the actual conditions under which the eggs are produced. "Animal Welfare Approved" is a voluntary, free certification that sets the highest standard for the treatment of hens used by the egg industry. It requires that hens are given access to pasture, nest boxes, and dust baths and prohibits debeaking.

There is no regulatory guidance from the USDA or FDA on the terms "pasture-raised", "farm fresh", "naturally raised", "animal friendly", or "happy hens".

Free Range

This is a confusing term. It implies the chickens producing the eggs roam freely outdoors. There are no requirements for the size or condition of the outdoor area or how much time the chickens spend outdoors. See *Understanding Food Labels.*

Cage Free

The USDA states eggs labeled as cage free "must be produced by hens housed in a building, room, or enclosed area that allows for unlimited access to food, water, and provides the freedom to roam within the area during the laying cycle." See *Understanding Food Labels.* USDA cage-free standards only require that hens are not kept in battery cages, which are designed for high denisty and stacked on top of each other. The living conditions for hens raised on cage-free farms can vary widely.

Pasture Raised

Pasture-raised hens are given the opportunity to roam on green, grassy pastures every single day. When accompanied by a third party verification from either "Animal Welfare Approved" or "Certified Humane", this means that hens in a pasture-raised flock can have anywhere from 35 to 108 square feet of pasture to roam.

Certified Organic

This means that chickens laying certified organic eggs were fed certified organic feed and grains and did not receive any antibiotics or hormones.

Organic vegetarian-fed: All certified organic eggs must come from chickens that receive a completely vegetarian diet

No Hormones or Hormone Free

This label is redundant. Hormones are never given to laying hens.

Omega-3 Enriched

When egg cartons bear this label, it means the chickens laying the eggs were fed an omega-3 rich diet, which is typically flaxseed.

Antibiotic Free

Eggs can only be labeled antibiotic free if producers do not use any antibiotics in their feed or water when the hens are growing or when they are laying eggs.

Pasteurized

Eggs are pasteurized in a warm water bath, which removes salmonella bacteria that may be present inside the shell. The letter "P" or the word "Pasteurized" will appear on the carton of pasteurized eggs. The American Egg Board advises that eggs that have been pasteurized in their shells are safe to use in recipes without cooking, like in Caesar salad dressing.

Storing and Using Eggs at Home

Refrigerate eggs immediately when you get home. Store them in the coldest part of your refrigerator, not in the door. Eggs should not be left out of the refrigerator for more than 2 hours. Keep eggs in their original carton. This helps cushion them from cracking.

When you open your egg carton, you will notice that producers place the eggs round side up and pointed side down. They do this because eggs have an air bubble in their rounded end, which helps the yolk stay centered, thus keeping the egg fresher longer. If you return an egg to the carton, place it pointed side down.

Do not put broken eggshells back into the carton with uncracked eggs. Used eggshells may have bacteria that can contaminate uncracked eggs.

If eggs crack on the way home from the store, you don't have to throw them out. Break them into a clean container, cover tightly, refrigerate, and use them within 2 days.

It is not necessary to wash eggs that you purchase from the supermarket. Washing eggs can remove their protective mineral oil coating and increase the possibility of bacteria on the shell entering the egg.

When combining eggs with other ingredients in a to recipe, cook immediately or refrigerate and cook within 24 hours.

Questions about Appearance

Blood spots are the result of small blood vessels rupturing in the yolk at the time of ovulation. The presence of blood spots does not mean the egg is unsafe.

A clear white is the sign of a fresh egg; a cloudy white is the sign of aging.

A pink, fluorescent, or greenish egg white or yolk indicates spoilage. If your egg smells like sulfur, it is past its prime and should be discarded.

The color of the yolk can vary depending upon the hen's diet. If she eats more yellow-orange plant pigment, the yolk will be a darker yellow than if she eats a diet of white cornmeal.

Hard-Boiled Eggs

A green ring around the yolk of a hard-boiled egg is a sign of overcooking. (Scrambled eggs cooked at too high a temperature may also develop a greenish cast.) The discoloration does not affect the safety of the egg.

Why are hard-boiled eggs sometimes hard to peel?

The fresher the egg, the harder it is to peel. When first laid, an egg has no air cell. This air cell, found at the larger end of the egg between the shell membranes, develops and increases in size the longer the egg is stored. Therefore, fresher eggs, once hard-boiled, are harder to peel as the air cell is smaller. Older eggs have a larger air cell, making them better candidates for peeling. To determine if an egg is just right for hard boiling, perform the float test in a bowl of water. If it sinks, it is fresh. If it stands on its side and wobbles, it is just right for hard boiling. If it floats, it is past its prime.

Safe Cooking

If eggs crack during the hard-boiling process, they are still safe for consumption. Hard-boiled eggs should be refrigerated within 2 hours of cooking and used within 7 days.

To cook eggs safely, whether poaching, frying, baking, or hard-boiling, yolks should be firm. Scrambled eggs should not be runny.

To make a recipe safe that calls for using eggs that aren't cooked, heat the eggs along with all the liquid from the recipe over low heat, stirring constantly, until the mixture reaches 160 degrees F. Then cool, if necessary, before combining it with the other ingredients in the recipe.

To determine if egg dishes like quiche are done, test the center of the mixture with a food thermometer. When the center reaches 160 degrees F, the dish is done.

Freezing Eggs

The price of eggs has risen significantly. If your supermarket has eggs on special, you can buy them in large quantities and freeze them. You can't freeze eggs in their shells or with their yolk intact, but you can freeze the whites and yolks separately as well as combined for dishes like scrambled eggs. Frozen eggs will keep about 12 months in the freezer.

To freeze eggs, you need an ice cube tray. Silicone ice cube trays work nicely.

To Freeze the Yolk and White Together

Crack open the eggs into a bowl. Using a whisk, gently beat the whites and yolks until they are just barely mixed. Pour the beaten egg mixture into the ice cube tray. Cover the tray with aluminum foil, parchment paper, or plastic wrap and place the tray into the freezer.

Once the eggs are frozen, remove them from the tray and transfer them to freezer Ziploc® storage bags. Use a marker to note the freezing date on the bag. Each section of the tray should equal about one half egg.

To Freeze the Yolk

Freezing yolks by themselves can be difficult as they tend to thicken. Adding salt or sugar to the yolks can help prevent this. Crack open the eggs and separate the yolks from the whites. Place the yolks in a bowl. Using a whisk, gently beat the yolks until they are liquid. To use yolks in savory dishes, add ½ teaspoon salt for 1 cup of yolks. For sweet recipes, add 1½ teaspoons sugar for each cup of yolks. Pour the yolks into the ice cube tray. Cover the tray with aluminum foil, parchment paper, or plastic wrap and place the tray into the freezer.

Once the eggs are frozen, remove them from the tray and transfer them to freezer Ziploc® storage bags. Use a marker to note the freezing date on the bag as well as whether you have added salt or sugar. Each section of the tray should equal 2 egg yolks.

To Freeze the Whites

Crack open the eggs and separate the yolks from the whites. Place the whites into the ice cube tray. There is no need to stir them. Cover the tray with aluminum foil, parchment paper, or plastic wrap and place the tray in the freezer.

Once the eggs are frozen, remove them from the tray and transfer them to freezer Ziploc® storage bags. Use a marker to note the freezing date on the bag. Each section of the tray will equal 1 egg white.

To Defrost Frozen Eggs

It is best to thaw frozen eggs overnight in your refrigerator.

Safe Refrigeration Times

Raw eggs in shell	3 to 5 weeks
Raw eggs unshelled	up to 2 days
Raw egg whites	up to 4 days
Raw egg yolks	up to 2 days
Hard-boiled eggs	1 week
Egg substitutes	unopened—10 days opened—3 days
Casseroles made with eggs	3 to 4 days frozen—3 months
Eggnog, commercial	5 to 7 days
Pies, custard, and chiffon	3 to 4 days
Quiche	3 to 4 days frozen—3 months

TEN

How to Select and Store Chicken

Fresh chicken has a clean smell.

Selecting Chicken

It doesn't matter if you are buying organic, free-range, cage-free, or just chicken; how to select and store it for maximum results will not vary. For more information about food labels, see my chapter on *Understanding Food Labels.*

When shopping, purchase your dry goods first and refrigerated items last. The less time items like chicken spend outside of refrigeration the better. Chicken should feel cold to the touch when it's in the supermarket cooler. Grocery stores do from time to time have trouble with refrigeration, so never purchase a chicken that feels warm.

Appearance

The skin of fresh chicken should have a yellow tint, and its meat should be a pink, fleshy hue. As chicken ages, its meat fades to a dull gray color. Avoid chicken that has a hint of gray. Fresh chicken should be plump. When you press its meat, it should be resilient but return to its normal shape. Fresh chicken has a clean smell. If it smells fishy, sour, or like sulfur or rotten eggs, it has past its prime. Avoid chicken that has bruises or tears in its flesh. This can affect its quality. Avoid chicken that is blotchy and dried around the edges.

Chicken breasts should be pale pink in color and possess little fat. Dark meat like thighs will be a darker pink and have more fat. If you are purchasing skin-on pieces that you want to sear, select pieces with ample skin that covers as much of the chicken as possible.

Although chicken meat is pinkish, it can have a white or yellow tinge. Its pigment does not affect its quality or nutritional value. If chickens are fed substances containing yellow pigment, then the color of their flesh will be more yellow than white. Look for meat that is not transparent.

Check Dates

Always check dates on packages. If the chicken has reached its "Sell-By" date, it will be safe to use 1 to 2 days past this date. Never purchase product that has past its "Use-By" date. It must be cooked or frozen by that day.

USDA Shield

Only purchase chicken that has been inspected by the USDA and bears a shield identifying it as US Grade A. Grades B and C are blemished and are normally used for frozen dinners, canned products, or ground chicken.

Individual Pieces Versus Weight

If you're cooking whole chicken breasts, hot wings, drumsticks, or bone-in thighs, and you want all your guest to get a specific number of pieces, buy chicken based on the number of pieces in the package. If you are going to shred the chicken or cut it into pieces, select a package based on weight.

Selecting Whole Chicken

Whole chicken is cheaper per pound than cut up chicken pieces. With inflating food prices, this may be a preferable alternative. When buying a whole bird, look for a well-shaped chicken. It should have more breast than leg meat. Both the breast and the chicken parts should be moist and plump. Make sure it has all its parts—2 legs and 2 wings. NEVER purchase a whole, raw stuffed chicken to cook at home. Poultry should be cooked immediately after stuffing. Some cooks prefer buying a chicken marked "roaster," which is an older chicken, and its meat will contain more muscle, flavor, and fat. Others prefer buying a "fryer" or "broiler."

Selecting Frozen Chicken

Buying frozen chicken can be more affordable than buying fresh. With inflating food prices, some of us will choose this alternative. If you are buying frozen chicken, it should be rock-hard with no signs of ice crystals or freezer burn inside the package. Always choose packages that are below the freezer line, which is usually 2 to 4 inches below the top of the freezer. Follow the same guidelines for fresh chicken. Avoid packages that contain product that is blemished or torn and packages that have a sour smell.

Chilling Process

Chicken must be brought to a temperature of 40 degrees F after feather removal. The industry standard immerses chicken in a cold-water bath. When chicken is cooled using this process, it will absorb some of this liquid. Once packaged, it may purge fluid into its tray, which dilutes the flavor and results in a soggy texture. Avoid buying chicken with an excess amount of liquid in its packaging.

Another process is air chilling, which circulates chicken through purified cold air to bring it to a safe temperature. Not all air chilling is the same. Some producers will use a combination of water and cold air and seek verification from the USDA that an air-chilling process was used. Labels will indicate if chickens are 100 percent air chilled.

In addition, if you love grilled or pan-seared chicken with crispy, golden skin, air-chilled chicken is a better choice. Because no water is used in the chilling process, chicken skin remains taut and never soggy.

Enhanced, Injected, or Plumped

Some chickens are enhanced, injected, or plumped with a solution of salt water or chicken broth. Processors are required by law to indicate the presence of an enhancer as well as its percentage. Some chickens are injected with up to 15 to 30 percent of their body weight. All the ingredients in the enhancer must also be listed on the label. Chickens can be classified as "natural" as long as the ingredients in the solution are considered "natural."

Chickens are Classified by Age and Weight

Roaster A *roaster* is less than 12 weeks old and weighs between 3 ½ and 5 pounds.

Broiler *Broilers* are 6 to 8 weeks old and weigh about 2 ½ pounds. This is the most common chicken found in supermarkets.

Fryer *Fryers* are 6 to 8 weeks old and weigh between 2 ½ and 3 ½ pounds.

Cornish Hen A *Cornish hen* is not a game bird. It is a small broiler chicken that is less than five weeks old and weighs between 1 and 2 pounds.

Stewing You may find chickens labeled *stewing chickens.* These chickens are older, and their meat is tough. They are best used in stews.

Capon *Capons* are castrated males that are fed a diet that is rich in milk or porridge. Capons are larger than regular chickens and smaller than turkeys. Their meat is tender, juicy, and flavorful.

Cocks and Roosters You will rarely find *cocks* or *roosters* in the supermarket. They are over 10 months old, and their meat is tough.

Types of Chicken Meat

White White meat is found in the breast, tender, and wing.

Dark Dark meat is found in the back of the chicken, the legs, and the thighs.

Labeling On Chicken Products

Fresh

Is fresh an important label? Chicken that is labeled fresh has never been held at a temperature colder than 26 degrees F, which is the freezing temperature for poultry. A good deal of the chicken sold in grocery stores is frozen during transport and thawed before it is sold. Frozen chicken has a different texture and taste than fresh chicken.

Use of Hormones and Steroids

Federal law prohibits the use of hormones and steroids in chicken, so no chicken you purchase in the supermarket is ever given hormones or steroids. In fact, chicken labels should state: “Federal regulations prohibit the use of hormones and steroids in the production of any poultry raised in the United States.”

Cage Free

This labeling is particularly confusing for chicken products. The majority of chickens raised for meat in the United States live in large, open structures called houses and are free to roam and eat and drink when they want. Therefore, most of the chicken products you purchase, with the exception of eggs, are, therefore, cage-free by default. If buying a cage-free chicken is important to you, look for a third party verification from either “Animal Welfare Approved” or “Certified Humane.”

Free Range

There is no precise federal government definition of “Free Range,” so the USDA approves free-range labeling on a case-by-case basis. The USDA generally permits chickens to be called free range if they have access to the outdoors for part of the day. The houses that chickens live in are equipped with advanced climate controls that keep the temperature inside the house at an optimal level, regardless of the temperature outside. In addition, their food and water are kept inside the houses. Chickens generally prefer to be close to their food and water, so, although they have access to the outdoors, how much time they spend outside is unknown. If buying a free-range chicken is important to you, look for a third party verification from either “Animal Welfare Approved” or “Certified Humane.”

Pasture Raised

Pasture-raised chickens are given the opportunity to roam on green, grassy pastures every single day of their lives. When also labeled with a third party verification from either "Animal Welfare Approved" or "Certified Humane", this means chickens are given 35 to 108 square feet of outdoor space. Pasture-raised chickens eat a diet of provided feed and foraged grubs and insects.

Organic

Chicken labeled as "organic" must also be "free range" (have access to the outdoors for some part of the day), but not all "free-range" chicken is "organic." To carry the USDA Certified Organic seal, chicken can only be fed organic food, which is generally corn and soybeans. Chickens can never be given any antibiotics, though they may have been vaccinated against common illnesses.

Processing of Organic Chicken

Any processing aids or sanitizers used in the processing of "organic" chickens labeled "organic" must be certified organic.

Checking Out

If you bring your own bags or request to have your order sacked in paper bags, it's best to ask the clerk to bag your chicken separately. Packaged chicken often leaks. Bagging chicken separately avoids the possibility of cross-contaminating other foods and keeps any leaking mess contained. Once home, I keep my chicken in plastic containers as well. This keeps any leakage from spilling out and cross-contaminating other foods in the refrigerator.

Storing and Using Chicken at Home

After purchasing, go directly home and put chicken immediately into the refrigerator. If you've purchased fresh chicken, it is best to use it within 1 to 2 days. If you've purchased frozen chicken, the USDA says frozen chicken will keep up to 1 year; but personally, I like to use my chicken within 1 to 2 months. Freezing poultry for an indefinite period of time results in significant moisture loss and affects its tenderness and flavor. Use a black marker to write the date of freezing on the product so you can keep track of the time it has been frozen.

Trimming and Deboning

You can save money trimming and deboning your own chicken, but this process requires following good sanitary procedures to prevent contamination of kitchen counters and utensils.

To debone a chicken: Rinse out the inside of the chicken and remove any innards. Scrap any remaining innards from the cavity. Pat the chicken dry with paper towels. Using a sharp knife, cut off the legs just below the breast at the natural crease between the leg and the body. Pull the leg out and pop the thigh out of the joint. Cut the leg off, slicing right through the joint. Place the chicken breast-side up and remove the wings. Using your fingers, find the joint and cut through it.

Place the chicken breast-side up. Using poultry shears and starting at the neck end, cut along one side of the backbone the entire length of the chicken. Repeat on the other side and pull the backbone out. Save the backbone and innards to make chicken stock. Make a slit through the cartilage in front of the keel bone. Fold the chicken breasts outward to crack the keel bone. Using your fingers, break the skin on either side of the keel bone and pull it out. Placing the chicken breast-side up, slice down the middle, cutting the breasts in half.

To debone chicken thighs: Lay chicken thighs skin-side down on a cutting board. Using a sharp knife, make small slices along both sides of the bone, gently cutting it away from the meat. Slip the knife under the bone and cut it free from the thigh.

To debone chicken breasts: If you are on a budget where every penny counts, it is cheaper to buy chicken breasts that still have their bones and skin. If the rib bones of the chicken are large, use a pair of poultry scissors to remove them. Cut out enough of the rib so that the breast will lie flat. Using a sharp knife, cut the breast away, keeping as close to the bone as possible. You should feel the bone with every cut. To remove the wishbone, simply cut around it and remove it. To remove the skin, simply slide your fingers underneath it and pull it off. Trim any excess fat.

Cooking tip: If you choose to debone a whole chicken or chicken breasts, save any bones or innards to make broth. Broth made from bones will be more flavorful than regular chicken stock and is full of L-glutamine, the most abundant amino acid in the body. Put the bones in a large kettle, with water, onion, celery, carrots, garlic, a bay leaf, and salt and simmer for 15 hours on the stove.

To clean a whole chicken: Remove the neck and chicken parts from its cavity. Wash the bird thoroughly, both its outside skin and inside its cavities. Remove any feathers or loose skin on the outside of the bird that were not removed during processing.

To truss a whole chicken: Use as 18-inch piece of kitchen twine and tie the center around the bird's ankles in such a manner as to fasten the legs together. You will have 2 equal lengths of twine to loop once around each wing at the elbow joint—the joint between the two meatiest parts of the wing.

Bring the ends of the twine over the lower third of the breast and tie as tightly as possible.

To carve a chicken: If the bird has been trussed, remove the twine. Remove any stuffing from the cavity. Place the bird on a cutting board. Using a large fork, hold the chicken in place. With a carving knife, cut through the skin where the leg is attached to the breast and push the leg off until the thighbone pops out of its socket. Detach the legs from the body and transfer to a cutting board. Separate the drumstick and thigh by cutting through the ball joint. You can carve the meat off of drumsticks and thighs or eat them like you would when you fry a chicken. Pry the wing from the body with your hand until the joint is exposed, then cut through the joint. To carve the breast, slice the meat parallel to the breastbone. Thinner slices of breast meat will dry out sooner.

Freezing Chicken

With inflating food prices, many of us have changed the way we shop and are buying chicken in bulk at warehouse stores. If you are buying chicken in large quantities and want to freeze it for later use, consider the following:

Freeze chicken as soon after purchase as possible. Separate the chicken into portions suitable for your family. Choose containers or wrapping appropriate for freezing—freezer foil, wraps, or bags or plastic containers made especially for freezing. Wrap the chicken tightly with a layer of plastic wrap or freezer paper and press out as much air as possible. Cover it with a layer of freezer foil, then place it in a freezer bag or airtight, freezer-safe container.

If you are freezing chicken in its original packaging, try over-wrapping it with freezer foil or putting it into freezer bags.

Proper wrapping prevents "freezer burn", which is caused by air getting to the surface of the food. Food that has been burned by freezing has grayish-brown, leathery spots. If your chicken becomes freezer burned, it's best to remove this part either before or during cooking as it will be dry and tasteless.

Defrosting Frozen Chicken

There are three safe ways to thaw chicken: in the refrigerator, in cold water, or in the microwave. Never set chicken out on the kitchen counter to thaw.

The best method is refrigerator thawing. Boneless chicken breasts will thaw overnight if placed in the refrigerator. Place frozen packages of chicken on the lowest shelf of your refrigerator. Whole chickens or chicken pieces with bones take 1 to 2 days or longer. It is a good idea to place the package in a plastic container or Ziploc® bag to prevent any leakage that could cross-contaminate other food. Once thawed, chicken may be kept in the refrigerator for 1 to 2 days before cooking. If you've had a crazy week and for some reason have not been able to cook thawed chicken, you must cook it before you can refreeze it.

Chicken can be thawed in cold water. Leave the bird in its airtight package and submerge it in cold water. Change the water every 30 minutes or so to ensure the water is cold. Allow 2 to 3 hours for a 3 to 4-pound package of chicken pieces to thaw and about 1 hour for a 1-pound package of boneless chicken breasts.

If you thaw chicken in the microwave, it must be cooked immediately. Bacteria begins to form when the meat is warm.

Not continuing to cook the meat until it is thoroughly cooked is dangerous.

Never cook frozen chicken in a microwave or slow cooker. You can cook it from its frozen state in the oven or on top of the stove. Allow 50 percent more time when cooking frozen chicken in this manner.

Using Deli Rotisserie Chicken

If you are buying rotisserie chicken from the deli, it should be stored in an oven-like area. Be sure it is hot at the time of purchase. Deli-roasted chicken should be eaten within 2 hours after bringing it home. If you'd like to refrigerate it to use the next day, cut it into several pieces and refrigerate it in shallow, covered containers. Rotisserie chicken must be eaten within 3 to 4 days and can be served either cold or hot. When reheating, it's best to bring the chicken to an internal temperature of 165 degrees F. Chicken should be hot and steaming. It is safe to freeze rotisserie chicken by placing it in freezer bags or airtight, freezer-safe containers. It will keep for 4 months, but I prefer not to keep it longer than 30 days.

Marinating

Chicken should not be marinated for more than 2 days in the refrigerator. If using marinade to baste chicken, bring marinade to a boil in a small saucepan over medium heat before reusing.

Safe Cooking

Whole chickens should be cooked to 180 degrees F. Test by placing a meat thermometer in the chicken's thigh. The USDA finds that chicken pieces, like thighs and wings, should be cooked to an internal temperature of 165 degrees F. They recommend that chicken breasts be cooked to 170 degrees F.

Safe Refrigeration Times

Fresh chicken	1 to 2 days
Cooked leftover chicken	3 to 4 days
Cooked chicken casseroles, dishes, or soup	3 to 4 days
Fried chicken	3 to 4 days
Deli-sliced chicken meat	3 to 5 days
Deli rotisserie or fried chicken	3 to 4 days
Chicken sausage	
opened package	7 days
unopened package	2 weeks provided not exceeding "Sell-By" date
Chicken salad	3 days

ELEVEN

How to Select and Store Turkey

Be extra careful when purchasing really cheap birds because often times they are defective.

Thanksgiving is my favorite holiday: tantalizing odors oozing from the kitchen, the laughter and gentle buzz of family gathered around the dinner table. It is a meal I prepare with loving care.

The centerpiece of the Thanksgiving meal is turkey. You want to serve your family the very best.

Fresh Versus Frozen

The debate over whether to purchase a fresh or frozen turkey can best be answered by the amount of space you have in your refrigerator for storage and the time required for safe thawing. If you shop ahead of time, it is safer to purchase a frozen turkey. If you purchase your turkey 1 to 2 days before cooking, you can feel safe purchasing a fresh bird.

A *fresh turkey* has never been held at a temperature colder than 26 degrees F. Even though water freezes at 32 degrees, turkey meat will remain pliable at this temperature. Fresh turkeys will cost more than frozen because their temperature needs require special handling. Your supermarket should keep fresh turkeys between 38 to 40 degrees F.

When shopping for a fresh turkey, check for indications that it has been stored at the proper temperature. Apply gentle pressure to check for signs of freezing. A fresh turkey will feel pliable. Examine the turkey for signs of ice crystals. Avoid fresh turkeys that have ice crystals. Supermarkets sometimes mound turkeys in refrigerated coolers above safe refrigeration levels. Select turkeys that have been stored at least 2 to 4 inches below the top of the cooler.

Commercially frozen turkeys are flash frozen. This is a process that cools them rapidly to 0 degrees F. Flash freezing ensures that the turkey will have the same level of freshness as the day it was frozen. There is, therefore, no difference in quality between fresh or frozen. Flash frozen turkeys will keep up to 1 year. They will maintain their quality better than turkeys frozen at home. If your supermarket has a sale on turkeys and you want to purchase several for later use, it is best to purchase flash frozen birds.

Frozen turkeys should be rock hard and show no signs of freezer damage. Avoid packages that have ice crystals, which may be an indication that the turkey has been stored at too cold of a temperature. Again, be sure your supermarket has stored frozen birds below the cooler's freezer line, which is usually 2 to 4 inches below the top of the freezer. Frozen turkeys stored above this line will begin to thaw and may be kept at inadequate temperatures, allowing bacteria to form inside the bird.

Turkeys are Graded

The USDA inspects most turkeys and grades them A, B, or C. You will know your turkey has been inspected if its wrapper bears a USDA shield. If a turkey is graded A, it is plump, has good body shape, and all its pin-feathers have been removed. It also lacks cuts, bruises, broken bones, and has no missing parts. Turkeys not graded A are safe to eat but their overall quality will be inferior. Natural turkeys are inspected but not graded. If you are buying a natural turkey, give it a good feel to be sure it has all its body parts. Nothing like putting a one-legged turkey on your table, especially when two members of the family are fond of drumsticks.

Turkeys are Classified by Age

Fryer-Roaster A *fryer-roaster* is usually less than 4 months old and weighs between 4 to 8 pounds.

Young Turkey Weighing between 8 to 24 pounds, a *young turkey* is between 4 to 8 months old. This turkey will be the most tender and have the most flavor. US supermarkets, for the most part, sell young turkeys.

Yearling A *yearling* is 12 months old. It will not be as tender and flavorful as a young turkey.

Mature Turkeys older than 15 months are called *mature.* Their meat will be tough and not suited for roasting.

Heritage Turkeys

Raised on small farms, the *heritage turkey* resembles the turkey our ancestors ate. These breeds have a longer body, smaller breast muscles, and are a bit leaner than commercial birds. Heritage turkeys require 2 to 3 more months to grow to proper size for processing, making them more expensive than commercially raised birds. Most heritage birds are purchased from small farms, specialty food markets, or online.

Some people like to buy their turkey from local farmers. Turkeys grown on local farms are raised with tender, loving care, are free-range, and fed a higher quality of feed than mass-produced turkeys. If you order your turkey from a small farm, the best turkeys are the *Broad Breasted Bronze*, also called the *Bronze*, or the *Broad Breasted White,* also called the *Large* or *Giant White.*

I personally prefer to purchase a name brand fresh turkey the day before I plan to use it. I have had good luck with Butterball®, Honey Suckle®, and Red Bird® brands. Many supermarkets advertise rock-bottom specials on turkeys at Thanksgiving. Be extra careful when purchasing really cheap birds because often times they are defective. I prefer to stick with well-known brand names to ensure a quality turkey.

Basted or Self-Basted Turkeys

Some bone-in poultry carries the term "*basted*" or "*self-basted*" on its label. I prefer to avoid these products because they are injected or marinated with a solution that contains butter or some other edible fat, broth, stock, or water plus spices and other flavor enhancers.

How Many Pounds Do I Need?

So, you've decided what type of bird you are going to purchase. The next question: How many pounds do I need? When calculating how much to buy, plan to purchase between 1 to 1½ pounds per person, depending on the amount of leftovers you'd like to have. If you're feeding 12 people, plan to purchase a 12- to 16-pound bird.

Labeling on Turkey Products

The decision to purchase a free-range, natural, organic, or kosher turkey is one of personal preference. Following is some information to help you understand their subtleties.

Organic

This label means the turkey is fed only organic feed and is allowed to roam outdoors. In order to be classified organic, it can never receive any antibiotics and must be processed without any added flavorings, coloring, or artificial ingredients. The federal government prohibits the use of growth hormones or steroids in any commercially raised poultry.

Natural

The term "natural" indicates that the turkey has had limited processing, which means the raw product was not altered during processing. In addition, no artificial ingredients, colorings, or chemical preservatives have been added. A "natural" turkey may or may not be free range, depending on the farm, and can be given antibiotics if it becomes ill.

Free Range

Free range means the bird has been allowed to roam outdoors, which is considered to have a positive effect on the flavor of its meat. Opponents of free-range birds believe that unless their environment is strictly controlled, they will scavenge on whatever they find. If buying a free-range turkey is important to you, look for third party verification from either "Animal Welfare Approved" or "Certified Humane."

Pasture Raised

Pasture-raised turkeys are given the opportunity to roam on green, grassy pastures. If buying a pasture-raised turkey is important to you, look for third party verification from either "Animal Welfare Approved" or "Certified Humane".

Cage Free

Turkeys are not raised in cages, so all turkeys are cage free.

Kosher

Kosher means the turkey is raised and processed following strict guidelines and under rabbinical supervision. A kosher turkey is free range, fed only grain, and never given any antibiotics.

Storing and Using Turkey at Home

Storing Fresh Turkeys

If you purchase a fresh turkey, store it in its original wrapper in the coldest part of your refrigerator, which is usually the bottom shelf near the back. Use a fresh turkey within 1 to 2 days of bringing it home. Fresh turkeys are readily available around the holidays but should be cooked within a few days of purchase.

Storing Frozen Turkeys

Frozen turkeys are available year-round. If I've bought a frozen turkey on sale, I never keep it in my freezer more than 2 months. Mark your purchase date on the wrapping with a black marker.

Thawing Frozen Turkeys

Turkeys must be thawed before cooking. The preferred method for thawing a turkey is in the refrigerator at a temperature of 40 degrees F or lower. Allow 24 hours of thawing time for every 5 pounds of turkey. A 16-pound bird will take a little more than three days to defrost.

Turkeys can also be thawed in cold water. Place the bird, breast-side down in its unopened wrapper, in your kitchen sink and fill it with enough cold water to cover the turkey. The water must be changed every 30 minutes to ensure it remains cold. Allow 30 minutes per pound if thawing in cold water. A 16-pound bird will take 8 hours to defrost using this method.

Tips on preparing turkey: The night before cooking your turkey, remove giblets from the cavity. Rinse the thawed turkey thoroughly, both inside the bird's two cavities and the outside skin. During rinsing, remove any pinfeathers or loose skin that might have been missed in processing. Scrape any remaining innards from the cavity. Pat the bird dry and place it in a roaster, cover with damp paper towels, and refrigerate until ready to stuff. Remove giblets from the wrapper, wash, place in a covered container, and refrigerate.

When you are ready to stuff the turkey, lightly salt the large cavity. Gently spoon in the stuffing, lightly filling both cavities to capacity. If the large cavity has a band of skin across the tail, push drumsticks under the tail. It is not necessary to fasten the opening. If there is no skin, close the opening by placing skewers across it and lacing it shut with a cord. Tie the drumsticks to the tail. Dental floss works well for lacing.

Roasting time by weights:

6 to 8 pounds	3½ to 4 hours
8 to 12 pounds	4 to 4½ hours
12 to 16 pounds	4½ to 5½ hours
16 to 20 pounds	5½ to 6½ hours
20 to 24 pounds	6½ to 7½ hours

Tips on carving the turkey: My Uncle Eddie was a butcher. The following is how he taught us to carve a turkey. His advice for making the task easier was to always use a very sharp knife and a fork with a guard.

Let the bird stand for at least 15 minutes so all the juices can be absorbed. Remove any trussing—skewers and cord. Remove any stuffing from the cavities and place in a serving dish, cover with aluminum foil to keep warm, and set aside. Place the turkey on a cutting board or platter.

Hold the drumstick with one hand, pulling it gently away from the turkey body. Removing the wings last helps steady your turkey, making it easier to carve. Using a carving knife, cut through the skin between the leg and body. Then cut through the joint that joins the leg to the backbone and push the leg off until the thighbone pops out of its socket. Separate the drumstick and thigh by cutting through the ball joint. You can carve the meat off the drumsticks and thighs or serve them whole. We like to serve the drumsticks whole and slice the thighs. To slice the drumstick, hold it upright at a convenient angle to the plate and cut downward. Rotate the drumstick so you get uniform slices. To slice the thigh, hold it firmly on a plate with a fork and cut slices parallel to the bone. To carve the breast meat, hold the bird in place with a fork. Cut the white meat parallel to the wing. Then make a deep cut into the breast all the way to the body frame. Halfway up the breast, cut slices of white meat down to the cut made parallel to the wing. The slices will fall away from the turkey as they are cut to this line. Thinner slices of breast meat will dry out faster. Pull the wings away from the body to locate the joint. Cut through the joint where the wing attaches to the body.

Storing Leftover Turkey

Refrigerate leftover turkey within 2 hours. Cut turkey into smaller pieces, slicing meat off the breast. Wings and legs may be left whole. Place in shallow containers and store in the refrigerator. Discard the carcass.

Freezing Leftover Turkey

To freeze leftover turkey meat, place it in airtight freezer containers or freezer bags. I prefer not to store a frozen turkey for more than 2 months.

Safe Refrigeration Time

Fresh turkey	1 to 2 days
Cooked leftover turkey	3 to 4 days
Cooked turkey casseroles, dishes, or soups	3 to 4 days

Leftover Turkey Soup

Save your turkey carcass to make soup.

1 turkey carcass
2 yellow onions, unpeeled and quartered
3 carrots, unpeeled and cut into thirds
3 celery stalks with leaves, cut into thirds
1 parsnip, unpeeled and cut into thirds
1 head garlic, unpeeled and cut in half crosswise
10 sprigs fresh parsley
10 sprigs fresh thyme
1 bay leaf
2 teaspoons salt
1 teaspoon black peppercorns

Using a sharp knife, remove turkey meat from the carcass and set aside. Remove the skin and any fat. Clean any stuffing off the bones. If your turkey is large, break it apart at the joints so it will fit into a kettle. In a large kettle, place turkey carcass, onions, carrots, celery, parsnip, garlic, parsley, thyme, and bay leaf. Fill the kettle with cold water, about 8 to 12 quarts, so that it covers the carcass. Add salt and peppercorns and stir to combine. Bring to a boil over a high heat. Lower the heat and simmer uncovered for 4 hours. Skim off any foam that comes to the surface. Take the kettle off the heat and let it cool. Using tongs, remove turkey bones. Using a slotted spoon, remove vegetables. Strain the contents of the kettle through a fine mesh sieve or a strainer, reserving stock.

TWELVE

How to Select and Store Pork

It is not safe to partially pre-cook pork and then refrigerate it to finish cooking later.

The majority of pork sold in your supermarket will either be cured—*ham, bacon, Canadian bacon, salt pork*—or fresh. Your supermarket may stock the following fresh pork products: *pork chops, pork loins, pork steaks, pork loin filets, pork ribs, spareribs, baby back ribs, country-style ribs, pork cutlets, tenderloins, crown roasts, Boston butt roasts, loin roasts, shoulder butt roasts, ground pork* and *sausage.*

Selecting Pork

When buying pork, look for cuts with a small amount of fat on the outside and meat that is firm with a pinkish red color. Pork will have better flavor and tenderness if it has a small amount of marbling, small speckles of fat within the meat. Choose packages that are cold and tightly wrapped without tears or punctures. Pork should not be blotchy. Spots indicate that it has begun to spoil. Avoid packages if the meat is pale in color or it contains liquid. Also, avoid meat that has dark-colored bones.

Make your pork selection, along with other perishables, last.

Bone-in pork roasts and bone-in pork chops will have more flavor than boneless.

Pork is Graded

Slaughterhouses can ask for their pork to be graded. Since they must pay for the grading, they often don't. Pork is graded by the USDA as either "Acceptable" 1, 2, 3, or 4 or "Utility", 1 being the best. Grading is based on the proportion of lean meat to fat. All pork for intrastate commerce must have a state or federal inspection for wholesomeness and to ensure that the slaughter and processing of the pork was done under sanitary conditions. Pork shipped interstate must be federally inspected. All fresh pork sold in supermarkets is "Acceptable." It does not have the quality grading differences that are available with beef products.

Heritage or Heirloom Hog Breeds

More chefs are using *heritage* or *heirloom* pork meat. The bloodlines of heritage pigs go back hundreds of years. Some names to look for are *Berkshire, Tamworth, Duroc*, and *Gloucestershire.* There may be some specialty markets that carry heritage or heirloom breeds, but, again, you may need to source it from local farmers.

Pork is Often Injected

Pork products are often injected with water, broth, salt, and extra flavorings. I avoid buying injected pork. To determine if pork is injected, read the ingredient label. Ingredients should be only pork. You may find the words "extra tender" and "juicy" on injected pork. It will also be high in sodium. If the nutritional label indicates a sodium count higher than 100 mg, the pork has been injected. Injected pork will contain too much liquid and may be difficult to sear. Once cooked, the meat may seem mushy and spongy. With the price of meat these days, who wants to pay for water?

Check Dates

Check dates on packages. The "Sell-By" date is the date the supermarket must remove the pork from the meat coolers. It will be safe to eat after this date, but you should confirm that the product is still good. If it has a slimy, sticky texture or has turned grayish, it is not safe to eat. Use or freeze products with a "Sell-By" date within 3 to 5 days of purchase. The "Use-By" date means the manufacturer believes the product will not be at its peak after that date. To save money on your food dollars, never buy product that has exceeded its "Use-By" date.

Labeling on Pork Products

Organic

Some specialty markets, like Whole Foods, will sell *organic* pork, but most of the pork sold in the United States is not organic. The USDA has specific regulations for raising organic pork, and pig farmers have found it difficult to comply. For their meat to be labeled organic, pigs must be raised in compliance with organic regulations starting at least 38 days prior to birth. It is interesting to note that a sow or gilt purchased from a conventional farm can give birth to organic piglets if the sow or gilt, a female pig that has not produced a litter, is managed organically for the last third of the gestation period. The sow or gilt, however, can never be classified as organic. Certified organic pigs must receive an organic diet of grains and protein sources and must have access to the outdoors. Raising pigs on pasture is not required by organic pork regulations. Certified organic pigs must be processed in a certified organic processing facility.

Pasture Raised

Pasture-raised pigs live in fields and woods and are free to roam. Farmers provide small shelters for them where they sleep in small groups. Pasture-raised pigs scavenge for food as they roam, and farmers give them feed, which may or may not be organic. If buying pasture-raised pork is important to you, there may be some specialty markets, like Whole Foods, that stock it; but you may need to source it from local farmers.

Crate Free

Different states are increasing regulations on pig farmers. The term cage free does not apply to pigs. They are placed in "gestation crates" prior to pregnancy because their hormonal changes can make them targets for aggressive sows. In addition, they are kept in gestation crates until pregnancy is verified. If buying pork from pigs that have not been confined is important to you, look for pigs that are raised in group housing and are crate free after pregnancy is confirmed.

Animal Welfare Certified

This label on pork products means the pigs were not raised using gestation stalls or farrowing (birthing crates), bedding is present in their housing, and they never received supplemental growth hormones.

No GMO

You may find pork labeled "Raised on a diet of no GMOs." This indicates the pork was not fed any genetically modified feed.

Checking Out

Ask the sacker to bag your pork separately in plastic bags to contain any leakage that might cross-contaminate other foods. Many grocery stores no longer provide plastic bags. Consider taking a separate bag for these types of products.

Storing and Using Pork at Home

Pork products should be refrigerated at 40 degrees F immediately upon your arrival at home. Use or freeze fresh pork within 3 to 5 days. You will find safe refrigeration times for individual products at the end of this chapter.

Freezing Pork

With inflating food prices, many of us have changed the way we shop and we buy pork in bulk. If you are buying pork in large quantities and want to freeze it for later use, consider the following:

Freeze pork as soon after purchase as possible. Choose containers or wrapping appropriate for freezing—freezer foil, wraps or bags, or plastic containers made specifically for this purpose.

If you are freezing cuts like pork chops, separate the pork into portions suitable for your family. It is safe to freeze pork in its original packaging or repackage it in Ziploc® freezer bags. If you are freezing pork in the original package, it is best to over-wrap the package tightly with aluminum foil or plastic wrap to avoid freezer burn. If using freezer bags, press as much air out of the bag as possible.

You can freeze whole pork roasts. Wrap pork roasts tightly with aluminum foil or plastic wrap or place them in freezer bags. If using freezer bags, press as much air out of the bag as possible.

Proper wrapping prevents "freezer burn", which is caused by air getting to the surface of the food. When air reaches the surface of food, it causes grayish-brown, leathery spots known as freezer burn. If your pork becomes freezer burned, it's best to remove the affected part either before or during cooking as it will be dry and tasteless. Frozen pork should be used within 3 to 4 months.

It is not necessary to wash raw pork before cooking, especially for freezing.

Mark the date of freezing on all packages with a black marker.

Thawing Frozen Pork

Pork can be safely thawed in the refrigerator, in cold water, or in the microwave. The preferred method is the refrigerator. Pork chops will thaw in 1 day. Whole roasts will take 2 days or longer. Once thawed, pork can be kept safely in the refrigerator for 3 to 5 days. To defrost in cold water, do not remove the packaging, which must be airtight.

If it is wrapped in butcher paper, place the pork in a leak-proof bag, then put it in a large bowl in your kitchen sink and fill it with cold water. The water should be changed every 30 minutes to ensure it stays cold. Small packages will defrost in about 1 hour using this method. A 3- to 4-pound roast may take 2 to 3 hours. If you use the microwave for thawing, the pork must be cooked immediately; however, I do not recommend this method.

It is safe to cook frozen pork in the oven, on the stove, or grill without thawing it first. Cooking times may take 50 percent longer. Frozen pork should not be cooked in a slow cooker.

Marinating Pork

Pork can be marinated in the refrigerator in a covered container for 3 to 5 days. Boil any marinade that has been in contact with raw meat before using it to baste cooked pork. Discard any leftover marinade.

Safe Cooking Temperatures and Practices

The most important factor in using pork safely is thorough cooking. Pork must be cooked to an internal temperature of 160 degrees F to eliminate disease-causing bacteria. For best results, use a meat thermometer. Whole roasts should be cooked to 145 degrees F, followed by a 30-minute rest before slicing.

It is not safe to partially pre-cook pork and then refrigerate it to finish cooking later. However, it is safe to partially pre-cook pork and then immediately transfer it to a hot grill to finish.

Pork chops will become tough if overcooked. Pay close attention to cooking times.

Cooking tip: Save pork bones to make broth. Roast the bones first in the oven. Put 4 to 5 pounds of bones in a large kettle, with water, onion, celery, carrots, garlic, a bay leaf, and salt and simmer for 15 hours on the stove.

Tip for cooking ham: Ham is labeled either "Partially Cooked" or "Fully Cooked". A smoked ham is fully cooked. To be fully cooked, the USDA requires that the ham's internal temperature reach 148 degrees F for 30 minutes. Smoking is the preferred method for accomplishing this, and it yields a very flavorful, tender ham. Whichever type you decide to buy, it is important to strictly follow the packer's heating instructions.

Quantity tip: When purchasing a bone-in ham, allow one-half (½ pound) pound per person.

Cooking tip: If you purchase an 8- to 10-pound smoked ham, cook it 2 to 2 ¼ hours. For a 10- to 14-pound smoked ham, cook 3 ½ to 4 hours at 325 degrees F.

Safe Refrigeration Times

Ground pork	1 to 2 days
Fresh pork roasts, steaks, chops, or ribs	3 to 5 days
Fresh pork variety meats	1 to 2 days
Home-cooked pork, soups, stews, or casseroles	3 to 4 days
Ham, fully-cooked, whole	7 days
Ham, fully-cooked, half	3 to 5 days
Ham, fully-cooked, sliced	3 to 4 days
Bacon	7 days
Uncooked sausages, smoked breakfast links, or patties	1 to 2 days 7 days
Summer sausage labeled 'Keep Refrigerated,' unopened	3 months
Summer sausage labeled 'Keep Refrigerated,' opened	3 weeks
Lunch and deli meats opened	3 to 5 days
Lunch meats unopened	2 weeks

Safe Freezer Times

Ground pork	1 to 3 months
Fresh pork roasts, steaks, chops, or ribs	3 to 6 months
Fresh pork variety meats	3 to 4 months
Home-cooked pork, soups, stews, or casseroles	2 to 3 months
Ham, fully-cooked, whole	1 to 2 months
Ham, fully-cooked, half	1 to 2 months
Ham, fully-cooked, sliced	1 to 2 months
Bacon	1 month
Uncooked sausages	up to 3 months
Smoked breakfast link or patties	1 to 3 months
Summer sausage labeled 'Keep Refrigerated,' unopened	1 to 2 months
Summer sausage labeled 'Keep Refrigerated,' opened	1 to 2 months
Lunch and deli meats opened	1 to 2 months
Lunch and deli meats unopened	1 to 2 months

THIRTEEN

How to Select and Store Beef

If buying pasture-raised beef is important to you,
ook for the American Grassfed or Certified Grassfed labels.

Your supermarket sells many cuts of beef steaks and roasts. Depending upon the part of the country you live in or the market you patronize, roast and steaks will have many names. When you read a recipe, it may call for using one cut of steak or roast, but when you get to the market, you might not find that particular cut in the case. Following is a guide to the many names roasts and steaks may have:

Steaks

- *boneless strip steaks,* also called Kansas City, Manhattan, and New York strip
- *flat iron,* also called shoulder top blade, top blade filet, top blade steak
- *ball tip*
- *top sirloin*
- *filet mignon,* also called tenderloin filet and tenderloin steak
- *Porterhouse*
- *T-bone*

- *flank*, also called London broil
- *skirt*, also called inside skirt, outside skirt, and Arrachera
- *rib eye*, also called Delmonico, Spencer, and Scotch
- *shoulder*, top round steak, also called butterball
- *round*, also called rump
- *cube steaks*
- *Denver*, also called bottom chuck and underblade
- *flap*, also called Bavette
- *Tomahawk*
- *tri-tip*

If you are pinching pennies, more affordable steaks will be the flat iron, strip, sirloin, flank, skirt, and tri-tip.

Roasts

- *chuck*, also called chuck eye, blade, pot, or chuck roll
- *clod*, also called arm chuck, arm pot, chuck primal, or pot roast
- *brisket*
- *rib*, also called standing rib or prime rib
- *strip loin*, also called top loin
- *tenderloin*
- *top sirloin*, also called top butt
- *top round*, also called inside round or London broil
- *bottom round*, also called rolled rump or eye of round
- *tri-tip*, also called triangle
- *sirloin tip*, also called knuckle

If you are pinching pennies, the bottom round, top sirloin, clod, and top sirloin roasts will be the most affordable.

Ground Beef

Some ground beef products are labeled "lean" and "extra lean". "Lean" means that for every 100 grams of beef, there are less than 10 grams of fat, 4.5 grams or less of saturated fat, and less than 95 milligrams of cholesterol. "Extra Lean" means for every 100 grams of beef there are less than 2 grams of saturated fat, and less than 95 milligrams of cholesterol.

Supermarkets will also label beef according to the meat/fat ratios: 73/27; 80/20; 85/15; 92/8; 93/7; 96/4. Select the type of ground beef that is appropriate for how you will prepare the beef. Ground beef with higher fat content will yield juicier grilled burgers. Leaner ground beef is good in recipes where the meat is crumbled—like spaghetti sauce or taco filling.

In addition, your supermarket may also sell cubed stew meat, fajita meat, beef back ribs, short ribs, oxtails, sweetbreads, tripe, and tongue.

Choosing a Meat Market

I like to shop at a reputable butcher shop where I can have my meat cut to order and where I can be assured of good quality beef. I prefer to purchase Choice meat; therefore, I look for markets that sell Choice meat.

Some chain stores will cut meat to order; however, experienced butchers will more likely work during the day. If you want meat custom cut, shop during the day if possible. Today, most chain supermarkets cut their beef in one central location and ship it packaged to surrounding stores. It is possible meat will have already been packaged for a few days before it arrives at its destination. If you buy your meat at a chain store, it is important to choose product that looks fresh.

Selecting Beef

Shop with your eyes. Look for bright cherry red meat that does not have brownish blotches. While some butchers may tell you spots don't affect the beef, spotting indicates the meat has started to spoil. If your market normally has several packages of spotted beef, it's an indication that meat is not selling quickly enough to ensure freshness. Be wary of these markets. Packages of spotted meat will often be on sale and marked "Manager's Special." Don't buy them.

When selecting beef, look for packages that are cold to the touch and tightly wrapped with no tears or punctures. Occasionally packages of meat may have a red liquid. This is not blood. Beef is about three fourths water. This liquid is natural moisture from the beef.

Check the dates on packages. Many stores mark packages with a "Sell-By" date. This is the date your supermarket must remove the beef from the meat cooler. It will be safe to consume past this date. If beef is slimy, sticky or smells bad, it is not safe to consume. To save money on your food dollars, never buy product that has expired. Frozen beef is safe to use if it has past its "Sell-By" date provided it was frozen prior to that date. "Use-By" dates mean this is the last day beef will be at its peak quality. It may be safe to use past this date.

If you are using beef past its "Sell-By" date, it is important to make sure it is safe to consume. Beef that is spoiled will look gray, green, or brown. It will smell like ammonia or sulfur and feel tacky to the touch.

When shopping, make your meat selection, like all perishables, last.

Beef is Graded

When buying beef, I consider three things—flavor, juiciness, and tenderness. The marbling in beef, white flecks of fat within the meat muscle, determines its flavor— the more the better.

Beef sold in retail outlets is graded by USDA inspectors as either *Prime, Choice, Select, Standard,* and *Commercial.* Beef is also graded *Utility, Cutter,* and *Canner*. These grades are not sold in supermarkets but are used in commercially ground beef and processed food.

Prime beef has more marbling and, therefore, more flavor. It is the most tender and juicy grade of beef; however, it is higher in fat content. Since only 2 to 3 percent of beef grades out as *Prime*, it is the most expensive. *Choice* beef is less expensive than *Prime* but still has good flavor and tenderness. *Select* beef has less marbling and is tougher and has less flavor than *Choice*. *Standard* and *Commercial* grades are even leaner than *Select*. They are often sold without a grading label or will be marked *"No Roll"* and will often bear your supermarket's private label.

Most supermarkets sell a combination of *Prime, Choice, Select, Standard,* and *Commercial.* If you are shopping for flavor, pay attention to the grade. When advertising special prices, chain stores usually discount *Select* or *Standard* grades.

I prefer purchasing *Choice*-graded beef. I never purchase *Select*. My palate finds it tough and flavorless. On special occasions, I will often spend the extra money for *Prime*. I never purchase a *Prime*-graded standing rib roast, as the *Choice* grade has enough marbling to ensure a tasty roast. I prefer tenderloins and filet mignons in *Choice* grade as well. *Prime* in these cuts is too mushy.

Beef is Aged

The best beef is aged. There are two processes for aging beef —dry and wet. *"Wet-aged"* means the beef is locked in plastic with a bit of water and left for 21 to 28 days. *"Dry-aged"* means the beef hangs in a cooler so that the blood drains out of the beef. Dry-aging takes from 10 days to 6 weeks. This process yields a very lean, tasty, and dense steak. If you're looking for the very best steak, purchase "dry-aged" Prime beef. It is not safe to age beef at home.

Breeds of Beef

You may find two breeds of beef in your supermarket. *Angus* beef is produced by the Angus breed of cattle. Black Angus beef is prized for its marbling, which makes the beef from Angus cattle juicy, flavorful, and tender. The USDA does certify Angus beef. Meat bearing the *Certified Angus* label must pass 10 quality standards.

These standards are based on various specifications which include but are not limited to the weight of the cow, the thickness of its fat, the size of its ribeye, superior muscling, and the amount of marbling in its meat.

Wagyu means "Japanese beef cattle." There are four breeds of Japanese cattle that produce wagyu beef: the *Japanese Black,* the *Japanese Brown,* the *Japanese Shorthorn,* and the *Japanese Polled.* This beef has a distinct appearance because it contains so much marbling. *Kobe* beef is produced from the *Tajima* breed of Japanese Black Cows. It is some of the most expensive beef in the world. Ranchers have crossbreed Angus cattle with the Tajima breed and are now producing American wagyu beef.

Labeling on Beef Products

Natural

The term *"natural"* or *"all natural"* means beef has been minimally processed and contains no preservatives or artificial additives. Since products like beef don't contain preservatives or additives, this label is meaningless.

Locally Grown

This term has no legal meaning and implies the beef comes from a *local farm.* If your supermarket stocks beef with this label, the meat department should be able to tell you which farm or ranch raised the cattle.

Organic

Certified organic beef must come from cattle that ate only organically grown feed, and this feed must not contain any animal byproducts. In addition, the animals can't be treated with synthetic hormones or antibiotics. Animals must have access to the outdoors and must have access to pasture. Organic animals cannot be cloned.

No Antibiotics And No Hormones

When cattle don't meet all the necessary requirements to be certified organic and they have not received antibiotics or hormones, producers may label them as such. To use these labels, producers must provide the USDA with documentation that the *animals did not receive antibiotics or hormones.* There is no testing to verify validity of this label. The letters "RWA" may appear on labels indicating the animals were "Raised Without Antibiotics."

Free Range

"Free range" labels on beef products mean the animals were given free access to the outdoors for a minimum of 120 days per

year. There is no requirement about how much space each animal has or what the conditions of the outdoor space are. This does not mean that the animals only grazed on range.

Pasture Raised

"Pasture raised" or *"pastured"* means cattle spend some time outdoors on pasture, feeding on grass or forage. There are no USDA standards for this label, including how much time the cattle spend on pasture. Some beef bearing this label will come from cows that spend time on pasture and then are fed grain before slaughter.

Grassfed

Grassfed means that, after the cattle are weaned, their source of food comes from grass or forage and not from grains like corn or soy. Some cattle raised as organic will eat grass but are sent to feedlots for the latter part of their life and fattened up on grain.

American Grassfed And Certified Grassfed

If buying free-range, pasture-raised, grassfed beef is important to you, look for the *American Grassfed* or *Certified Grassfed* labels. Beef bearing these labels was produced from animals that were grassfed throughout their entire lives. The label also certifies and verifies that the animals had continuous access to pasture and were not raised in confinement. In addition, the Certified Grassfed label indicates that cattle were managed according to highest welfare and environmental standards.

Checking Out

Ask the sacker to bag your meat separately, to contain any leakage that might cross-contaminate other foods.

Storing and Using Beef at Home

Beef should be refrigerated at 40 degrees F immediately upon your arrival at home and should be used within 3 to 5 days (1 to 2 days for meats like sweetbreads, tongue, or tripe). If you do not plan to use beef within this time frame, freeze it.

It is not necessary to wash raw beef before cooking. Any bacteria present on the surface will be destroyed in the cooking process.

When exposed to oxygen, ground beef will become a rosy red color. Sometimes you may find the center of a package of ground beef has darkened. This is not harmful. This is the result of lack of exposure to oxygen. If you have concerns about ground beef, check the smell. It should be fresh, not sour, and the meat should feel moist, not slimy.

Many recipes suggest bringing steaks to room temperature before grilling. Steaks should not be removed from the refrigerator more than 30 to 40 minutes before grilling. This should be sufficient time to bring them to the appropriate temperature for even grilling.

Freezing Beef

It is safe to freeze beef in its original packaging or repackage it in reusable or plastic Ziploc® freezer bags. Beef freezes best when your freezer is set at 0 degrees F. If you are freezing beef in the original package, it is best to over-wrap the package with aluminum foil, freezer paper, or plastic wrap to avoid freezer burn. When frigid air reaches the surface of food, it causes grayish-brown, leathery spots known as freezer burn. Portions damaged by freezer burn should be cut away, either during or after cooking. If you are repacking beef, freeze it in meal-size portions. Place it in a reusable or a plastic Ziploc® freezer bag. Press as much air out of the bag as possible. Frozen beef should be used within 4 to 6 months.

Thawing Frozen Beef

Beef can be safely defrosted in the refrigerator, in cold water, or in the microwave. Never thaw beef on the counter. The preferred method is the refrigerator. Ground beef, stew meat, and steaks will thaw in 1 day. Bone-in parts and whole roasts will take 2 days or longer. Once thawed, beef is safe to keep in the refrigerator for 3 to 5 days.

To defrost in cold water, do not remove the packaging. For this method, the packaging must be airtight or the package must be put into a leak-proof bag. This method is not suitable for product wrapped in butcher paper only. Place the beef in a large bowl in your kitchen sink and fill it with cold water. The water should be changed every 30 minutes to ensure that it stays cold. Small packages of beef will defrost in about 1 hour. A 3- to 4-pound roast may take 2 to 3 hours.

Only thaw beef in the microwave if you are pressed for time or in an emergency. Thawing beef in the microwave changes its texture and consistency. If you use the microwave for defrosting, the beef must be cooked immediately.

Marinating Beef

Beef is normally marinated for 6 to 24 hours. It can be marinated for up to 2 days in the refrigerator. After that time, beef may begin to break down. Boil any used marinade before brushing it on cooked beef. Discard any uncooked marinade.

Cooking tip: Save beef bones to make broth. Roast the bones first in the oven. Put 4 to 5 pounds of bones in a large kettle, with water, onion, celery, carrots, garlic, a bay leaf, and salt and simmer for 15 hours on the stove.

To carve a prime rib: Remove any string from the roast. If you have cooked a bone-in roast, place it on a cutting board on its side so that the bones are on your left-hand side. Using one hand, steady the roast with a fork. Cut a serving slice from the roast by slicing horizontally across the meat toward the bones. Then remove the slice from the roast by cutting downward parallel to the bones. Slices are normally ½-inch thick. Transfer slices to a serving platter. You can serve the rib bones with the meat if your guests like that.

Safe Cooking Times

Hamburger should be cooked to an internal temperature of 160 degrees F. Use a meat thermometer to ensure that meat has reached an adequate temperature. It is safe to cook steaks and roasts medium rare (145 degrees F). If you are using a meat thermometer, the following temperature readings indicate doneness: 145 degrees F for medium rare; 160 degrees F for medium; and 170 degrees F for well done.

Safe Refrigeration Times

Beef products will remain fresh for a few days after their "Sell-By" date. If you don't use beef products within that time frame, you should freeze them. Check all product that is past its "Sell-By" date to ensure it is still good. When beef has gone bad, it will feel slimy or tacky and smell bad.

Fresh beef roast, steaks, chops, or ribs	3 to 5 days
Fresh beef liver or variety meats	1 to 2 days
Ground beef	1 to 2 days
Home cooked beef, soups, stews, or casseroles	3 to 4 days
Deli-prepared convenience meals	1 to 2 days
Beef hot dogs, unopened package Beef hot dogs, opened	2 weeks 7 days
Lunch meats, opened package	3 to 5 days
Canned beef products, opened	3 to 4 days
Jerky refrigerated	2 to 3 months

FOURTEEN

How to Select and Store Lamb

The Spring Lamb label is no longer significant since lamb products are now available and produced all year long.

Lamb (often referred to as *regular lamb*) is the meat from young sheep that are slaughtered when less than 1 year old. *Baby lamb* are slaughtered between 6 and 8 weeks of age; *Spring lamb* is usually 3 to 5 months old. Lamb between 12 and 24 months of age are referred to as *yearlings*. Sheep over 2 years old are called *mutton*. Their meat will be tougher and have a stronger flavor. Most lamb sold in the supermarket is "regular."

Your supermarket may sell lamb as chops, legs, or roasts. Lamb chops will include *sirloin chop, shoulder chop*, or *loin chop*. Legs will include *BRT* or *boneless leg, bone-in leg*, or *shank*. Roasts may include *rack of lamb, Frenched rack*, or *crown roast*. Your supermarket may not stock more expensive or specialty cuts like rack of lamb or crown roast, but you can ask your butcher to order them for you. In addition, supermarkets will sell cut-up *lamb stew meat, cubes for kabobs*, and *ground lamb*.

Selecting Lamb

The meat of lamb should be a rosy, pink or red color and contain white marbling, the white flecks of fat within the meat muscle. The fat trim around cuts of lamb should be firm, white, and not too thick. Lamb meat will be fine textured and firm. Lamb meat that is darker than rosy, pink is old and will not be as tender and flavorful. Packages of lamb should feel cold to the touch and be tightly wrapped with no tears or punctures. Do not purchase lamb that is dried around the edges or has a bad odor.

Your supermarket may not always have lamb in stock. If you want to serve lamb, it is best to order it ahead of time at the meat counter.

As with any other perishable, make your lamb purchase at the end of your shopping trip.

Check Dates

Check the dates on packages. Many stores mark packages with a "Sell-By" date. Never buy product that has expired. Frozen lamb is safe to use if it has past its "Sell-By" date provided it was frozen prior to that date. "Use-By" dates mean this is the last day lamb will be at its peak quality. It may be safe to use past this date.

Lamb is Graded

Lamb is graded *Prime, Choice, Good, Utility,* and *Cull*. Your supermarket will sell *Prime, Choice,* and *Good* graded lamb. *Utility* and *Cull* grades are used in processed meat products or for ground. The USDA grades lamb meat based upon maturity, color, firmness, and texture. *Prime* lamb will have more fat marbling, and, therefore, higher fat content, and be more tender and flavorful than *Choice* or *Good. Choice* will still have good marbling and flavor, but not as much as *Prime. Good* will have less marbling and flavor than *Choice.* Eighty (80) percent of the lamb sold in US supermarkets is graded *Prime* and *Choice.*

Labeling on Lamb Products

Fresh American Lamb

Lamb bearing this label was raised in the United States. An *American lamb* weighs about 135 pounds, which is considerably larger than lamb grown in other countries. This yields larger cuts of meat and a higher meat-to-bone ratio. Although grassfed, a good percentage of US lambs are finished on grain. Lamb producers believe this makes the lamb more tender and gives them a milder, less gamey flavor.

Spring Lamb

If lamb is labeled *Spring Lamb*, it was produced between March and October. This term was important in the past but has lost its significance since lamb products are now available all year long.

Organic

Certified organic lamb must come from sheep that ate only organically grown feed, and this feed must not contain any animal byproducts. In addition, the animals can't be treated with synthetic hormones or antibiotics. Animals must have access to the outdoors and must have access to pasture. Organic animals cannot be cloned.

While there is organic lamb sold in the United States, the USDA organic standards prohibit sheep farmers from using anthelmintics, an anti-parasitic drug. Organic standards in the British Isle allow the use of this drug. While alternate methods of controlling parasites in sheep are being researched, most US sheep farmers find the need to use anthelmintics for the health and welfare of their flocks.

Natural

The term *"natural"* or *"all natural"* means lamb has been minimally processed and contains no preservatives or artificial additives. Since products like lamb don't contain preservatives or additives, this label is meaningless.

Pasture Raised

"Pasture raised" or *"pastured"* means lamb spend time outdoors on pasture, feeding on grass or forage. There are no USDA standards for this label, including how much time the lamb spends on pasture. Some lamb bearing this label will come from lamb that spend time on pasture but also receive a grain supplement.

Grassfed Versus Grain Fed

Most all the sheep raised in the US graze on pastures for part of their life. Some sheep are 100 percent grassfed, while others receive a grain supplement. If buying grassfed only sheep is important to you, investigate the farmer's practices. Many sheep farmers contend that a partial grain diet makes lamb meat more tender and flavorful, with a less gamey taste.

Animal Welfare Approved

If buying pasture-raised and grassfed lamb is important to you, look for the "Animal Welfare Approved" label. This verification means lambs were raised with outdoor access, had freedom to roam, and were given no hormones. They receive antibiotics only when sick. In addition, the lamb were raised humanely.

Country of Origin

Country of Origin Labeling (COOL) is a labeling law that requires grocery stores, supermarkets, and warehouse stores to inform their customers about the county of origin of many products, including lamb.

Storing and Using Lamb at Home

Lamb should be refrigerated at 40 degrees F immediately when you arrive home. Chops and roasts should be used within 3 to 5 days, and ground lamb, stew, and kabob meat should be used within 2 days. If you do not plan to use lamb within this time frame, freeze it.

Many recipes suggest bringing lamb to room temperature before grilling or cooking. Lamb should not be removed from the refrigerator more than 20 to 30 minutes before grilling or cooking. This should be sufficient time to bring it to the appropriate temperature for even cooking.

Due to residual heat, lamb will continue to cook after it is removed from the oven. Take it out of the oven when it is 5 to 10 degrees short of its desired cooking temperature. It will continue to cook. Lamb is best if it is allowed to rest for 15 to 30 minutes before eating.

Cooking tip: To stretch your food dollars, save your lamb bones and make broth. It is a great substitute for beef broth. Roast the bones in a 400 degree F oven for about 30 minutes until well browned. Place them in a large kettle with onion, carrots, celery, garlic, salt, and water and simmer 12 to 15 hours.

Freezing Lamb

It is safe to freeze lamb in its original packaging or repackage it in Ziploc® freezer bags. Lamb freezes best when your freezer is set at 0 degrees F. If you are freezing lamb in the original package, it is best to over-wrap the package with aluminum foil, freezer paper, or plastic wrap to avoid freezer burn. When frigid air reaches the surface of food, it causes grayish-brown, leathery spots known as freezer burn. Portions damaged by freezer burn should be cut away either during or after cooking.

If you are repacking lamb, freeze it in meal-size portions. Place it in a reusable or plastic Ziploc® freezer bag. Press as much air out of the bag as possible. Frozen lamb should be used within 4 to 6 months.

Thawing Frozen Lamb

Lamb can be safely defrosted in the refrigerator, in cold water, or in the microwave. Never thaw lamb on the counter. The preferred method is the refrigerator. Ground lamb, stew or kabob meat, and chops will thaw in 1 day. Bone-in parts and whole roasts will take 2 days or longer. Once thawed, lamb is safe to keep in the refrigerator for 3 to 5 days. Stew and kabob meat and ground lamb should be used in 1 to 2 days. Lamb that is defrosted in the refrigerator can be refrozen.

To defrost in cold water, do not remove the packaging. To use this method, the package must be airtight or put into a leak-proof bag. This method is not suitable for product wrapped in butcher paper only. Place the lamb in a large bowl in your kitchen sink and fill it with cold water. The water should be changed every 30 minutes to ensure that it stays cold. Small packages of lamb will defrost in about 1 hour. A 3- to 4-pound roast may take 2 to 3 hours. Lamb that is thawed in cold water must be cooked before it is refrozen.

Only thaw lamb in the microwave if you are pressed for time or in an emergency. Thawing lamb in the microwave changes its texture and consistency. If you use the microwave for defrosting, the lamb must be cooked immediately.

Safe Cooking Times

The USDA recommends cooking lamb to 145 degrees F. Use a meat thermometer to ensure that the meat has reached an adequate temperature. Most chefs prefer their lamb on the rarer side. They recommend 115 to 120 degrees F for rare, 125 degrees F for medium rare, 130 degrees F for medium, 145 degrees F for medium well, and 150 degrees F for well done. The USDA recommends cooking ground lamb and lamb patties to an internal temperature of 170 degrees F.

Safe Refrigeration Times

Lamb products will remain fresh for a few days after their "Sell-By" date. If you don't use lamb products within that time frame, you should freeze them. If you are using lamb past its "Sell-By" date, it is important to ensure it is still safe to eat. Lamb has past its prime if it has turned gray or smells bad. It will feel sticky or slimy to the touch and will have mushy or moldy spots.

Fresh lamb roasts or chops	3 to 5 days
Ground lamb	1 to 2 days
Home cooked lamb, soups, stews, or casseroles	3 to 4 days

FIFTEEN

How to Select and Store Fish and Seafood

To ensure fish are parasite free, the FDA established guidelines that fishmongers are expected to follow called the parasite destruction guarantee.

Fish and seafood are very perishable, making it important to get the freshest products available. Depending upon where you live, buying fresh fish and seafood may not be easy. It is, therefore, important to buy your fish and seafood from a reputable source.

When selecting a fish market, pick a store that is clean and well organized. The fish should be displayed in a manner that keeps them fresh—in a refrigerated case and on ice.

What is more important, however, is finding a knowledgeable fishmonger. You want to purchase your fish and seafood from someone who knows the product and can answer your questions. A good fishmonger will know where the fish was harvested, whether it is farm raised or wild, when it arrived at the store, and whether or not it was previously frozen. Cooking fish can be a tricky proposition; therefore, you also want a fishmonger who can give you advice on how to prepare your purchase.

General Rules

Always buy fresh fish or seafood that has been refrigerated or properly iced. The best seafood is the freshest, no more than 2 to 3 days out of the water. When shopping, purchase your dry goods first and refrigerated items last. The less time items like fresh fish spend outside refrigeration the better.

Selecting Whole Fish

Depending upon where you live and shop, the following fish might be available to purchase whole at the supermarket you patronize: *rainbow trout, snapper, catfish, tilapia, orange roughy, white roughy, branzino (bronzini), sea bass, red snapper, red fish, walleye, mackerel, hake, sea bream, anchovies*, and *striped bass*. Regardless of the variety, the same general guidelines apply.

When shopping for fresh fish, shop with your eyes and sense of smell. The skin of whole fish should be shiny, almost metallic. As fish decompose, the skin coloring becomes less distinct, but the scales should be brightly colored and tightly attached to the skin.

The gills of fresh fish should be bright red or pink and free from slime. Gills on fish that have past their prime have faded to a light pink color and may appear gray or somewhat brown or green.

If the head is still on the fish, the eyes should be bright, clear, and full, and will bulge slightly. As fish age, their eyes become cloudy and pink.

Fresh fish never smells "fishy" but has a fresh, mild odor. Fish only smells "fishy" or like ammonia when it starts to decompose.

Selecting Fillets and Steaks

As with whole fish, general rules apply to buying fish fillets and steaks. Depending upon where you live and the supermarket you patronize, the following fish may be available to purchase in fillet or steak portions: *Chilean sea bass, cod, halibut, swordfish, tilapia, Artic char, sablefish, mackerel, hake, sea bream, yellowtail, carp, pike, herring, tuna, Dover sole, catfish, rock fish, orange roughy, white roughy, flounder, red fish, steel head trout, grey sole, branzino, bluegill, crappie, striped bass, haddock, monkfish, mahi-mahi, red snapper, salmon, pollock, lionfish*, and *pagnasius.*

Fillets and steaks should have firm, elastic flesh and a moist, fresh appearance. Avoid fish with browning around the edges. Fillets and steaks should not have separated from the bones. If kept too long in the case, fillets will separate.

When pressed, the flesh of fresh fish should spring back. It should be almost translucent with no evidence of bruising or reddening. Avoid buying fish packaged in liquid. They deteriorate more quickly.

Salmon

Because salmon is a popular fish in the US, I have included more information about the different varieties. When you are standing in front of the fish counter at your supermarket, do you ever wonder, "Which variety of salmon should I purchase?" It can be quite puzzling. What exactly is the difference between wild and farm-raised salmon and between Pacific and Atlantic salmon?

Wild salmon is caught in its natural environment like oceans, rivers, or lakes and eats a diet consistent with its surroundings. *Farm-raised salmon* is farmed using a process called aquaculture, where the fish are given a processed feed that is high in fat and protein, designed to make them grow larger.

Pacific Salmon

Salmon connoisseurs agree that wild salmon is the most flavorful; nutritionists find it contains more minerals than farm-raised fish and is a good source of Omega-3's; and food purists believe it contains the least contaminants. It is also pricier than Atlantic salmon. In 2022, the *Cordova Times* reported that king salmon could sell for as much as $80 per pound and sockeye as much as $54 per pound.

King or Chinook is one of the rarest varieties of salmon and, with its rich, buttery flavor, is considered the best salmon money can buy. A king salmon can weigh anywhere between 40 to 130 pounds. Because of its size, this variety is cut into thick fillets; and if you are looking for a fish that contains lots of Omega-3's, choose this variety. King salmon is found along the coast of Central California all the way to Alaska and even into Asia. When caught in prestigious rivers like the Columbia or Copper, king salmon can be very pricey. If the price per pound doesn't break your pocketbook, purchase king salmon.

Sockeye or Red salmon are mostly caught in Alaskan waters and are generally smaller and leaner than kings. They possess a striking red-orange flesh, a salmony taste, and a moderate amount of fat. Because they are generally less expensive than king or coho, sockeye salmon are very popular with salmon lovers.

Coho or Silver salmon has a bright silver skin and a more subtle, delicate flavor. Because it is smaller than some salmon, cohos are used when cooking a whole fish. While their flavor is similar to king salmon, their texture is more delicate; and they have less fat content.

Pink or Humpback salmon have a distinctive hump on their back that develops when they spawn. The pink or humpback salmon is typically processed and sold in cans or pouches.

Chum or Silverbrite (Keta or Dog), mostly found in Alaskan waters, is a light to medium-colored fish that is most prized for its roe, which is considered a delicacy in many cuisines. Chum's roe can be bigger and tastier than the roe of other varieties of salmon. This salmon gets its name from its dog-like teeth.

Atlantic Salmon

Atlantic salmon is normally the most reasonably priced. While there are salmon lovers who prefer the taste of Atlantic salmon, its price point is its strongest suit. Nutritionists find that farm-raised salmon is higher in vitamin C, saturated fat, and calories than wild salmon. Both are excellent sources of Omega 3's. Atlantic salmon has a milder flavor than Pacific salmon and is often larger in size because of the diet it is fed.

There are very few wild Atlantic salmon in existence today; it is mostly farm-raised. Dams in the Northeast US have prevented salmon from swimming upriver and spawning.

While there are a few Atlantic fish farms in the US, most of our Atlantic salmon is imported from Canada, South America (primarily Chile), or Europe (primarily Norway). Norwegian salmon are raised in a natural habitat, unlike Chilean salmon which are raised in cramped pools. Also, Norway is committed to stricter regulations.

While fish farming has improved over the years with more fisheries feeding their fish plant-based food better formulated for good health, if I am buying Atlantic salmon, I prefer Norwegian.

Storing Fish

The best fish is the freshest, no more than 2 to 3 days out of the water. Therefore, I always buy fresh fish the same day I use it. Fish will keep 1 to 2 days in the refrigerator. Once cooked, fish will keep for 3 to 4 days in the refrigerator.

Storing Smoked Fish

Smoked fish, like lox, will keep up to 14 days refrigerated.

Storing Canned Fish

Once cans have been opened, canned fish or seafood should be discarded after 3 to 4 days in the refrigerator. Note: do not store in the original can.

Selecting Frozen Fish

If fish has been frozen and thawed for retail sale, it should be labeled "Previously Frozen." If you're buying frozen fish, again shop with your nose. There should be no "fishy" odor. Avoid packages that are torn or perforated. Frozen fish should be solidly frozen and show no signs of discoloration which may indicate freezer burn. Look for wrappings that are tight, with no air spaces between the fish and the wrappings.

Wild Caught versus Farm Raised

The decision whether to purchase wild-caught or farm-raised fish and seafood can be difficult. There are pros and cons to both.

Wild Caught

Wild-caught fish, shellfish, and seafood are harvested directly from oceans, rivers, or lakes and have never lived in captivity. Because wild-caught fish roam freely, they have a more diverse diet than farm-raised fish, which makes their flesh more colorful and gives them better flavor. Some chefs prefer wild-caught fish because its brightly colored flesh makes for a more attractive presentation when the fish is cooked and plated. Because wild fish are constantly on the move looking for food and avoiding predators, their meat is leaner and less fatty.

There is a downside. Wild-caught fish populations are shrinking, but demand for them is staying at the same level. Meeting the demand is unsustainable. Many species of fish are diminishing because of overfishing; and bycatch (when unintended species are caught during fishing) makes this a less sustainable choice. Because fish populations are shrinking and demand remains high, wild-caught fish are pricier than farm raised.

Wild fish are sometimes only available during certain seasons of the year and must travel a great distance to reach many consumers. In addition, wild fish contain higher levels of mercury. While wild fish do not contain enough mercury to be harmful to humans, their mercury levels are higher than their farm-raised counterparts.

Farm Raised

Farm-raised fish, often referred to as *"ocean raised,"* are grown in floating net pens in oceans, rivers, and lakes or in man-made pens on land. Some consider ocean-raised fish to be a more sustainable option because it reduces stress on wild fish populations, allowing them time to reproduce. Farm-raised fish, often called aquaculture, are available year-round and are less expensive than wild because it costs less to harvest, process, and ship them. Farm-raised fish have lower levels of Omega 3s than wild-caught fish, one of the main health benefits from eating fish and seafood. Therefore, farm-raised fish may not be as healthy.

Where the fish are raised and how the farm is operated can determine whether it is a viable choice. Some fish farms don't adhere to good environmental practices and harm the surrounding environment by spreading chemicals and waste. This can negatively affect local wildlife as well as wild fish populations. If you are concerned about eating antibiotic-free fish, farm-raised fish are more likely to get sick and are often fed antibiotics because they are raised in captivity.

Know the Source of Your Fish

Knowing the source is the best way to choose fish and seafood. Seafood should always have two labels: one that tells you where and when it was caught or farmed, and one that tells you where it was packaged. Aquaculture in the United States is held to higher inspections standards, so buying fish and seafood farmed in the US may be a better choice.

The Marine Stewardship Council is working to address the negative impact of wild-caught fish, and Global Seafood Watch is working to address the negative effects of farm-raised fish.

Selecting Sustainable Fish and Seafood

A growing number of consumers want to purchase fish and seafood that is caught or farmed following *sustainable* and *ocean-friendly practices* and with minimal social and environmental impact. If this is important to you, look for the *Marine Stewardship Council* blue label or a *Best Aquaculture Practices* certification on the products you purchase.

Marine Stewardship Council

The Marine Stewardship Council blue label is open to any wild-caught seafood or fisheries that meet MSC standards. This label ensures there will be enough stock in the sea so that fish can reproduce indefinitely, that there is minimal environmental impact, ensuring the marine environment can flourish, and that fisheries have good management practices in place so they can respond quickly to change. You will also find the MSC blue label on canned fish. A complete list of major retailers carrying MSC labeled fish can be found on the Marine Stewardship Council website.

Best Aquaculture Practices

The Best Aquaculture Practices Certification is a program undertaken by the Global Seafood Alliance. This certification is verification that producers follow best practices in the entire production chain including the processing plant, farm, hatchery, and feed mill. It also ensures that employees in these facilities are treated fairly and that animal welfare is a top priority. A complete list of major retailers carrying Best Aquaculture Practices products can be found on their website.

There are other conservation programs that provide guides on sustainable seafood: Monterey Bay Aquarium Seafood Watch, Oceana, Audubon G. U. L. F., Environmental Defense Fund Seafood Selector, and World Wildlife Fund Seafood Guides. The organizations producing these guides focus on different geographical regions and may have different values or goals.

Can You Buy Organic Fish?

Although you may find *organic* labels on fish, the USDA does not currently certify organic aquaculture production; but they are in the process of developing organic standards for farm-raised fish. Wild-caught fish have been excluded from the organic label, because since they roam free, there is no certainty about what they have ingested.

There are some fish and seafood that require more detailed comment.

Selecting Seafood

Clams

There are two varieties of clams—hard shell and soft shell. Clams eat by filtering water through a siphon. Hard-shell clams have a small, short siphon which allows them to close their shell. They are the most common type of clams sold in the supermarket. When buying hard-shell clams, look for *little neck, cherry stone, top neck,* or *quahog.*

Soft-shell clams dig themselves deeper into the sand; therefore, they need a longer siphon to filter water. A longer siphon means the clam never completely retracts into its shell, so its shell never completely closes. Understanding this is important in selecting good quality clams. When buying soft-shell clams, look for *steamers, geoduck,* or *long necks.* The siphon on soft shell clams tends to be tough.

Selecting Clams

Clams are kept on ice in the seafood case and are either sold individually or in mesh bags. If you buy clams in a mesh bag, the bag will bear a "harvest tag," which indicates the date and location of harvest as well as a "Use-By" date. If you buy individual clams, you can ask the fishmonger to show you the "harvest tag."

Inspect the shells. Discard clams with chipped, smashed, or cracked shells. Clams should never smell fishy but fresh like the ocean. Their shells should be tightly closed. If you find a hard-shell clam open shell, tap on it lightly. If it does not react, it is dead and should be discarded. Since soft-shell clams never fully close their shell, their shells will be slightly open. To determine if soft-shell clams are still alive, tap on the shell lightly. If the clam does not react, it is dead and should be discarded.

Storing Clams

Remove the clams from the mesh bag so they can breathe. Place them in a bowl, cover them with a damp cloth, and refrigerate them. Although they will keep 2 days in your fridge, it is best to use clams within 24 hours of purchase.

Tips on cleaning clams: Clams can be quite sandy. Because the shells of soft-shell clams do not close completely, it is essential to clean them before cooking. Although some clams are cleaned or purged before you purchase them, I prefer to clean them anyway as I do not want any sand remaining in the recipe I prepare. To clean clams, soak them in salted water for a couple of hours. Add ⅓ cup of kosher or non-iodized sea salt to 1 gallon of water. After placing clams in salted water, sprinkle ½ cup of corn meal over them. The clams will ingest the cornmeal and expel sand. Use a slotted spoon to remove the clams from the water so any sand remains on the bottom of the bowl.

Tips on eating clams: If clams don't open during the cooking process, they should be discarded.

Selecting Pre-Shucked Clams

Some supermarkets will sell pre-shucked clams in a lidded container. The container will contain liquid that was inside the clam's shell. Look for plump clams. The liquid should be creamy white or light tan.

Storing Pre-Shucked Clams

Pre-shucked clams will keep 3 to 5 days when kept in their original container and refrigerated. To check for freshness, use your sense of smell. Pre-shucked clams should smell like the ocean. If they smell sour, they are past their prime and should be discarded. You can freeze pre-shucked clams.

Tips on shucking clams: Make sure shells are tightly closed. Place clams under cold running water and scrub their shells with a stiff brush to remove any loose grit or barnacles. If you have not soaked the clams, do so before shucking. Place a bowl underneath your workspace to catch any liquor. Hold the clam with an oven mitt with the hinge side out. If you are right-handed, hold it in your left hand.

Position the clam's hinge in the area where your thumb meets your palm. It is important to use an oven mitt to protect your hand in case the knife slips. Insert the tip of a clam knife about ½-inch into the clam near one side of the hinge. Hold the clam firmly and slide the knife around the lip of the lower edge of the top shell to cut the clam's abductor muscles. Once the abductor muscles are cut, the shells should open easily.

Freeze clams that are difficult to open for 15 to 20 minutes. Slide the knife around inside the shell to loosen the meat. Remove the black siphon before eating.

Tips on making clam chowder: I like buying canned clams for my chowder. Each can only costs $2.79 in 2023, making it an inexpensive weeknight meal. Since canned clams are already cooked, add them after the potatoes are done. If you cook them separately before adding them to the chowder, they will become chewy. Three (6.5-ounce) cans yield two cups of clams and juice. I don't drain the clams but put the clam juice into the chowder, adding more flavor.

Oysters

There are two varieties of oysters—*East Coast* and *West Coast*. Supermarkets will sell canned, frozen, live, and pre-shucked oysters. Pre-shucked oysters are sold in lidded containers, especially around the holidays. If you purchase pre-shucked oysters, check the "Use-By" date and follow it closely.

Selecting Live Oysters

Live oysters bear a "harvest tag" indicating where and when they were harvested. Never buy an oyster with a harvest date older than 5 to 7 days. Shop with your nose. Oysters should smell like the ocean and never smell fishy. Fresh seaweed on an oyster is a sign of freshness. In addition, small crustaceans often attach themselves to oysters. If they are present on an oyster shell, they should smell fresh, never fishy. The shells of oysters should be closed. An open shell means the oyster is dead. Liquid inside the shell is also a sign of freshness. If the liquid has dried out, the oyster is past its prime. Live oysters should feel heavy for their size and full of water.

Storing Live Oysters

Place oysters in a bowl and cover them with a damp cloth and refrigerate them. Do not place live oysters in an airtight container. This will kill them. If you want to store them on ice, be sure they do not come into contact with water. This will, also, kill the oyster.

Tips on shucking oysters: Place the oyster under cold running water and scrub the shells with a stiff brush to remove any loose grit or barnacles. Hold the oyster (in your left hand if you are right-handed) with an oven mitt with the hinge side out. It is important to use an oven mitt to protect your hand in case the knife slips. The flat side of the oyster should be up. Insert the tip of an oyster knife about ½-inch into the oyster near one side of the hinge. Hold the oyster firmly and slide the knife around the lip of the oyster until you come to the other side of the hinge. Place a bowl underneath your workspace to catch any liquid that might spill. Using your fingers, pry the shell apart. Using the oyster knife, detach any muscle that clings to the inside of the top shell. Remove the top shell. Carefully remove any grit that is on the inside of the oyster. Do not wash a shucked oyster as this will affect its flavor.

Tips on cleaning oysters: For pre-shucked oysters purchased from the supermarket, place in a colander and rinse with cold water. Drain. For oysters in the shell, fill the sink with cold water. Place the oysters in the sink. Wearing kitchen gloves, whirl oysters in the water, removing any grit. Repeat this process if necessary. Scrub shells with a brush if needed. Drain immediately as oysters don't like to be kept in water.

Selecting Pre-Shucked Oysters

Supermarkets will sell pre-shucked oysters in lidded containers, especially around the holidays. When selecting pre-shucked oysters, look for ones that are plump and a glossy tan color. Do not buy pre-shucked oysters that are dry and withered or have a cloudy appearance. Pre-shucked oysters should smell fresh and mild and never fishy.

Storing Pre-Shucked Oysters

Fresh, pre-shucked oysters should be refrigerated in their liquor and kept no more than 1 or 2 days.

Crab

Selecting Crab

You can purchase crab either alive or cooked and processed —picked crabmeat or crack-and-eat legs.

Selecting Live Crab

If you are buying live crab, the crab should be alive. If you touch it and it doesn't move, pass. When you pick it up, it should move its claws and eyes. Never buy dead, raw crab. If the crab smells like ammonia, pass. If you purchase a live crab, it is recommended you cook it within 10 to 15 minutes after its death. A good crab will have a hard, firm underbelly. Although many crab connoisseurs believe female crabs have a better taste, it is best to purchase male crabs. Because of dwindling populations, it is better to keep females in the ocean to reproduce. Male crabs have blue tips on their claws, and female have red tips.

Selecting Crab

Cooked, ready-to-eat crab is available at your supermarket either fresh, frozen, or pasteurized in cans. Crab should feel cold to the touch when you purchase it. Any exposed meat should be white. If you are buying frozen crab, check the package for ice crystals. This is a sign of freezer burn. Avoid fresh, picked crabmeat that smells or has pockets of blue or gray. This discoloration means it has not been stored properly.

Selecting Soft-Shell Crabs

When the hard shells of a crab grow, crabs shed their shells and must exit them. This is called molting. After leaving their shells, crabs remain soft for two to three hours before their shells begin to harden. When selecting soft-shell crabs, look for ones that have all their legs and claws and are very soft. Avoid soft-shell crabs that are wrapped in plastic wrap. This means they were previously frozen. Do not buy them if they have been cleaned. Soft-shell crabs should be cleaned just before cooking. Soft-shell crab season runs from April through October.

Tips on cleaning soft-shell crabs: Rinse the crab under cold water. Using cooking scissors, with the crab shell-side up, make a ½-inch cut behind the eyes. Discard any gooey matter. With shell-side up, lift up each side of the shell and remove the feathery-looking gills. Turn the crab over so that the white meat is exposed. Lift up the pointed flap, which is called the apron, and remove it. Rinse.

Storing Crab

If you purchase live crab, use it the day you buy it. To store live crab until you cook it, place it in an open container lined with wet newspaper and store it briefly in your refrigerator or a cooler. Keep live crab moist and cool but not wet.

Fresh crabmeat should be refrigerated and eaten within 2 days of purchase or frozen. Keep frozen crab frozen until you are ready to heat it.

Pasteurized crab sold in cans has an 8- to 18-month shelf life. Once cans have been opened, the crab will keep for 7 days in your refrigerator.

Tips on thawing crab legs: You can thaw frozen crab legs by placing them in the refrigerator overnight (about 8 hours) or by placing them in your sink and running cold water over them. If you thaw them in your refrigerator, place them on a rack in a water-tight container so that any water drains to the bottom during defrosting.

Mussels

Selecting Fresh Mussels

Look for clean, whole shells that have not been chipped, broken, or smashed. Good mussels should look wet and smell like the ocean—salty and clean. If they smell bad, pass. Shells should be tightly closed and never open. A gaping shell means the animal is dead. Ask the fishmonger to pack shellfish on ice for the ride home. It is best to buy mussels the same day you plan to use them.

Storing Fresh Mussels

Mussels need to be kept cold and moist until they are cooked, but they also need to breathe. Once you arrive home, remove mussels from the package and place them in a large bowl. Cover with a wet paper towel and refrigerate until ready to use.

Cleaning fresh mussels: Frozen mussels are usually cleaned before freezing. If you are buying fresh mussels, they need to be cleaned before cooking. Fill a large bowl with cold water and 1/3 cup of flour. Add the mussels and soak them for about 30 minutes. They will take in fresh water and expel any dirt that's settled inside. After soaking them, place mussels under a slow stream of cold water and scrub the shells using a stiff brush. Each mussel has a beard, the stringy group of fibers located between the shells, which must be removed. Gently pull the fibers from the mussel. If the beard is stubborn and difficult to remove, a pair of piers works nicely.

Tips on eating mussels: If the shells of mussels do not open after cooking, discard them. They are not safe to eat.

Scallops

Selecting Scallops

Fresh scallops will look moist but not milky. A feathery white surface is a sign of freezer burn. Scallops should smell sweet and a bit like seaweed. Buy "unsoaked" or dry scallops. Pass on scallops that smell like iodine. Avoid scallops that appear dry or have brown edges. Fresh scallops are very perishable. Buy them the same day you plan to use them. The off-white, cork-shaped *northeastern bay scallop* is thought to be the most flavorful. It is found in a small area between Long Island and Cape Cod and has a short season—November through February. This is the best scallop for eating raw.

Storing Scallops

Some fresh fish, especially scallops, often leak on the way home from the supermarket. Placing them in plastic bags or a separate shopping bag avoids leaks that can cross-contaminate other foods and keeps any leaking mess contained. Once home, I usually store scallops in plastic bags in the refrigerator as well for the same reason. If the scallops you purchase are in a plastic container, place it in a bowl of ice and store it in the coldest part of your refrigerator. Don't let the scallops come into contact with the ice as it will destroy the texture and flavor of the fish.

Tips on handling scallops: Scallops must always be rinsed before using.

Shrimp

Shrimp are sold according to the number in a pound, known as the count. *Jumbo* shrimp range from 21–25 per pound; *extra-large* 26–30; *large* 31–35; *medium* 36–42; *small* 51–60; *extra small* 61 and over. When making peel-and-eat shrimp or shrimp cocktail, larger shrimp are preferable. For shrimp salads or other dishes, a smaller shrimp is better. When shrimp is on sale, be sure to check the count your grocer advertises.

Selecting Shrimp

Fresh versus *Frozen*. Fishermen put shrimp on ice as soon as they are caught. This preserves the shrimp, freezing them so they are just-caught fresh until they are thawed. The fresh shrimp you see on ice in the seafood counter at your supermarket were most likely once frozen and are thawing in the counter. The longer they are in the counter, the less fresh they will be. Unless you know that the fresh shrimp you are buying is fresh off the boat, frozen shrimp is a better choice.

Wild Caught or *Farm Raised*: Wild-caught shrimp have a sharper, more shrimpy taste; however, they are pricier and harder to find. Ninety percent of shrimp sold in the US are imported from Southeast Asia, Ecuador, and India; and the majority of that is farm-raised. Your supermarket is required to divulge the country of origin and whether shrimp is wild or farmed. Check the label.

If you have doubts, farm-raised shrimp cultivated under cleaner standards will bear a "Best Aquaculture Practices" label. The certification label to look for when buying wild shrimp is "Marine Stewardship Council Approved".

The most common imported shrimp sold in the supermarket are *white vannemei* and *tiger shrimp* from Asia. The most common domestic varieties are *white* and *pink* shrimp from the Gulf of Mexico. If I have a choice, I prefer pink shrimp.

Do not purchase frozen shrimp that have dry spots on their shells. This is a sign of freezer burn. Except for the *black tiger* variety of shrimp, black spots on shells are an indication of spoilage. Signs of yellow or grit on the shells could mean the shrimp have been bleached to remove black spots. Avoid shrimp that smell like ammonia or feel soft or slimy.

Selecting Unsoaked Scallops and Shrimp

Scallops and shrimp are often soaked in a solution of water and tripolyphosphate to extend their shelf life, but this hurts their flavor. Your supermarket is required by law to tell you whether fish has been soaked in this solution. If available, buy the unsoaked or "dry" variety. They have a superior taste.

Tips on deveining shrimp: Unless you are cooking with very small shrimp, they must be deveined. The intestinal tract on medium to large shrimp runs down their back and is quite unappetizing. To devein shrimp, hold them under a slow stream of cold water and run the tip of an ice pick, sharp knife, or toothpick down their back, scraping out the intestine, yet leaving the shrimp intact. Rinse gently to remove any black from the shrimp.

Crayfish

Crayfish, also called crawfish and crawdads, come from fresh waters in Louisiana and are either caught in the wild or farmed. Crayfish die and spoil very quickly, so it is important to handle them properly. Crayfish are in season midwinter to late spring, but are cheaper and more abundant in March, April, and May. Like shrimp, crayfish are available in a variety of sizes from extra small to jumbo.

Supermarkets will sell frozen crayfish. Most frozen crayfish have been cooked and peeled with their tails removed.

Selecting Live Crayfish

Live crayfish should be active and frisky. Discard any uncooked crayfish with cracked bodies or ones that smell bad. Before they are cooked, crayfish are a translucent sandy yellow, green, red, blue, or brown in color. It is only after they are cooked that they turn the same color as lobsters.

Storing Live Crayfish

To keep crayfish alive until you cook them, place them in a plastic bag and store then in an ice-filled cooler. The ideal temperature for keeping them alive is between 46 to 48 degrees F. Keep the lid of the cooler ajar.

Tips on cleaning crayfish: Crayfish need to be cleaned before cooking. Fill a tub with cold water and soak the crayfish for about 5 minutes. Remove the crayfish, empty the tub, and refill it with clean water. Repeat the soaking process until the water is clear. This should not only remove any dirt from the shell but also remove the intestinal tract. Discard any dead crayfish.

Serving tip: Plan for 12 medium-sized crayfish per person. When shelled, 6 to 7 pounds of crayfish yields 1 pound of meat.

Tip on eating crayfish: Cooked crayfish with straight tails should not be consumed.

Lobster

Your supermarket will sell fresh, live, frozen, and canned lobster. Often called the king of the crustacean family, lobsters have a jointed body and limbs that are covered with a hard shell. There are two varieties that are most often found in the supermarket.

The *spiny* lobster is clawless and comes from the warm water of the Caribbean and off the coasts of Florida, Southern California, Mexico, Australia, New Zealand, and South Africa. Since it has no claws, most of the meat of the spiny lobster is found in its tail. The majority of spiny lobster sold in the US are tails and labeled "rock lobster tails."

The *Maine* lobster comes from the cold Atlantic waters and is sold live. This lobster has five pairs of legs, the first of which is heavy claws. The Maine lobster contains a great deal of meat.

Lobsters shed their shells at least once a year, revealing a softer shell underneath. After shedding their shells, lobsters puff themselves up with water to fill up the new shell, which eventually hardens. To tell the difference between a hard-shell and a soft-shell lobster, give the lobster a gentle squeeze. A soft-shell lobster will give slightly. Unlike soft-shelled crabs, these shells are not edible.

Selecting Lobster Tails

Avoid buying lobster tails that have discoloration, black spots, or yellowing on their flesh. Check the label. If the tails have been soaked in sodium tripolyphosphates, pass. (This fact should be on the label.) If the tails are gray, it may mean that the lobster was dead before it was processed, and it will not be good quality. Tails between 5 and 12 ounces in size will yield the most meat and have a better taste and texture.

Selecting Live Lobsters

To select a live lobster, pick it up. A healthy lobster will lift its claws, raise its tail, and move its legs. Avoid lobsters with limp claws and ones that do not move. Lobsters eat each other's antennae. Pass on lobsters with no antennae. If you look into a tank of lobsters and see a lobster's antennae have been nibbled down to the base, it has been in the tank a long time.

Tips on steaming lobster tails: Choose a kettle large enough to hold the lobster tails and large enough to allow steam to circulate around the tails. Place a steamer basket or an upturned colander in the bottom of the kettle. You do not want the lobster tails submerged in water. Fill the kettle with water to a depth of 2 inches.

Cover the kettle and bring the water to a boil over a high heat. When the water is boiling, place the lobster tails into the steamer basket and steam until the tails are cooked through.

The weight of your lobster tails will determine the cooking time. See recommended cooking times below. You do not want to overcook your lobster tails. When you have reached the estimated cooking time, use a cooking thermometer to test for doneness. Lobster meat should be cooked to 140 degrees F. Using tongs, remove lobster tails from the kettle.

The following steaming times will work for cooking two to six tails at the same time:

Weight of Tail	Cooking Time
3 to 6 ounces	4 to 6 minutes
6 to 7 ounces	6 to 8 minutes
8 to 10 ounces	8 to 10 minutes
10 to 16 ounces	9 to 11 minutes
16 to 10 ounces	10 to 12 minutes
20 to 28 ounces	10 to 13 minutes

Tips on removing the tail from the shell: Hold the tails so that the shell faces down. Place your thumbs on each side of the shell. Pull back on both sides to crack the shell open and remove the meat. Rinse the meat under cold running water to remove the tomalley (the green substance found in the body cavity) and pat dry with paper towels. You can also place a small knife under the meat, loosen it from the shell, and gently remove it.

Tips on steaming whole live lobsters: Add 2 to 3 inches of water to a large pot. Season the water generously with sea salt. If you have a steamer basket, you can place it in the pot, but it is not necessary. When the water comes to a rolling boil, carefully add the lobsters to the pot and cover with a tightly fitting lid. Make sure the lobsters are alive when you put them into the pot. A general rule of thumb is to cook 10 minutes per pound for the first two lobsters. Add an additional 3 minutes per each additional lobster you place in the pot. Lobsters are done when they are a bright red color. When you remove the cooked lobsters from the pot, place them in an ice bath to cool. This will make them easier to handle when you are ready to eat them. Remove the bands from the claws.

Storing Live Lobsters

To keep lobsters alive, wrap them in damp newspapers or seaweed and store them in the coldest part of your refrigerator. It is best to cook live lobsters immediately, but they can be kept alive for 1 to 2 days. Do not remove the bands around the claws.

Tips on quantity: You should plan on buying 5 lobster tails to yield one pound of cooked lobster meat. A 1½ pound lobster will yield 6 to 8 ounces of meat.

Tips on thawing frozen lobster tails: To thaw, place frozen tails in your refrigerator 24 hours before you want to cook them.

Langoustines

Langoustines are similar to crayfish, but crayfish grow in fresh water and langoustines grow in saltwater oceans and seas. The majority of langoustines today come from waters off the coast of Scotland. *Langoustino* means "little lobster" in Spanish. Langoustines are smaller than lobsters, never growing over 10 inches. Their shells are a bright shade of orange but don't change color when cooked, like lobsters do.

The meat of langoustines tastes very similar to lobster. Most good seafood markets will carry langoustines either frozen or thawed and ready to cook. Langoustines are hard to keep alive once they are caught, so most langoustines are quick frozen on the boat. Since langostines are sold frozen in packages, selection is limited.

Squid

Finding fresh squid in a supermarket may be difficult. Your supermarket will sell frozen squid tubes, which are the bodies, cut rings, and tentacles.

Selecting Fresh Squid

Squid should have bright, clear, shiny eyes. Its flesh should be firm and plump. Squid will have a white flesh that is covered with a reddish, purplish pigmentation. Avoid squid with dark pigmentation, which indicates that it is is older. Fresh squid should smell like the ocean and never smell "fishy." If you want the squid to cook quickly, choose smaller specimens.

Selecting Frozen Squid

Avoid packages with ice crystals or other signs of freezer burn. Squid that has a reddish tinge was not properly frozen.

Storing Fresh Squid

Cover fresh or thawed squid tightly and store it in the coldest part of your refrigerator. Fresh or previously thawed squid should be used in 2 days.

Tips on thawing frozen squid: Place frozen squid in your refrigerator and thaw it overnight. You can also thaw it by placing it under cold running water or in a bowl of cold water.

Tips on cleaning squid: Cleaning squid can be a messy process, so work over the sink. Using your hands, carefully pull out the head and stomach. Remove and discard the ink sac, being careful not to break it. If it breaks, rinse the squid. Using a paring knife, remove the innards and discard. With the tip of the knife, cut out the beak, the center of the tentacles. Cut beneath both eyes and remove them. Remove the cuttlebone from the body and discard. At the tip where the body and fins intersect, lift the thin layer of skin, twist it, and pull it down. Peel the skin off the body and the fin. If you are cleaning a large number of squid, keep cleaned squid on ice.

Octopus

Most octopus' connoisseurs believe the best octopus comes from Portugal.

Selecting Fresh Octopus

If octopus smells like ammonia, it is past its prime. A fresh octopus will not smell. Its tentacles should feel firm to the touch and a bit slimy. Most all octopus you purchase will have been previously frozen. Some believe the freezing process helps tenderize the meat.

Storing Fresh Octopus

Frozen octopus will keep 9 months. If refrigerated, fresh octopus will last no more than 72 hours. It is best to use octopus within 24 hours.

Tips on cleaning octopus: The beak and eyes will need to be removed. You can ask the fishmonger to remove them for you. In most cases the head of an octopus will already have been cleaned. If the head has been cleaned, there will be a large slit. This slit needs to be rinsed and cleared of any innards or debris.

Selecting Fish For Sushi

Most of the fish for sale in your supermarket is not safe to eat raw. If you want to make sushi, look for fish labeled *sushi-grade* or *sashimi-grade*. Fish with this label are cleaned and deep-frozen while still on the boat.

It is better to purchase farm-raised fish for sushi as it is less likely to contain parasites. The only fish that do not contain parasites are fish that are aquacultured and fed parasite-free pellets.

The best fish for sushi is fish that has been previously frozen. To ensure fish are parasite free, the FDA established guidelines that fishmongers are expected to follow called the parasite destruction guarantee. Following these guidelines, fish are frozen at very low temperatures (–31 degrees F), which kills the parasite. This process is called deep-frozen.

Checking Out

When checking out, it's best to ask the clerk to bag your fish separately. Consider bringing a separate bag from home for fish. Some fresh fish often leak, especially scallops. Placing fish in a separate bag avoids leaks that can cross-contaminate other foods and keeps any leaking mess contained.

Cooking tip: When you make shellfish at home, save the shells and make seafood stock. It is really quite easy. You need 6 to 8 cups of shells to make stock. Place discarded seafood shells in a Ziploc® bag and keep them in your freezer until you have enough to make stock.

Seafood Stock

6 to 8 cups seafood shells (any combination of shrimp, lobster, and crab shells)

1 yellow onion, quartered

2 carrots, unpeeled and coarsely chopped

2 celery stalks, coarsely chopped

2 cloves garlic, smashed

10 sprigs fresh thyme leaves

10 sprigs fresh parsley leaves

1 bay leaf

1 teaspoon peppercorns

2 teaspoons salt

¼ cup tomato paste

1 cup white wine

Salt for seasoning

Place seafood shells in a Ziploc® plastic bag and break them into smaller pieces with a meat cleaver or a rolling pin. Smaller shells yield more flavor.

Preheat the oven to 400 degrees F. Line a baking sheet with parchment paper. Place seafood shells on the baking sheet and roast for 10 minutes.

Transfer roasted shells to a large kettle. Add onion, carrots, celery, garlic, thyme, parsley, bay leaf, peppercorns, and salt. Add enough water to cover the shells. Add tomato paste and wine and stir to combine.

Bring the liquid to a boil over a medium high heat, then reduce the heat to a simmer. Skim off any foam that forms on top of the stock. Simmer for at least 1 hour. Season to taste with salt.

Let the stock cool. Line a large strainer with cheesecloth. Place the strainer over a large bowl and strain the stock into the bowl, removing shells, veggies, and herbs. Transfer the stock to a covered container to store in your refrigerator for 3 to 4 days or freeze in an airtight container for 2 months.

Freezing Fish

If you are freezing fish in its original supermarket packaging, it's best to over-wrap it with aluminum foil to prevent freezer burn. Fish fillets freeze nicely in sealed Ziploc® freezer bags. Before closing the bag, force the air out through a small opening and then quickly finish closing the bag, locking the zip tightly. To freeze whole fish with the skin on, dip them in ice water to form a protective glaze over the fish and then wrap them in freezer paper.

Frozen fish should be used within 1 to 2 months.

Freezing Shellfish

If you are freezing shellfish in its original supermarket packaging, it's best to over-wrap it with aluminum foil to prevent freezer burn. Seafood should be frozen as rapidly as possible; therefore, it is important to thoroughly pre-chill seafood before freezing. Have the temperature of the freezer at 0 degrees F. Place seafood in small packages and spread them out to allow the cold air to circulate evenly.

If it is not in its original packaging, shellfish must be prepped before freezing. See the chart below for individual preparation techniques. After prepping, place shells in a freezer bag or an airtight freezer container. If using a freezer bag, press as much air of the bag as possible. This helps prevent freezer burn. Leave a ½-inch headspace in freezer containers. Label the date of freezing on the package.

Shellfish	Preparation	Recommended Freezing Times
Clams in the Shell	Discard any clams with broken, chipped, or open shells. Rinse shells under a cold stream of running water.	3 months
Pre-shucked Clams	Wash the meat by running it under a cold stream of water. If you buy the clams pre-shucked from the supermarket, drain them first. It is important to clean clams individually as they can be quite sandy.	3 months
Oysters in the Shell	Discard any oysters with open shells. Clean shells.	3 months
Pre-shucked Oysters	If you have purchased pre-shucked oysters from the supermarket, place the meat in a colander and rinse.	3 months
Live Crab	Live crab must be cooked before freezing. This will preserve the flavor and texture of the meat. After cooking, place the crab in an ice bath to retard the cooking process. Wrap the crab with paper towels to prevent the shell from piercing the freezer bag.	3 months
Refreezing Supermarket Crab Legs	Alaska's Seafood Marketing Institute advises against refreezing crab legs.	
Soft-Shell Crabs	Rinse and clean the crabs	3 months

Shellfish	Preparation	Recommended Freezing Times
Mussels	Discard any chipped, broken, or smashed mussels or ones with open shells. Clean them thoroughly.	3 months
Scallops	Pat scallops dry with paper towels. Most scallops purchased at the super-market are previously frozen. You can refreeze these scallops, but their quality will diminish.	2 months
Shrimp	Shrimp can be frozen either cooked or raw, with or its shell. For best results, remove heads but leave shells on. Wash and drain shrimp before freezing. Most shrimp purchased at the supermarket are previously frozen. You can refreeze these shrimp, but their quality will diminish.	3 to 6 months
Live Crayfish	Clean the crayfish. Dis-card any dead specimens. Remove the tails and place them in a colander. Rinse under a cold stream of water. Wrap each tail with freezer paper before storing. Frozen crayfish from the supermarket can be refrozen, but its quality will diminish.	2 months
Fresh Squid	Clean fresh squid before freezing. Squid can be frozen whole or cut into pieces. Place the squid on a baking sheet lined with parchment paper so that the pieces don't overlay. Place the tray in the freezer until the pieces are frozen, about 2 to 3 hours.	3 months

Thawing Frozen Seafood or Fish

It is best to thaw frozen seafood or fish in the refrigerator overnight, especially if you need to refreeze it. If you need to speed up the process, place fish in its package in a large bowl in the sink. Fill the bowl with cold water and keep a slow stream of cold water running into the bowl. Removing fish or seafood from its package and thawing it directly in cold water may damage its color and flavor.

Tip on cooking: Fish should be cooked until it's opaque, or until it flakes easily when pierced with a fork.

Tip on using fish: Washing your hands in cold water before handling fish helps prevent your hands from smelling fishy.

SIXTEEN

How to Select and Store Deli Products

To ensure your deli meat is cut to the thickness you desire, ask the deli clerk to show you the thickness of the first slice before completing your order.

Supermarkets will have a deli section where you can buy cut-to-order meats and cheeses, prepared salads, ready-to-heat meals, grab-and-go meals, party and sandwich platters, fruit and veggie trays, rotisserie and fried chicken, and side dishes. Some supermarkets will also have an olive bar, soup bar, and salad bar.

Deli Meats

Deli meats can be classified into three groups: whole meat, sectioned and formed, and processed.

Whole deli meats refer to a section of meat or poultry that has been cooked and flavored with salt, spices, or sugars. It is an all-meat product.

Sectioned and formed deli meats are prepared from several chunks of meat and are bonded together using non-meat additives.

Processed deli meats include any type of meat that is chopped, seasoned, and formed into a symmetrical shape, like bologna. Sectioned, formed, and processed deli meats will contain more artificial flavorings and ingredients.

Your supermarket will sell deli meats in two locations—the deli and either the meat or dairy department. The meat sold in the deli will be cut to order or cut ahead of time and packaged into 1-pound bags. You will find packages of deli meats hanging in either the meat or dairy section depending upon which supermarket you patronize. This deli meat will be prepackaged.

Because it is a whole-meat product, I personally prefer purchasing Boar's Head® deli products and having my meat cut to order. There are as many opinions about the quality of deli meats as there are people. Even experts disagree. What is important is to select the product that meets the needs of your family based on the quality of the food you want to serve them as well as your budget constraints.

Selecting PrePackaged Deli Meats

Some things to consider when purchasing prepackaged deli meats: Always read the label of prepackaged deli meat. It is required by law that manufacturers list all the ingredients in the products they produce. Ingredients are listed on the label based on weight in descending order. Labels may list preservatives and additives like carrageenan, corn syrup, sodium nitrate, monosodium glutamate, and sucrose. Do not purchase products with these ingredients if that does not meet the needs of your family. Federal law does not require manufacturers to list individual spices. They need only state "spices" or "flavorings."

Prepackaged deli meats will include labels like, "Humanely Raised", "Organic", "Pasture Raised", "Grassfed", "No Added Nitrates", etc., that indicate how the animals were raised and processed. You can decide which brands to purchase based on what is important to you. For more explanation about this terminology, see the chapter on "Understanding Food Labels".

Some deli meat will be injected with a water or brine. The percentage of liquid allowed is regulated by the USDA according to the type of product, but that percentage must be indicated on the label.

Prepackaged deli meat will be dated. Always check dates and buy deli meats that have as much shelf life as possible.

Storing PrePackaged Deli Meat

Deli meat should be placed in the meat drawer of your refrigerator immediately after you come home. If unopened, prepackaged deli meat will be good for 7 to 10 days past its "Sell-By" date. Once opened, it is good for 5 days. Be sure to reclose opened packages tightly. Deli meat that is slimy or iridescent or smells bad has past its prime.

Selecting Cut To Order Deli Meat

Your deli may sell *salami, mortadella, pancetta, prosciutto, pepperoni, pastrami, corned beef,* various flavors of *ham, turkey,* and *chicken* as well as *roast beef.*

Once its package has been opened, cut-to-order deli meat will have a short shelf life. Buy your meat from a market that is busy and turns their product quickly.

If you want to purchase freshly sliced meat from the deli counter, observe the following to ensure your deli meat is fresh:

Deli meats and cheeses should be sliced on different slicers; slicers are dedicated to either meat or cheese. Deli employees should not use the same slicer for both meat and cheese. Slicers should be cleaned after every use. With the shortage of staff these days, this may not occur; but slicers should be cleaned on a regular basis. If you have allergies—for example, you are allergic to beef—alert the deli clerk and make sure the slicer is cleaned before your order is sliced. The towels used to clean the slicer should also be changed after every cleaning. Observe whether or not meat is returned to the deli case immediately after slicing. Deli employees should change their gloves after slicing each customer's order. If addition, they are required to change gloves during the same order if they are slicing both a meat and cheese item. In you don't feel the deli employees are following these safety procedures, consider buying prepackaged sliced meats.

Thickness

When cutting meat to order, every supermarket will have its own definition of thickness. Also, the slicers at different stores may vary significantly from one another. Deli meats can be shaved, sliced very thin, thin, medium (sandwich cut), or thick (dinner cut). The thicker the meat is sliced, the fewer slices there are per pound. Some stores may have a slicer guide posted on the service counter to help you determine desired thickness. To ensure that your meat is cut to the thickness you desire, ask the deli clerk to show you the thickness of the first slice before completeing your order.

Meats like prosciutto, salami, pastrami, corned beef, and meat for sliders are best shaved. Thinly sliced deli meats are best for charcuterie boards. Thin cut meats are best for sandwiches where more than one type of meat will be used. Medium cut is the cut most often used for single-meat sandwiches. Thick cut meats are used for dinner plates or to cube for salads and pastas.

Quantities to Purchase

For sandwiches: One pound of deli meat will make 3 to 5 sandwiches depending upon the amount of meat you prefer in your sandwich. I generally put one-quarter (1/4) of a pound of meat on each sandwich. If you are adding cheese to your sandwich, plan a ratio of 3 to 2—meat to cheese.

For charcuterie boards: If you are serving a charcuterie board as an appetizer, plan 3 ounces of both meat and cheese per person. If you are serving it as an entrée, plan 6 ounces of both meat and cheese per person.

Storing Cut-To-Order Deli Meat

Deli meat should be placed in the meat drawer of your refrigerator immediately after you get home. Salami, mortadella, prosciutto, chicken roll, pastrami, and corned beef will keep for 2 days. Ham, chicken, turkey, and roast beef deli meats will keep for 5 days. Your supermarket will place cut-to-order deli meats in a Ziploc® bag. Always be sure to tightly reseal the bag after each use. Deli meat that is slimy or iridescent or smells bad has past its prime.

Freezing Deli Meats

You can freeze deli meats, but processed meats like bologna and sausage are better candidates for freezing. If you want to freeze unopened, prepackaged deli meats, wrap the package in aluminum foil before freezing. Use a black marker to indicate the date of freezing. If you want to freeze cut-to-order deli meats, consider separating the meat into sandwich-size portions. Placing a piece of wax paper between each slice makes the thawing process easier. Place each serving-size stack of meat into a reusable or Ziploc® freezer bag and press as much air out of the bag as possible. Use a black marker to indicate the date of freezing. Use frozen deli meats within 2 months. Processed meats will keep for up to 3 months in the freezer.

Thawing Frozen Deli Meat

Place frozen deli meats in the refrigerator overnight to thaw. If moisture is present on thawed meat, use paper towels to pat it dry. Deli meat may lose some of its texture and flavor once it is thawed. If this occurs, add it to casseroles, omelets, or to pizza as a topping.

Deli Cheeses

For more information, see *Cheese.*

Deli Rotisserie and Fried Chicken

If you are buying hot rotisserie or fried chicken from the deli, your supermarket should store it in an oven-like area. Be sure it is hot at time of the purchase. Do not purchase lukewarm foods. Deli-roasted and fried chicken should be eaten within 2 hours after bringing it home.

If you'd like to refrigerate rotisserie chicken to use the next day, cut it into several pieces and refrigerate it in shallow, covered containers. Refrigerated rotisserie chicken must be eaten within 3 to 4 days and can be served either cold or hot.

When reheating, it's best to bring the chicken to a temperature of 165 degrees F. Reheated chicken should be hot and steaming. It is safe to freeze rotisserie chicken by placing it in freezer bags or airtight, freezer-safe containers. It will keep for 4 months, but I prefer not to keep it longer than 30 days.

Use fried chicken within 3 to 4 days. Store leftover fried chicken in the refrigerator in covered containers. Reheat fried chicken to a temperature of 165 degrees F or eat it cold if you prefer.

Selecting Hot Prepared Foods

Depending upon the deli you patronize, your supermarket will sell a variety of hot foods like macaroni and cheese, mashed potatoes, and pizza. If you purchase hot prepared foods from the deli, make sure they are hot. Avoid lukewarm food. Supermarkets are required to keep hot foods at 140 degrees F. Bacteria begins to form when the temperature of food is between 41 and 135 degrees F. Shop with your eyes. Does the food look appetizing? Avoid food that looks dry or overcooked.

Using and Storing Hot Prepared Foods

Hot foods from the deli should be consumed within two hours of purchase. Keep containers sealed until you are ready to serve. If you will not consume it immediately upon arriving home, place it in a 200 degree F oven until you are ready to serve it. Covering it with aluminum foil will prevent it from drying out. If you have leftovers, place them in covered containers and refrigerate them within two hours of opening. Use any leftovers within three days.

If you don't plan to consume hot foods that day, refrigerate them. To reheat them, bring to an internal temperature of 165 degrees F or until steaming hot.

Selecting Prepared Entrées, Side Dishes, and Salads From the Deli Counter

Depending upon the supermarket you patronize, the deli case will be stocked with a variety of entrées and side dishes—like salmon and green beans—and salads—like potato, coleslaw, and chicken—which are either produced in house (chef-prepared), manufactured by a third party like Home Chef® or Resers®, or produced in your supermarket's corporate centralized kitchen and shipped to various stores. In addition, some products you might think are fresh or chef-prepared have been shipped to your supermarket frozen and then reheated. Food that is prepared in house should be labeled "chef-prepared".

If you are buying chef-prepared, ready-to-heat foods from the deli counter, ask the deli clerk if they are, in fact, prepared in house. Chef-prepared foods have the same shelf life as foods you prepare at home—3 to 4 days. Your supermarket can sell these foods for 3 days. Since you don't know when the chef-prepared meals were prepared, it is best to consume them the same day of purchase.

When purchasing food from the deli case, shop with your eyes. Does the food look appetizing? Avoid food that looks dry or is lukewarm. Cold foods should be stored at 40 degrees F.

The FDA requires supermarkets to provide nutritional information for all prepackaged food. In addition, they require that nutritional information be available for food that is intended to be "eaten on the premises, while walking away, or soon after arriving at another location." For example, if you purchase macaroni and cheese from the deli case or a piece of pizza, nutritional information for that item may be displayed on the case. If it is not, the deli clerk should be able to provide that information to you.

Grab-and-Go Meals

Often times leftover chef-prepared food is repackaged for sale and sold as grab-and-go options. Always check and closely follow expiration dates on all grab-and-go purchases. Inspect the food carefully. Does it look fresh?

Selecting Ready-to-Heat Prepared Meals and Salads

All packaged foods are required by law to have a nutritional facts label, which also includes a list of ingredients. If you are buying packaged ready-to-heat meals or salads, read the nutritional label. Make sure its ingredients and nutritional facts meet your needs. Look for a calorie count of 350 to 500, saturated fat of 3 grams or less, and sodium of no more than 600 mg per serving. Check the number of servings per container as well as the expiration date. Buy product that has enough shelf-life so it won't go to waste. Cold foods should be kept at 40 degrees F or lower. Avoid lukewarm product. Never purchase packages with broken damaged lids, seals, or wraps.

Using Deli Food at Home

Never leave food at room temperature longer than two hours. Keep cold foods refrigerated at 40 degrees F or lower until ready to serve.

Deli/Sandwich Trays and Other Catering Orders

Before ordering fruit, veggie, and sandwich trays from your supermarket, ask how much advance notice they need. This will vary between companies, but a good rule of thumb is 48 hours. I suggest placing orders seven days prior to pick up. Deli clerks get busy and can misplace orders, so I recommend calling the deli and confirming your order is in the queue.

Fruit and veggie trays are always popular items for special occasion buffets. With rising food costs, you may not want to spend the extra dollars to purchase them. It's easier than you might imagine to assemble attractive fruit platters. And it's lots of fun. When I first started, I was uptight about the finishing touches. An experienced deli professional advised, "Just relax and have fun. When it's time to add the garnish, let your creative juices flow. Do something funky." You can purchase deli platters with fitted covers at good party stores. Directions for both follow:

Fruit Platters

Fruit	**Approximate Yield**
1 pineapple (3 to 4-pounds)	40 chunks
1 cantaloupe (4-pounds)	36 chunks
1 honeydew (2-pounds)	36 chunks
1 seedless watermelon (4 to 5-pounds)	48 chunks
1 pound seedless green grapes	12 to 15 clusters
1 pound seedless red grapes	12 to 15 clusters
1 pound strawberries	20 berries

Selecting: The most important part of serving a fruit platter is fresh fruit. For tips on selecting fresh fruits, see *How to Select and Store Fresh Fruit.*

Serving pineapple in the rind: Place the pineapple on a cutting board and with a large knife cut it into fourths from the base through the green top. Remove the core and loosen the pineapple from its rind using a sharp paring knife. Slice each quarter into 5 triangular-shaped wedges. Cut each wedge in half by slicing the wedges down the center. Place frilly picks in each pineapple piece. If you are making a large tray, pineapple prepared in this manner makes an attractive centerpiece.

Prepping fruit: Cut cantaloupe and honeydew melon in half with a large utility knife and scrape out the seeds with a spoon. Remove the peel and cut the fruit into bite-size chunks or use a melon baller to make nice round balls. Cut the watermelon in half with a large utility knife and remove the peel. Cut into bite-size chunks. If the watermelon is not seedless, use a paring knife to remove the seeds. Wash grapes thoroughly. Remove any shriveled or dried grapes. Using cooking scissors, snip grapes into small clusters. Wash strawberries, leaving the stems on.

Arranging fruit on tray: Delis typically line platters with leaf lettuce or romaine before arranging the fruit on top. I like using kale leaves to separate the different fruits into sections. Kale helps prevent the juices from running into other sections. Kiwifruit, star fruit, and berries are fun to use as garnish. When cutting your cantaloupe for the tray, try cutting it in half using a zigzag pattern. This zigzag bowl makes an attractive centerpiece for serving dip.

Vegetable Platters

Vegetable	Weight	Approx. Number of Prepared Pieces
Asparagus	1 pound	30 spears, ends removed
Broccoli	2¾ pounds	45 (1¼-inch) florets
Carrots	1 pound	65 (3 X ½-inch) sticks, peeled
Cauliflower	4¾ pounds	75 (1¼-inch) florets
Celery	1¾ pounds	100 (4 X ½-inch) sticks
Cherry Tomatoes	1 pint (¾ pound)	25 (1-inch) tomatoes
Cucumber	1¾ pounds	45 (4 X 3¾-inch) spears, unpeeled and unseeded
Green Bell Pepper	7 ounces	24 (3½ X ½-inch) sticks
Jicama	1¼ pounds	40 (4 X ½-inch) sticks, peeled
Mushrooms	1 pound	20 whole (1 to 1½-inch) caps
Pea Pods	¼ pound	30 pods
Jerusalem Artichokes	1 pound	50 (1¼-inch) slices, unpeeled
Zucchini	1¼ pounds (three 6-inch)	35 (½-inch) slices, unpeeled
Yellow Squash	1¼ pounds (three 6-inch)	35 (½-inch) slices, unpeeled

Selecting: Use any combination of vegetables you prefer. When shopping, select firm, unblemished vegetables, e.g., avoid cauliflower that has black spots. Mushrooms should have closed caps and not be wrinkled, spongy, or spotted. For tips on selecting vegetables see, *How to Select and Store Fresh Vegetables.*

Prepping vegetables: What is most important when serving crudités is clean, crisp vegetables. Wash and cut the vegetables into the desired shapes and sizes. Blanch asparagus, broccoli, and pea pods for a brighter color. To blanch, plunge vegetables into a saucepan of boiling water for no more than 2 minutes. Remove the vegetables and immediately plunge them into ice water to retard cooking. Drain and then pat the vegetables dry with paper towels. A hint for celery: My mother taught me to de-string celery by using a small paring knife and lifting the strings from the celery ends by pulling them up and off. Soak celery and carrot sticks in ice water for 30 minutes to make them extra crispy. Soak Jerusalem artichokes in a solution of 1 tablespoon lemon juice and 1 quart water for about 10 minutes to prevent darkening. Drain and pat dry with paper towels.

Serving: Allow 4 to 8 pieces per person. If you are using the crudités as a relish, plan on 4 pieces per person. If they are used as a salad, increase that number to 8 per person. Delis typically line platters with leaf lettuce or romaine before arranging the veg-etables on top. I like using kale to separate the different vegetables into sections. Cherry tomatoes, olives, and cherry peppers make fun garnishes. Try hollowing out a green, red, or yellow bell pepper to use as a container for serving dip. Using both a green and a red bell pepper makes a nice color contrast.

When your Kitchen Caters a Large Gathering

Many supermarkets will also provide catering services. With today's rising food costs, you may prefer to prepare the food yourself. Entertaining a crowd is manageable with proper planning. One of the hardest parts about entertaining is knowing how much food to prepare. Following are guidelines we used in our delis to calculate the amounts necessary to feed a crowd of 25. If you are hosting a gathering of 50, double the quantities.

Food	Amount Per Serving	Approx. Amount for 25
Coffee	one (6-ounce) serving	½ pound
Punch	one (6-ounce) serving	4 to 5 quarts
Rolls	1½ per person	3 dozen
Butter		½ to ¾ pound
Finger Sandwiches	4 per person	8 dozen
Soup	one (6 to 8-ounce) serving	1½ to 2 gallons
Palate Refresher	⅓ cup per person	9 cups
Ham (boneless-cooked)		
Meal	1 (4-ounce) serving	6 pounds
Reception	2 to 3 ounces per serving	4 to 5 pounds
Beef (boneless top round for roasting and slicing)		
Meal	about 6 ounces per serving	10 pounds
Reception	3 to 4 ounces per serving	5 to 7 pounds
Meat and cheese trays		
Meat	2 ounces per serving	3 pounds
Cheese	1 ounce per serving	1½ pounds
Main course entrée (boneless meat or fish, depending upon richness or units or parts of units)		
	4 to 8 ounces per serving	6 to 13 pounds
Sauce for entrée	1 to 2 ounces per serving	½ to ¾ gallon
Pasta as a small course (dry pasta)		
	6 to 8 servings per pound	3 to 4 pounds

Chicken salad		
Meal	1 cup serving	1½ gallons
Reception	½ cup serving	¾ to 1 gallon
Tossed green salad		
	1 cup serving	5 heads (25-ounces) iceberg 5 bags (10-ounces) spinach
Salad Dressing	2 ounces per serving	½ gallon
Side dishes—Potato Salad, Cole Slaw, Baked Beans		
	½ cup per serving	¾ to 1 gallon
Cooked Starch	2 ounces per serving	3 pounds
Vegetable	½ cup per serving	¾ to 1 gallons or 6 pounds
Cheese Course (one cheese or a selection of cheeses)		
	3 ounces per serving	4 to 5 pounds
Crackers	4 per serving	1 to 1¼ pounds
Potato Chips	1 ounce per serving	1 ½ pounds
Olives or Pickles		1 quart
Mixed Nuts		¾ pound
Mints		
Pillow		½ pound
Wafer		¾ pound

For Desserts

Ice Cream	½ cup	1 gallon
8 to 10-inch Cake White or lemon (serves 8 to 12 people)		3 cakes
Rich Cakes, like cheesecakes or dense chocolate cakes (serves 14 people)		2 cakes
Fruit Tart (serves 6 people)		4 to 5 cakes
Cookies, petit fours, or dessert truffles	2 per person	4 to 5 dozen

The previous suggestions work well if you are plating your meals and are in charge of portion control. If you plan to serve buffet style, increase portions by about 10 percent to ensure you'll have adequate amounts.

Olive, Soup, Salad, and Hot Food Bars

Supermarkets may have self-service olive, soup, salad, and hot foods bars. These bars should have a clean, sanitary appearance. Cold foods should look fresh and appealing, and hot foods should not look dried out. Avoid any self-service food where flies or insects hover about. This is a sign the food has started to decay.

Cold foods should be cold and kept at 40 degrees F or less. Hot foods should be hot and kept at temperatures above 135 degrees F. Bacteria begins to form when foods are held at temperatures between 41 degrees F and 135 degrees F. If you are concerned that the food has not been stored at proper temperatures, pass. An observation: deli foods stored in shallow containers will hold their temperature better than deep containers.

Each food item that is displayed in the bar should have its own separate container and utensil. Utensils should always be placed into the container with their handle up. Deli employees should dispose of any food that falls out of its bowl, and the bar should have a neat, tidy appearance. Cross contamination can occur when food falls into the wrong container or when a utensil is placed in the wrong container. Bacteria can begin to form when cross contamination occurs. When a utensil is dropped on the floor or placed in the wrong bowl, it should be replaced.

Self-service bars should have a sneeze guard. Neither employees nor customers should duck underneath the guard. Avoid any self-service food if you see that a customer or employee has put their hands into the food.

When stocking the bar, employees should wear gloves and hairnets. When a container is almost empty, the entire container should be replaced. New salads or hot foods should not be spooned over food that has been sitting in the bar.

Selecting Sushi

Sushi is either made in-store by sushi chefs or is manufactured in commercial kitchens and shipped to grocery stores. Companies that produce sushi for resale in supermarkets include Fuji Food Products, Advanced Fresh Concepts, Genji, and Snow Fox. I personally prefer to purchase sushi that is made in store.

Sushi should look fresh. Avoid packages where the fish looks discolored or slimy. Never buy sushi that smells fishy. Fresh seafood and sushi should smell like the ocean. Always check expiration dates. If refrigerated, raw fish should be safe to eat for three days. Never buy sushi that is over three days old. It is best to eat sushi the same day you buy it. If you are concerned about the freshness of sushi for sale in your supermarket, ask if the in-store chef can make your roll to order.

Index

T

U

V

Bibliography

BOOKS

Green, Aliza, *Field Guide to Produce,* Philadelphia: Quirk Books, 2004.

Herbst, Sharon Tyler, *Food Lover's Companion,* Hauppauge, Barron's Educational Series, Inc., 2001.

Kates, Carol Ann, *Secret Recipes from the Corner Market,* Fort Collins: Penny Lane Press of Colorado, 2006.

WEBSITES

A Greener World. *www.agreenerworld.org.*

Alaska Seafood Marketing Institute. *www.alaskaseafood.org.*

American Grassfed Association. *www.americangrassfed.org.*

Best Aquaculture Practices. *www.bapcertification.org.*

Certified Humane. A Project of Humane Farm Animal Care. *www.certifiedhumane.org.*

EDF Seafood Selector. *www.seafood.edf.org.*

Environmental Working Group. *www.ewg.org.*

Food Alliance. *www.foodalliance.org.*

Food and Drug Administration. *www.fda.gov/food/new-nutrition-facts-label.*

Food and Water Watch. *www.foodandwaterwatch.com.*

Global Animal Partnership. *www.globalanimalpartnership.org.*

Global Fishing Watch. *www.globalfishingwatch.org.*

Global Seafood Alliance. *www.globalseafood.org.*

Marine Stewardship Council. *www.msc.org.*

National Cattlemen's Beef Association. *www.ncba.org.*

National Lamb Feeders Association. *www.lambfeedersusa.org.*

National Pork Producers Council. *www.nppc.org.*

The National Center for Appropriate Technology. *www.ncat.org.*

The Non-GMO Project. *www.nongmoproject.org.*

The Whole Foods Diet. *www.wholefoodsdiet.com.*

The Whole Grains Council. *www.wholegrainscouncil.org.*

United States Department of Agriculture. *www.ams.usda.gov/rules-regulations, www.fsis.usda.gov/oa/pubs, www.usda.gov/our-agency/about-usda/laws-and-regulations.*

University of Georgia Extension Office. *www.exension.ugs.edu.*

US Poultry and Egg Association. *www.uspoultry.org.*

Vegan Awareness Foundation. *www.vegan.org.*